India's Working Women and
Career Discourses

India's Working Women and Career Discourses

Society, Socialization, and Agency

Suchitra Shenoy-Packer

LEXINGTON BOOKS
Lanham • Boulder • New York • London

Published by Lexington Books
An imprint of The Rowman & Littlefield Publishing Group, Inc.
4501 Forbes Boulevard, Suite 200, Lanham, Maryland 20706
www.rowman.com

16 Carlisle Street, London W1D 3BT, United Kingdom

British Library Cataloguing in Publication Information Available

Library of Congress Cataloging-in-Publication Data

Shenoy-Packer, Suchitra.
India's working women and career discourses : society, socialization, and agency / Suchitra Shenoy-Packer.
pages cm
Includes bibliographical references and index.
ISBN 978-0-7391-8477-6 (cloth : alk. paper) -- ISBN 978-0-7391-8478-3 (electronic) 1. Women--Employment--India. 2. Work and family--Inida. 3. Sex discrimination in employment--India. 4. Women--India--Social conditions. I. Title.
HD6189.S54 2014
331.40954--dc23
2014016279

Printed in the United States of America

This book is dedicated to my research collaborators—my participants, for their inspiring work, stories, and life lessons.

Contents

Acknowledgments

This book is based on research I conducted as a graduate student at Purdue University, U.S.A. I will forever be grateful to my advisor and mentor, Patrice M. Buzzanell, for seeing the potential in this study and encouraging me to pursue an interdisciplinary topic of personal interest. I am also grateful to my committee members Karen K. Myers (University of California, Santa Barbara), Stacey L. Connaughton (Purdue University), and Gregory Hundley (Krannert School of Management, Purdue University)

At Purdue, thank you to the Purdue Research Foundation Dissertation Grant that allowed for an extended stay in India for data collection. Thank you to my students, particularly those from my COM 224: Communicating in the Global Workplace (Fall 2007), and COM 320: Small Group Communication (Spring 2008) classes. I taught these courses during the semesters I wrote my preliminary examination and defended my prospectus. My students have supported me, encouraged me, and cheered me on through this entire process. I thank you for making even my most stressful day full of learning and laughter.

At DePaul, thank you to DePaul University Research Council's Competitive Research grant award. Thank you to my colleague and friend, Paul Booth, for patiently answering my many questions. Thank you Katherine Leone for your meticulous research assistance.

Thank you to the *Journal of Communication and Religion*, and the *Iowa Journal of Communication* for permitting portions of previously published content to be republished in this book.

Thank you to my father, Vijendranath, and mother, Maya, for more things than I can enumerate in this space and especially for your excitement, support, and unflagging belief in my work and my project. Most importantly, thank you for your positive spirit and energy, for your love and unflinching faith in raising your feminist daughter, and for always respecting my resistance and questioning of archaic traditions and the logic-less socio-religious-cultural dictates of our society. Thank you to the amazing women I consider my role models and inspiration; Prema Kini, Ratna Mallya, and Sumithra Shenoy; and Tara Kulkarni and Madhuri Shenoy. Thank you, Sam and Reni Packer. Your encouragement and support of my many research endeavors makes me want to continue to do and be better.

Thank you, Matthew Packer, for the amazing person you are. I cannot believe I get to walk this journey of life with you. Your kindness, generosity, patience, and love are more than I ever hoped for but everything I ever wished. Thank you for making my wishes come true.

In India, a big thank you to the many people directly responsible for the completion of this project: Sunalini Satoor, for helping translate English consent forms into Marathi and introducing me to some key personnel affiliated with the University of Pune; Anil Tambe, for typing up the Marathi translations into a formatted consent form for approval by Purdue's Institutional Review Board (IRB); Pramod Kulkarni, for providing an official note to the IRB attesting to the culturally sensitive nature of my study; Mangala Murali for hundreds of pages of transcriptions; Padmaja Deshmukh, Uma Karve-Chakranarayan, Mridula Kolhatkar, Aulokita Mane, Radha Gokhale, Himani Kolhatkar, Ravjot Chumber, Bhagyashree Desai, Smita Tribhuvan, Vinita Deshmukh, Ratnakar Bhat, Revathi Bhat, Jayanti Bhat, and Vipin Dongre, for helping with recruitment.

At Lexington Books, thank you Jana Hodges-Kluck and Natalie Mandziuk for understanding life's many commitments and working with me throughout the publication process. Your conviction for this project helped birth into reality a five-year-old dream.

Finally, I would like to thank the women who breathed life into this idea of a research project. Thank you for your candor in sharing your lives with the readers and me. The integrity with which you lead your lives is truly inspirational.

Chapter One

Introduction

Who is the 21st century Indian working woman? What makes her excited about going in to work every day? Why *does* she work? What does she consider as meaningful work? What motivates and inspires her to participate in the nearly 150 million strong female Indian workforce? How does childhood socialization direct the course of her life or does it? How do Indian traditions, culture, and society influence her agency in career decision-making? Answers to these questions are fundamental to gaining at least a modicum of understanding of today's Indian working women. Of course, "today" is represented by women across generations and socio-economic status who collectively embody a force that has been pivotal to ongoing social change. Even though reams of newsprint and reels of video have been expended heralding the "new" Indian woman—popularized in media as a "Power Goddess" who is "Smart and Sassy," and a "Mistress of Choices" capable of "Doing it all" (*India Today* cover stories, 2005; 2006; 2007)—this sudden spotlight on Indian women does not discount the fact that India's women have always worked. The globalizing forces that swept India off her feet in the early 2000s and continue with some sustained strength this decade, have gradually transitioned from catapulting the woman of the new millennia as an agent of social change to a matter-of-fact partner in nation building to more recent refocusing of energies on the perils and constraints faced by India's working women in light of the Delhi rape case.[1]

Indian women, paradoxically worshipped as goddesses while being victimized by rape, infanticide, and discrimination, have always struggled against an archaic system that continues to privilege age-old patriarchal social structures, characterized by male dominance, and patrifocality, defined as kinship and family structures and ideology that give precedence to men over women (Mukhopadhyay & Seymour, 1994). The cliché that surrounds Indian nation-

1

al reputation—that of it being a land of contradictions—is perhaps most poignantly experienced in the everyday lives of women. As subjects of this book who go about their everyday juxtaposed lives with an awareness of their social surroundings, constrained agency, and strategic resistance, Indian women excel at walking the delicate tightrope of socio-cultural expectations and personal-professional ambitions.

The complex brew of economic disparities and social inequalities stemming from centuries of customs, traditions, and norms inherent in India's dominant Hindu culture are an inseparable part of people's lived realities and, as will be seen in this chapter, have been particularly harsh on India's women. These socially constructed nuances of everyday existence influence every aspect of an Indian's life, including career choice and implementation. Throughout the book, unless otherwise specified, career will be defined as "the evolving sequence of a person's work experiences over time" (Arthur, Hall, & Lawrence, 1989, p. 8; also see chapter 5). Understandably, women end up becoming disadvantaged in the public domain of work, and also subjugated to social control in their private spheres under the garb of value constructs determined by men. Caste and class have been other key issues responsible for relegating women to a lower social position.

Caste in India has typically been defined in terms of family and kinship ties. One is always born into a certain caste with pre-determined occupational responsibilities and confinements. Prevailing norms suggest that society could not function without the contribution of any single caste. Historically, the division of labor, based on caste, was clearly demarcated and everybody knew their place in this social hierarchy. Such explicit distribution of occupations, however, has been especially detrimental to Indian women because of their traditional lower position in patriarchal Indian society vis-à-vis men. Even though caste-based sexual division of labor was typically the case in Indian society, as dynamic as this society is, things have been changing, and rapidly.

Today, more than hierarchal or ritual status as bestowed by caste, it is social mobility, a rising standard of living, and an embracing of consumerist values and lifestyles that distinguishes people from one another. In fact, Nijman (2006) contends that caste as a stratisfactory system is almost absent in urban, educated India even as it continues to remain significant in other parts. It is membership into the new middle class that most people strive for, a class that is not based merely on education and merit as was the case with the old middle class, but one that is based more on money, drive, and the ability to accomplish things (Das, 2002).

Expectedly, these social changes have influenced the traditional norms of women's work and behavior, especially among educated Indian women. Not only have more women entered the urban workforce, particularly business process outsourcing (BPO) centers, but women have now ventured into unorthodox career paths such as bartending, taxi cab driving, and priesthood (Shenoy-Packer, 2013) which previously were male domains. While these occupational choices receive media attention, more scholarship has investigated issues concerning urban, educated Indian women in the workplace such as stress, discrimination in hiring practices, lack of upward mobility in management, and inequity in reward and pay structures (e.g., Chanana, 2003; Dasgupta, 1998; Gupta & Sharma, 2003; Gupta, Koshal, & Koshal, 1998; Kaila, 2004). Understandably, new ways of working and embodiment of prescribed work cultures bring new challenges and strongly impact policy and research agendas. For example, even though Indian women have engaged in paid employment for decades, it is only recently that the Indian parliament passed *The Sexual Harassment of Women at Workplace (Prevention, Prohibition, and Redressal) Bill*, entitling women to a safe and harassment free workplace (Parliament passes, 2013). Albeit late, the bill is a step in the right direction toward at least legally ensuring a safe work environment for women. More provisions and legal mandates are of course needed so these protections can be integrated into a larger systemic endeavor to make workplaces favorable and inclusive of women. An important characteristic of this bill is that it accounts for the often invisible work of domestic helpers and agricultural workers in the informal sector. The provisions of this bill are applicable to women working in formal workplace structures as well as transient work spaces such as an employer's home, construction sites, farmlands, and so on. This is especially important because in a country like India, despite the fact that the majority of the female workforce is engaged in work in the informal economy, only limited attention is given to the concerns of these key contributors of the economy in the larger work-life-society conversations. The current research project is one exception because it encompasses women across socio-economic status.

THIS BOOK

Even with the substantial promise, potential, and contributions made by scholarship on India's working women, we know little in the way of qualitatively rich personal data collected directly from women across and at the intersections of occupations, generations, and income levels—an important omission, which this book will fulfill. Inkson (2007) has argued that studying individual careers is flawed unless they are also understood from a wider perspective. The life experiences and realities of Indian women differ along the lines of social and occupational class, and studying these areas within any one demographic provides only a partial view of their lives. Furthermore, as has been briefly explained above, it has traditionally been the case that one's caste has strongly determined the nature of work and occupation in which one could engage. Because men and women could only work certain jobs, they were limited in the scope and opportunities they had in pursuing upward mobility. Invariably, one's caste had consequences on individuals' attainability of higher social class status. One aim of this project, therefore, is to investigate the work lives and careers of India's women within a historical context influenced by India's cultural and traditional realities. This project is interested in how society, family socialization, and individual agency influence women's career discourses and decisions. This project will also explore the meanings Indian women associate with work, which is defined here as paid employment.

To understand and explore the contemporary lives of India's working women, I conducted face-to-face interviews with seventy-eight women across socio-economic status and income categories; low-income women who often work in marginalized and "informal" occupations such as street sweeping and domestic work; middle-income women employed in occupations like teaching, social work, and journalism; and highly educated women in high-income professions such as business, engineering, and medicine. By incorporating women from different occupational classifications and across incomes, this project contributes to a holistic understanding of women's work lives in India. However, in order to do justice to the project, I had to appropriate two specific limitations, which in some ways, always worked as strengths. First, the data for the project were collected from a single urban Indian city—Pune, Maharashtra. My native familiarity and own work experience in the city allowed for the understanding of local nuances, cultural and linguistic expertise, and the convenience of a network of personal and professional contacts which enabled the recruitment of participants. Second, data were only collected from Hindu working women. My religious and cultural upbringing as a middle/upper-middle class, upper-caste Hindu provided for a more intimate, insightful, empathetic, and better interpretation of participants' experiences.

In the following sections, first, I will discuss the context of India's position in the global economy along with its implications on Indian working women. Second, I present the contexts of women's work in India by tracing its brief history and highlighting the contemporary climate for women and work. Third, I provide a brief overview of the study's theoretical framework as well as the study's research objectives. This introductory chapter concludes with an overview of the project and upcoming chapters.

GLOBALIZATION AND INDIA

On August 14, 1947, on the eve of India's independence, the first prime minister of free India, Jawaharlal Nehru, gave his famous speech on India's

"Tryst with Destiny," where he called on the people of India and its elected officials to "redeem our pledge, not wholly or in full measure, but very substantially" to fulfill the responsibility of serving India by laboring and working hard "to give reality to our dreams . . . dreams for India but also for the world . . ." (A tryst, 1997; Tryst, 2008). On August 15, 2012, India celebrated her 65th year of independence. In the 21st century, few would dispute that India is well on her path to realizing that tryst with destiny promised by Nehru. The journey to get to this point of economic growth has been an eventful one. In the decades immediately following independence, the country's socialist policies pushed India into her "darkest economic decades" (Das, 2006, para 7). In the 1980s, with the introduction of modest liberal reforms, the government's attitude toward the private sector began to change and by the 1990s, India had abandoned her past policies. The post-independence socialist-oriented policies initiated by Nehru gradually gave way to urban industrial and agricultural development. When Rajiv Gandhi took over as prime minister in 1984, he pushed for science and technology and slowly developed policies to depart from socialist ones. Various governments that succeeded Gandhi after his assassination in 1991 implemented a liberalization policy that transitioned India into high macroeconomic growth (Corbridge, Harriss, & Jeffrey, 2013). With the opening of its market to foreign investments, privatization, and subsequent globalization, India thus began her journey of integration into the world economy (M. Ali, 2006; Das, 2006).

Then, at the turn of the 20th century came the dot-com boom and bubble, both of which benefited India (Friedman, 2005). Along with upgrading American computer systems to handle the Y2K bug to conducting e-commerce activities, to handling the back offices of some of the biggest businesses worldwide, India had more than a foot in the door of the new world order. As Friedman (2005) observes, "Any service, call center, business support operation, or knowledge work that could be digitized could be sourced globally to the cheapest, smartest, or most efficient provider" (p. 109) and this meant new opportunities, competitive paychecks with perquisites, and a promising new lifestyle for thousands of well-educated Indians. A contagious change of momentum was sweeping India, especially its youth and had in its path, begun to tug at the fabric of Indian life, transforming it, perhaps forever. For the casual observer India had finally arrived on the world stage. In fact, Thomas Friedman, in his popular book *The World Is Flat*, had credited India as one of the main reasons behind the flattening of the world (Friedman, 2005).

India's new globalizing economy posed challenges along with the numerous opportunities it created (M. Ali, 2006). Realistically speaking, just as one cannot help but notice the rising number of skyscrapers, malls, and multiplexes dotting the skylines of major Indian cities today, one cannot ignore the reality of a nation that is home to 33% of the world's poor according to the World Bank (Lalmalsawma, 2013; The state of the poor, 2013), and had a little over 269 million citizens living below the poverty line in 2012 (Kala, 2013; Poverty estimates, 2013). Some scholars argue that India is "poised at a key moment in history" (Das, 2006, para. 4). The poise of a country undergoing large-scale socioeconomic transformation notwithstanding, it is a challenging reality to acknowledge the economic disparities that go hand in hand with social inequalities in a country with its history that spans centuries, ancient civilizations, deeply religious and mythology, induced mindsets, and traditionally dictated normative structures and systems. Corbridge et al. (2013), who agree with this observation, maintain that while India is undergoing great change, it is impossible to overlook what has not changed—"enduring inequalities of Indian society, and the continuing prevalence of great poverty, in spite of such successful economic growth . . . the persistence of hierarchical values . . . of patriarchy . . . and the continuing deep disadvantages of Indian women" (p. 304). It is to this discussion, I turn to next.

WOMEN AND WORK IN CONTEXT

The status of women in India has always been somewhat of an ambiguity for cultural outsiders. Even as one hears tales of how India has the second largest workforce in the world—478 million (Inderfurth & Khambatta, 2012), we hear about how the country is failing to capitalize on its population dividend (Corbridge et al., 2013; Crabtree & Pugliese, 2012; Madgavkar, 2012). Furthermore, consistent studies conducted by Indian and international organizations alike, paradoxical to initial reports from the early 2000s, highlight the declining female labor force and the economic loss the nation is suffering as a result; this, despite the fact that a recent study estimated that the country's female workforce is likely to make the country richer by 25% by 2025 (Heikkila, 2012). Unfortunately, more studies and economic indicators show that the unprecedented growth India experienced in the early 2000s that led to millions of women entering the workforce has gradually dropped. Mazumdar (2007) argues that even though some of the forces of globalization have led to more women stepping out of their homes to engage in paid employment in the services sector, there simultaneously has been a decrease in work participation rates among women in general causing higher rates of unemployment. One wonders why Indian women, who comprise 48% of the country's 1.2 billion-plus population make up only 25% of the country's total workforce (Census of India, 2011). Several speculations have abounded to make sense of these numbers.

According to the findings of a Gallup Poll presented by Crabtree and Pugliese (2012), traditional cultural expectations and social norms often work to the detriment of women's active workforce participation. The study also held India's higher fertility rates and lack of reliable access to education as responsible for the lack of female participation. The International Labor Organization (ILO) added other factors such as rising household incomes that allowed for women to withdraw from the workforce, erroneous data collection methods, limited opportunity in non-traditional sectors of employment, and challenges to re-entering the workforce after childbirth as other reasons that contributed to India's inability to increase female employment participation. While cautioning that India needs to make more concerted efforts toward gender equality and strive for more than superficial changes, however, both the Gallup and ILO studies were optimistic that in years to come India's falling fertility rate, historic migration of rural workers to urban areas with access to more education and employment opportunities, women's assertion for autonomy, and higher school enrollment will work constructively to advance the position of women in the country and fortify their place in the workforce.

Part of the issue with enumerating women's participation in the overall Indian workforce is that just as their place in Indian society is often invisible, their non-economic work activities are simply not recognized as work by members of the household or the women themselves (Chandrashekhar & Ghosh, 2011). Even when they are employed in income-generating work, according to the Self Employed Women's Association, a significant proportion of these women are undocumented and unregistered laborers who comprise the informal sector in both rural and urban areas. In fact, three of the top industries Indian women engage in are farming (68.5%), tobacco products and clothes manufacturing (10.8%), and construction (5%). A viable reason to add to the declining female workforce participation rates is also the fact that because the Indian manufacturing and export-oriented sectors were hugely hit in 2009–10 due to power shortages, and reduced international export demands, 3.7 million jobs were lost, 80% of which were held by women (Thomas, 2013).

Some reports do suggest that despite the challenges Indian women face in the workforce, their numbers, at least in the urban areas have been steadily increasing even though this difference is not significantly obvious between the census reports of 2001 and 2011. This reported growth is anecdotally and observationally more apparent in the IT industry. If India is celebrating its entry into the new world economy and the rise of its new middle-class, it is largely based on the IT-enabled services and a different class of urban, educated, women workers employed in the service sector such as business process outsourcing centers or BPOs (Mazumdar, 2007). This new class of highly visible women does not truly represent all of India's working women.

The true picture is much more complex, multilayered, and contradictory than one is led to believe. The careers and work lives of Indian women are at an interesting juncture today. The "new" and neo-globalized Indian woman is often defined in terms of income, growth of female labor participation, desire to chart non-traditional and unconventional careers, and so on (e.g., Divakaruni, 2005; Bamzai, 2006; Butalia, 2007). However, such images of urban Indian women continue to co-exist with the realities of poor women working in the informal sector as will be examined in an upcoming chapter.

To understand Indian women's work lives, it is important to learn about the gendered socialization and enculturation that takes place in their lives from a young age. *Socialization,* a sociological construct, refers to "the deliberate shaping, by conscious and active training of the individual to imbibe and adapt to the more, values, and expectations of the society" (Berry, Poortinga, Segall, & Dasen, 1992; cited in Saraswathi, 1999, p. 13). *Enculturation,* a related term, was developed by cultural anthropologists to imply that "the individual is encompassed by his [sic] culture, immersion in which results in spontaneous learning" (Berry et al., 1992; cited in Saraswathi, 1999, p. 14). Dube (1988) has extensively argued that Hindu Indian girls are strategically socialized into the culture's patrilineal and patrifocal milieu through rituals, ceremonies, prescribed gender rules, and other practices. These will be discussed in more detail in upcoming chapters. Thus, growing up, individuals are influenced by the purposeful socialization they receive, grooming them to become active, responsible, and participating members of a particular society. This way, socially constructed norms, mores, and values get produced and reproduced over time.

According to Ganesh (1999), it is not possible to study Indian women outside of a patriarchal society in which patriarchal principles get actualized through socialization into governing rules for gendered behavior. Gupta and Sharma (2003) argue that unlike the use of the term "patriarchal" in Western societies, the term that best describes the Indian context is "patrifocal," a term first used by Mukhopadhyay and Seymour (1994). Specific to an agricultural social context, the structural features of patrifocality emphasize lineage purity by controlling marriage and female sexuality in addition to patrilineal descent, patrilineal inheritance and succession, and a male dominated family hierarchy. Ganesh (1999) argues that such patrilineal principles derived from Hindu normative traditions are responsible for structuring rules and molding behavior in the Indian family. This sociocultural complexity profoundly impacts women's lives (Eapen & Kodoth, 2004). Although some scholars have expressed their preference for the term "patrifocality," patrifocal, patriarchal, and patrilineal are used interchangeably in this book. Some of the aspects of a patrilineal Hindu Indian family include (in varying degrees):

restrictions on women's mobility, anxiety regarding early and appropriate marriage of daughters, the high valorization of chastity and fidelity which generates stringent and intricate rules for appropriate behavior of girls, severance of ties with natal kin which reduces the support network in times of stress and crisis. (Ganesh, 1999, p. 241)

Traditionally, Hindu families have controlled or limited the visibility of women in public spaces but as more and more women demand their own place in the world outside their homes, parents are relenting. Parents of a previous generation may have been forced to give in to traditional dictates, but this generation of parents is far more accepting of nontraditional career paths and lifestyles for their daughters. These changing career and life aspects for working women include: living alone or with roommates, moving away to different cities for work, late-night work hours due to the 24/7 call center operations, decisions to stay single or marry late, and not spending holidays or weekends with extended family (Bharadwaj 2007a, 2007b; Butalia, 2007; Pai, Krishnamurthy, & Sen, 2007; Pal & Buzzanell, 2008; Vasudev, 2005).

It *has* been argued that even in the past, women were not passive in their acceptance of societal impositions. They are in fact considered active recipients of socialization messages and the exercising of their agency is seen as "reflecting a position for themselves by (among other things) drawing upon alternative conceptions of gender available in the larger culture, as well as by making use of structural lags and ambivalences within patriliny" (Ganesh, 1999, p. 236). Even though Ganesh (1999) observes a gap between patrilineal norms and their practice among groups lower in a social hierarchy, they influence normative restrictions on some aspects of women's lives, including their work lives. For example, regardless of a woman's position in the social hierarchy, the idea of household responsibilities being a woman's job is so deeply institutionalized in the patriarchal system that it is beyond negotiation (S. Kapadia, 1999).

Employed and unemployed upper-class women have the benefit of hiring lower-class women to do their household tasks while lower-class women have no such advantage (Qayum & Ray, 2003; Uberoi, 2005). Additionally, occupational gender typing—the labeling of occupations as appropriate for individuals based on their sex instead of on their ability (Bhogale, 1999)— has traditionally had far-reaching consequences on women's career choice. In fact, the ILO's Global Employment Trends report (2013) categorically mentioned how India's occupational segregation engendered by gender-typing, leads women to be relegated to industries and occupations such as agriculture, sales, and handicraft manufacturing; because there has been no significant employment growth in these occupations, female employment has essentially stalled. There is, however, some evidence to show that occupational gender typing in urban areas at least is no longer as limiting in current times as it was once. This change is exemplified by the increasing number of women working in traditionally male-dominated jobs such as driving an auto-rickshaw or taxi, bartending, or priesthood (Bamzai, 2006; Bharadwaj, 2007a, 2007b; Raina, 2005; Shenoy-Packer, 2012).

Along with gender, the communicative negotiation of societal discourses surrounding class and caste are important social processes in career research in India. The particular caste, community, and religious groups to which women belong, the extent to which their caste and class overlap, as well as the extent to which these are embedded in social formations and structures influence their participation in the workforce. Therefore, to understand the nature of women's careers, it is important to study the myriad circumstances that surround their choices and inform their decisions.

IMPLICATIONS FOR WORK AND CAREERS IN INDIA

Women in India have traditionally been assigned secondary position vis-à-vis men due to the rigid social system stratified by caste and class. In fact, argue Liddle and Joshi (1989), the subordination of women was crucial to developing a caste-based hierarchy. The higher the caste of a woman, the more her independence was constrained. Caste also had irrevocable influences on class. Caste in India has an over 2000-year-old history and its impact on the lives of women, both in the private and public domains, has been far-reaching. A caste-based division of labor has traditionally existed in India, reinforced by the ensuing cultural norms and rituals, often specific to the particular caste. However, contradictory reports of which came first, whether it was the ancient, historically, and mythologically learned cultural norms that formalized a caste system or whether it was the caste system that determined cultural norms, is an unresolved issue (see Liddle & Joshi, 1989).

Because it was assumed that attainment and maintenance of upper-caste status was only possible through following the three requirements of purity essential for an upper-caste status—vegetarianism, abstinence from intoxicants, and control of women's sexuality—upper-caste Brahmins enforced these tenets strictly. Those desiring upper-caste status reportedly started following the Brahmins in adopting their rituals. Even though caste status was determined at birth, it was believed that access to a higher caste was possible through sexual access to upper-caste women. This flexibility necessitated the need for upper-caste women to be controlled and confined to their homes so that caste supremacy could prevail. As a result, lower-caste women had more freedom and mobility concerning their work and could work as maids or field workers while upper-caste Hindu women were restricted in movement and secluded at home (D'Aluisio & Menzel, 1996; Dirks, 2001; Lebra, Paulson & Everett, 1984; Liddle & Joshi, 1989; M. Mohanty, 2004).

According to Liddle and Joshi (1989), the middle-class in India emerged out of the British colonizers' need to hire English-educated Indians to administer the country. Dirks (2001) argues that caste ended up becoming the "product of an historical encounter between India and the Western colonial rule" (p. 5). The opportunities to be educated in English and work for the British were available almost exclusively to upper-caste Brahmins, while other occupations such as money-lending and business/commerce were based on caste-based divisions. By segregating work on the basis of caste, the British colonizers extended and gave new interpretation to the traditional divisions of society. Dirks (2001) further holds the British responsible for systematically organizing the diversity of social identities and community memberships to which Indians belonged by using caste as an "identifiable (if contested) ideological canon" (p. 5) and as a powerful institution for ruling the country for over 200 years. By allowing for caste to be used as a measure for all social things, by allowing the social to become political, by transforming caste into a religious system, and by creating a hierarchical and ordered difference, the British recruited eligible and elite Indians to become participants in the new order to construct and spread colonial knowledge (Dirks, 2001). These "opportunities" had contradictory effects on women's work such that despite social and economic advantages afforded by the existing system, a number of educated, middle-class women continued to stay home. The norms of behavior that were imposed on upper-caste women also came to be applied on urban, middle-class women. Despite being refused entry into administrative occupations at the time, middle-class educated Indian women are reported to have served their communities as teachers and doctors. These women realized their unique position in being able to step out of their houses, acquire an independent source of income, and survive the patriarchal caste structure (Liddle & Joshi, 1989). These possibilities posed problems for traditionalists of the Indian society since economically independent women were considered "difficult to control" and capable of undermining the social structure and hierarchy. It is no surprise, argue Liddle and Joshi (1989), that women's organizations, activism, and resistance rose from middle-class working women. Thus, caste and class have always affected women's work in Indian society.

Caste and the Emergence of the "New" Class in India

In the Indian context, caste is often explained and understood in terms of familial and kinship ties, membership to which can only be achieved by birth. With its roots in the Latin word *Castus* meaning "pure," Ketkar remarked in 1909 that it was the Portuguese derivation of the word, *casta,* meaning "lineage" or "race" that had come to be used in India (Dirks, 2001; Ketkar, 1909). According to Ketkar (1909), used as an abstract noun, "caste" means "either the caste system or any of its supposed peculiarities, like exclusiveness, hierarchy, fixed order of things, greater regard to the ancestry of a person than to his individual merits, pretensions of the purity of blood, feeling of superiority and inferiority or customary manifestations thereof" (p. 18). Even though there are thousands of castes and sub-castes in India, the four castes (of which others are derivations) in the Hindu society are: Brahmins (nonviolent, spiritual, educated, and the only caste to which priests could once belong), Kshatriyas (strong and aggressive, suitable as warriors), Vaishyas (businessmen and entrepreneurs), and Shudras (servants, scavengers, shoemakers) (Ketkar, 1909). A last group of people known as Dalits or the untouchables, were considered to be undeserving of even a low-caste status.

The relationship between one's caste and occupation is unmistakable to the culturally trained eye and to followers of the implications of British rule in India. In fact, castes have traditionally been associated with specific occupations and occupational specialization. Caste-based occupational segregations affect women the most as they end up becoming twice disadvantaged because of their caste and sex. Because the caste system is known to determine not only the social but also the sexual division of labor, segregation of work tasks is considered normative. For example, due to the concepts of purity and menstrual "pollution," women in agriculture are allowed to work in transplanting and removing weeds but not in ploughing (Deshpande, 2011). Similar unfounded "rules" are imposed on women in construction as well, which will be described a little later in the chapter. Since most low caste people are also poor and illiterate, the combination of caste and its many implications deny women their rightful access to preferred jobs and occupational selection. Dirks (2001) reminds us that "caste remains the single most powerful category for reminding the nation of the resilience of poverty, oppression, domination, exclusion, and the social life of privilege" (p. 16). This social dimension of Indian societ—that of dividing society on the basis of one's caste—influences "values, beliefs, prejudices, and injunctions, as well as its distortions of reality, [and] become part of the individual's mind and contents of his [sic] conscience" (Kakar & Kakar, 2007, p. 26).

In urban Indian discourse the topic of caste is often conspicuous by its absence—perhaps a reflection of "deep sensitivities and a desire to circumvent possible prejudice" (Nijman, 2006, p. 762). In the new liberalized economy, caste, according to Sheth (1999) has been subject to "de-ritualization" (p. 2502) due to the loss of a support system that in the past perpetuated caste in every aspect of Indian life. In contemporary India, people of all castes feel the desire of upward mobility, individually as well as collectively, argues Nijman (2006). Even though one cannot successfully argue that caste-based discrimination across India is nonexistent, at least in the case of urban cities with an overwhelming educated population, caste as a marker of social stratification has been replaced by class (Nijman, 2006). Sheth (1999) observes that people no longer aspire to higher ritual status, instead amassing wealth, political power, and consumerist lifestyles is what drives people on their way to becoming socially mobile. Scholars argue that in India today there is an emergent stratisfactory system that is a fusion between the old closed-status system and the new open and fluid system of social stratification (e.g., Mukherjee, 1999; Nijman, 2006; Sheth, 1999).

The new open system addressed by these scholars is social class. Caste and class share a complex relationship (Nijman, 2006). Nijman (2006) observes that with the rise of post-structuralism, social sciences in the last 25 years have focused on race, gender, and ethnicity, at the cost of class identity, an observation supported by Cheney (2000). Smith (2000) argues for the revival of class as a social and political lens.

Economists and political commentators have written about the rising "new" Indian middle class for a while now (e.g., Beinhocker, Farrell, & Zainulbhai, 2007; Fernandes, 2000; Varma, 1998). Typically, India's urban middle class has been the educated and employed demographic that rose slowly in its path to upward mobility. Today, with the opening of the economy and IT jobs driving the labor force, a new and rich middle-class, considered a cultural and political phenomenon (Nijman, 2006) has emerged. This rising new middle-class structure has "cut across the caste hierarchy, forming new alliances and antagonisms" (Mukherjee, 1999, p. 1761). The current middle class is "new" in the sense that it has emerged in direct contrast to the hierarchical caste system that had traditionally been a determinant of social class. Membership into this new middle class is associated with "new life styles (modern consumption patterns), ownership of certain economic assets, and the self-consciousness of belonging to the middle-class" (Sheth, 1999, p. 2509). Thus, along "with economic growth, economic class is increasingly salient for overall social status: caste-based status and ritual purity are slowly declining in importance" (Kapadia, 2002a, p. 151).

Indians of all castes have participated in nation building by acquiring a good education, taking to non-traditional, non-caste specific occupations, changing lifestyles, and developing modern mindsets (Sheth, 1999). However, people of lower-castes are often only able to access the opportunities of the upper-castes because of economic and political resources such as legal provisions provided by affirmative action programs entitling them to a reserved quota in education and employment, due to which class always carries some elements of caste within it (Sheth, 1999). Even though the Indian Constitution abolished caste discrimination so equal rights could be afforded to all its citizens alike, it discernibly authorized "a system of positive discrimination that is based on caste" (Hancock, 1999, p. 41). Caste quotas and

reservations allow for members of lower castes to avail of positions in institutions of higher education and the public/government sector. Thus, caste
gets embedded within the new class structure. Caste-based issues continue to
be extremely controversial in nature especially when intertwined with politics (see Bidwai, 2006; Nigam, 2002).

Thus far, the discussion on caste and class has been relatively gender-
neutral. There is reason to speculate that women of different castes are differently treated because of their caste membership. Often times, though, caste is
not the only factor fueling discriminatory behavior. Lack of appropriate resources or knowledge of government-sponsored allocations such as in education and employment dovetails with the existence of illiteracy and continued
belief in traditional patriarchal Hindu ideologies. In the next section, I discuss the concepts of work and career, with a look at how caste influences the
sexual division of labor briefly introduced above.

Caste, Class, Gender, and Women's Work

Srinivas (1978) defined caste as being hereditary and as having traditional
associations with a specific occupation. The root of caste representations is
based on cultural, moral, and social philosophies. Even though the caste
groups were created equal in status and dignity, the hierarchical division of
society led to barriers and a more consolidated institution of caste that came
to be predetermined in work, family, marriage, and social lives of everybody
concerned (Mohan, 1999). Mohan (1999) observed that caste structure gave
people psychological, social, and occupational stability but affected both
geographical and social mobility. Gradually, the distinction among the castes
became associated with division of labor justified on ideological and cultural
terms (Mohanty, 2004). Career choice and vocational pursuits came to be
decided at birth in a pre-determined occupational structure. Agency and conscious decision-making regarding picking a career of one's liking was absent
in such a society. One's family unit became the source of career preparation
and one's career aspirations came to revolve around one's limited world of
work and occupational set up.

An interface of caste, class, and gender and its importance to this study
can be illuminated through a brief summary of Mohanty's (2004) discussion
of the same in his book, *Class, Caste, Gender.* According to Mohanty (2004),
the image of women as dependent on men, mainly performing household
tasks, and as producing and raising children was enforced as a result of a long
period of the country's feudal and capitalist social history that looked upon
men as playing crucial roles in the society's production system and therefore
as yielding more power. This image came to be reinforced due to Hindu
scriptures and religious and caste ideologies with the latter gaining control
over women's labor. Desai and Krishnaraj (2004; also see Deshpande, 2011)

argue that caste not only determined social division of labor but also the sexual division of labor such that tasks came to be regarded as essentialized male and female jobs. Thus, the caste system not only legitimized the feudal relation of production existing at time, but also provided a justification for the subordination of women (Desai & Krishnaraj, 2004). This system was most discriminatory toward women of the upper and middle castes (Mohanty, 1999) not only in terms of what tasks they could or could not do but also in terms of restrictions on their behavior (Lebra et al., 1984). Moreover, it came to be considered a sign of prosperity and high social status if the women of a household did not work—it represented the ability of men to provide for their women. On the other hand, women of the lower-castes did not have an option. Even though the caste hierarchy confined them to specific tasks, they continued to work since their work status did not further condemn their social standing, or its lack thereof. However, Deshpande (2011) asserts that the caste-class dynamic has had interesting implications on the workforce participation of urban women. Upper-caste and upper class women have been consistently able to break away from social and cultural controls of their mobility, abandon traditional caste dictates, and successfully pursue higher education, professional ambitions, and navigate marriage choices.

Even as these transitions may be celebrated, it is important to remain mindful of caste's convoluted place in Indian women's history, occupational or otherwise. Dirks (2001) reminds us that:

> community is always segmented by class, gender, and region . . . that all claims about community are claims about privilege, participation, and exclusion. Caste has been the site of collisions between patriarchy and tradition; in its valorization of Brahmanic ideal around the status of women and the general subservience of women to marriage rules and domestic conditions, caste has simultaneously preserved the patriarchy of premodern society and worked to sanction the continued oppression and exclusion of women in nationalist reimaginings of the past . . . Caste may be the precipitate of the modern, but it is still the specter of the past. (pp 17–18)

It is with this knowledge above that I offer an overview into women's work histories below.

Tracing the Roots of Women's Work

Several scholars have argued against the existence of a representative Indian woman (e.g., Bijapurkar, 2007; Lebra et al., 1984; Nagaich, 1997). While the diversity of India on ethnic, religious, and linguistic lines, in addition to caste, and cultural norms has divided the women of this country, they are united by traditions and ideals (Lebra et al., 1984). In order to understand the

context of women's work today, it is important to learn the historical perspective from which their informed normative behaviors and feminine ideals
emerged.

It has been proposed that the Indus valley civilization (around 1500 BC),
before the advent of the Vedic Aryans into India, worshipped the Mother
Goddess and considered her as superior to a male deity. It is also speculated
that as a result, it may have been the case that a matrilineal system existed at
the time (Lebra et al., 1984). A matrilineal structure is evident among several
co-cultures and tribal groups in India even today. Women during the Vedic
age were known to have enjoyed a high position in family and society,
participated in religious rituals, got educated, married late, and pursued
knowledge and scholarship for its own sake (Nagaich, 1997). Persian and
Greek invaders who arrived from Central Asia in the years BC were considered the earliest Hindus. Baker (1990) posits that these northern Aryans
forced India's Dravidian inhabitants southwards. Thus gradually, with the
advent of Aryans who were also known to be patriarchal, the fabric of Indian
society began to change. In order to attain superiority over the existing pre-
Vedic Dravidians or the indigenous inhabitants, Aryans introduced the concept of hypergamy (marriage upward) for women to prevent intermarriage
with Dravidians.

These beliefs started manifesting themselves into more restrictions related
to ritual pollution, which is believed to have eventually led to the creation of
a caste system. Research indicates that Aryan women were prohibited from
marrying below their caste and a strict control of chastity and fidelity was
imposed, resulting in practices of child marriage, and *sati* (burning of a
widow on husband's funeral pyre). These restrictions were unyielding on
Brahmin women at the top of the caste hierarchy and if members of the
lower-castes desired to raise their lot in the hierarchy, they too had to adopt
these rigid mores. The process of people of the lower-castes adopting the
rituals, and practices of an upper-caste is known as *Sanskritization,* a term
first used by M. N. Srinivas (1978).

Even though the historic data on this issue is not clear, it is speculated that
soon after the status of women started deteriorating. Around 6 BC the privilege of performing religious ceremonies and rituals came to be reserved to
Brahmins. Sons became indispensable to the performing of religious rites
and sacrifices toward family ancestors and the existence of daughters became
a liability. Women were not permitted to attend religious functions as a result
of their "monthly pollution" (Lebra et al., 1984, p. 6). These restrictions,
along with the custom of dowry, made them economic, social, and cultural
liabilities, report Lebra and colleagues. It was only after giving birth to a son
that a woman could redeem herself in a patriarchal system, they argue. The
arrival and subsequent invasion of India by the Arabs and later by the Mu-
ghals in 16th century introduced Islam to India, which did little to change

women's status in society. The Mughal Empire remained in power until the arrival of Europeans in the 18th century.

In reviewing the history of women's work, Lebra and colleagues note that during India's colonized history under the British (and the French, Dutch, and Portuguese in some parts), several educated Indian elites worked for the betterment of women by bringing about social reforms. They assert that the Social Reform Movement in the 19th century and the Nationalist Movement in the 20th century were catalysts in spreading awareness of women's status and working toward bettering the position of women in Indian society and that Gandhi's mass mobilization of people during the independence struggle included women in large numbers. The authors note that Gandhi used his message of non-violence and *satyagraha*—"the search for truth through non-violent resistance" (Nagaich, 1997, p. 33) to appeal to what he believed was natural to women, given their ability to endure suffering and sacrifice (Lebra et al., 1984). In 1947, India won her independence from the British. Women had played an active role in the national struggle. Desai and Krishnaraj (2004) consider this pre-independence period as marking the "beginning of awareness of the suffering of women due to oppressive social customs" (p. 311). In other words, just prior to independence,

> an awareness of the need to remove social disabilities of women was created, the doors of education were opened for them; women's organizations emerged to represent the needs and cause of middle-class urban women; political partic-ipation of women increased women's mobility. Finally through several legal enactments, women's unequal position was being rectified. (Desai & Krishna-raj, 2004, p. 312)

The Indian Constitution that was promulgated three years after indepen-dence, in 1950, guaranteed equality to women. Soon after, additional acts were passed: the Hindu Marriage Act, 1955; the Special Marriage Act, 1954, permitting secular and mixed marriages; the Hindu Succession Act, 1956, providing sons, daughters, widow/mother equal share to inheritance; Dowry Prohibition Act, 1961; and Termination of Pregnancy Act, 1972, legalizing abortion.

Women and Work in Independent India

Independence and legislation, however, did little to eradicate caste-based hierarchies and bring about any material changes in the lives of women. As has been mentioned earlier, the normative restrictions on upper-caste women were stricter than they were for their lower-caste sisters. Working for pay, for an upper-caste woman, was blasphemous and demeaning to the family. The norms that affected their work for pay outside their homes were severely influenced by their position in the caste hierarchy and social stratification

(D'Aluisio & Menzel, 1996; Deshpande, 2011; Raju & Bagchi, 1993). In fact, "exclusion of females from the labour force outside the familial domain" was a symbol of high social status (Raju & Bagchi, 1993, p. 21). Not governed by the social taboos that applied to upper-caste women, lower-caste women, led by the need of poverty alleviation, took up any work they could get (Bardhan, 1993; Desai & Krishnaraj, 2004). The ability to work, however menial the job may be, according to Lebra et al. (1984), gave these women economic advantage over upper-caste women.

In the rural areas, women's work became largely restricted to agriculture (cultivation, weeding, and harvesting), and home-based jobs (such as making handicrafts, pottery, and basket weaving, among others), even though technological changes and modernization have reduced the demand for such labor in recent times (Lebra et al., 1984; Nagaich, 1997). Illiteracy and a lack of awareness of their constitutional rights often put these women at a disadvantage. For example, the Equal Remuneration Act of 1976 provides equal pay for equal work, for men and women including in the informal sector, and yet because women's income is seen as insignificant and supplementary to that of men's (B. N. Singh, 1989), even today, in such occupations as mentioned above, the pay discrimination is quite high. In the urban areas, due to education and an awareness of their rights, women have generally been treated better. Even though women make a disappointing 62% of the salary men earn (Inderfurth & Khambatta, 2012), there has been a steady growth in women's employment in white-collar jobs (Nagaich, 1997) when jobs have been available. Women working in urban areas in organized occupations have the benefit of not only a labor legislation that employers are more conscious of observing, they are also relatively better paid than their sisters in the informal economy, have better access to child care and health services, and a stronger family support system (Lebra et al., 1984).

As urban Indian society became more progressive, upper-caste women started engaging in occupations that gave them little scope for vertical mobility or promotions (Raju & Bagchi, 1993) so as not to ruffle too many sociocultural feathers at the same time. Upper-caste women's employment engagement was allowed within the confines of limited mobility. In other words, these women could only engage in "respectable" jobs such as teaching and medicine that did not require them to relocate or travel for work (Bardhan, 1993). Raju and Bagchi (1993) succinctly summarize the discussion above:

> [I]n the South Asian context, mere presence of economic opportunities is inadequate in explaining the extent and nature of female participation in the labour force; b) while poverty and related attributes may enforce females to enter the labour market, the extent to which they can do so is constrained by their memberships of particular caste, community and religious groups; c)

however, the extent to which caste assumes importance depends upon the class/caste overlap: in situations where this overlap is substantial, caste identities cease to be very important and vice versa; further, existing caste mores can be reinforced/modified by the presence of certain religious groups and/or communities; and d) notwithstanding localised specific details, an overall regional context is vital in explaining the broad regional variation in female workforce participation. (pp. 24–25)

Nature of Women's Work

Traditionally, a majority of India's working women have been employed in the unorganized or informal sector in both rural and urban areas, a fact that holds true even today. Over the years, however, Indian women have been stepping out of their homes to work in culturally respectable occupations such as teaching, medicine, and social work, considered the organized, formal sector. Because of changes in legislation, and a dynamic society where very slowly but surely normative control over women's behaviors began to relax, more and more urban women started entering into the workforce, stepping beyond their traditional roles as wives and mothers (Liddle & Joshi, 1989). Dhawan's (2005) paper on Indian women's role expectations and identity development proposes that Indian society is undergoing a restructuring as it reorients itself to the new roles of women. This was not always the case and, in many ways, perhaps, is still not. Taking a different view from scholars who argue that the position of Indian women is improving as a result of evidence from rising levels of education, paid employment, and declining fertility rates in some states, Kapadia (2002b) asserts that women's access to education and jobs has been limited compared to men, and therefore such positive indicators of women's progress may not necessarily be accurate.

Banerjee (2002) argues that although women belonging to the poorest classes in India enjoy greater physical mobility and personal autonomy, they are restricted to low-income jobs as a result of a lack of education, even as a small section of urban women have used availability of education and training to have successful careers in the "professions, in the public services, and even in business" (p. 58). The visibility of these middle-class women in public arenas is not surprising, she says, because "middle-class parents of girls, especially in large cities, are aware of the fast expanding opportunities for lucrative careers that are now open to qualified young people" (p. 58).

The visibility of middle-class women in public spaces, however, is not a complete indication of women's participation in the labor force. Depending on one's social status and position, women continue to get a raw deal in the labor market. In fact, Banerjee (2002) argues the reason women continue to be economically disadvantaged is because of the "tight controls that families still impose on their bodies, their sexuality and their labour" (p. 54). In other words, even though middle-class parents may "allow" their daughters to work, the women are constrained by the familial and societal mores imposed on their choices of jobs. Therefore, as a result of their location in the class structure, and the traditions, training, and socialization imparted to them, women remain disadvantaged when entering the work force (Banerjee, 2002).

Several scholars have argued how development and modernization of an economy, including through globalization, is detrimental to women's economic growth and progress (e.g., A. Datta, 2005; Mazumdar, 2007; Pande, 2007; Ruether, 2005). Despite the negatives that an emerging phenomenon or development process brings with it, one cannot deny the emergence of a "new" Indian woman amidst all the brouhaha that has been enveloping India since the beginning of the 21st century.

The "New" Indian Woman

In educated, urban India, the status of working women is changing rapidly if popular media reports are to be believed. The question regarding "Who is the 'new' 21st century Indian woman?" is what this discussion hopes to answer.

Women in India have been "worshipped as divine, celebrated as mother, eulogized as martyr, and devalued systematically," reflecting "ancient, mythological prescriptions" (Hegde, 1995, p. 177) of the Indian society. Given these parameters, it is interesting to note that the 21st century Indian woman has been found to indulge in guilt-free materialism, renegotiate parental ties, disregard norms of an appropriate marital age, and pursue single-minded careerism (*BusinessWeek*, 2005*)*. Bharadwaj (2007b) observes that with the growth of the BPO and biotechnology industries, India's women are no longer content teaching or "living the office receptionist cliché." They want careers and are willing to go the extra mile by attending vocational training schools. In the process of reaching for their ambitions, they are not discouraged by the head start men have had over them and they are willing to dispel the traditional mindset of women's careers as temporary detours on the destined road to marriage, observes Bharadwaj. Even though these journalistic reports do not specify the particular caste or class of the interviewed women, based on cultural understanding it is not difficult to imagine that these stories mostly relate to women from the middle- and upper classes.

Undeterred by the traditionally dictated norms of appropriate occupations for women, urban, educated women of today are taking up unconventional professions into which girls from "decent" families were previously not allowed (Sengupta, 2007). In marriages and other relationships, Indian women are increasingly taking a dialogical approach as opposed to one of non-confrontational acceptance, delaying marriages, postponing motherhood, and not shying from being primary petitioners in divorce cases (Vasudev, 2005). As daughters, they are vocal on several issues. They want to continue to care for their parents after marriage. Typically, active caregiving of parents ceased to occur once daughters were married off; then it was their job to take care of their in-laws, making the parental desire for a son that much more relevant. Women also want to understand their inheritance rights and are not afraid of lighting the father's funeral pyre (something only sons could do) (Bala, 2003; Vajpeyi, 2003) blurring at once, "social, emotional, religious, and familial" (Vasudev, 2005, para. 4) boundaries.

Writing in the early 1980s, Lebra et al. (1984) had commented about how virtually every Indian woman marries. Today, one can easily argue that nearly every Indian woman works (paid employment). With delayed marriages, the group of single women who rearrange their priorities based on what *they* want, are termed by Bharadwaj (2007a) as EVES, short for Employed, Very Educated Single women. She defines these women as:

> professionals who are putting off marriage to pursue career ambitions. Armed with a degree, they are 'work gypsies' by choice and follow promising job opportunities to new cities where they set up home. It is the final step towards real independence-a life where they are their own chief wage earners as well as moral guardians. (para.1)

In order to stay competitive and be taken seriously in what continues to be a male-dominated workforce, these EVES underplay their vulnerabilities by projecting an assertive, gender-neutral manner, a strong personality, picking up strong language, and developing interests in traditional male interests such as sports and automobiles (Bharadwaj, 2007a). Thus, it is a brave new world for women who seek that adventure and want to capitalize on the rising opportunities for young women in a growing economy. At heart and in essence, however, this urban, educated Indian woman continues to remain very much Indian as demonstrated by "independence with social acceptance, success and autonomy that set its boundaries but do not require a complete break from the traditional, extended, semi-feudal family structure" (Divakaruni, 2005, para. 2). A decade earlier, Hegde (1995) had concluded her analysis of *Femina*'s (an Indian women's magazine mostly targeted at working women) portrayals of women achievers, an observation that still applies today.

> Achievers all epitomize the new Indian professional woman, a woman who is aware, assertive, and more vocal. Collectively, women have found places in their respective fields and share traits of motivation for and commitment to work. She is a superwoman reincarnated but not in the traditional sense, and she is busy, integrated, unflappable, and controlled. Women who have entered male-dominated fields—as scientist, pilot, electrical engineer, veterinarian, slum developer, doctor, educator, social worker, small business entrepreneur—are featured. They are from elite ranks, and each emphasizes that she has faced no professional discrimination. Given their background, they depart sig-

nificantly from the experiences of ordinary women. Hence, a sense of dissocia-
tion from others permeates the discourses about them. They seem to return to
the fold, however, when they discuss the barriers society erects in their lives
and the mythological models of womanhood that exert control over their personal and social interactions (Chowdhury, 1990, p. 185)

In Hegde's analysis above, it is apparent that a new and professional woman
exists, in all her multiple manifestations. As has always been the case with
Indian women, this woman does not represent all working women and has
obvious differences between her and her other less advantaged sisters.

The economic reforms introduced into the country in the 1990s integrated
a liberalized Indian economy with world capitalism, bringing sweeping
changes in the lives of middle- and upper-class Indians, while devastating the
lives of the poor, the unskilled, and the uneducated, especially women, by
increased economic and social exploitation (Mazumdar, 2007). Mazumdar
argues that much of the celebration of globalization among the business and
middle-class Indians has been based on the employment of a different class
of women in new forms of IT-enabled services. These forms of employment
in the digital age posits Mazumdar (2007), "are seen by globalizers as being
singularly important for employment generation as well as in terms of the
potential to transform India from a still largely backward and overwhelming-
ly poor country into the 'superpower' league" (p. xxii). However, in reality,
such employment, particularly at call centers, with its night shifts, cultural
degradation as a result of employees' having to learn new accents, and take
on "new" names, constant work surveillance, health hazards, and burnout, is
evidence more of corporate colonization (Deetz, 1992) and hardly a cause for
celebration (see Basu, 2006; Freeman, 2001; Mazumdar, 2007; Pal & Buzzanell, 2008; Shome, 2006; Townsley, 2006). Mazumdar (2007) puts the above
employment trend among women into perspective:

> The overall picture that emerges from the studies points to the emergence of
> multilayered contradictions in the sphere of paid work by women. On the one
> hand, some processes associated with globalized organization of production
> have led to the drawing in of women into forms of employment to which they
> might earlier not have had such access, but such a phenomenon has tended to
> be highly circumscribed by the larger trend of falling work participation rates
> among women and higher levels of unemployment. (p. xxiii)

Thus, it appears that while globalization, seen as represented in the form of
the boom in IT-enabled services, has opened new avenues for educated wom-
en in cities, the other side of globalization, which is represented by mechani-
zation and opening up of international food chains and products, among
others, has almost eliminated the jobs of poor, uneducated women. There is
no denying that globalization has provided numerous opportunities, but the

provision of these opportunities has advantaged the educated women while being disproportionately unfair on the employment of poor women within the same local urban setting.

As opposed to the argument about the loss of employment for poor women made above, Datta (2005) uses a unique lens to show how globalization is leading to a McDonaldization of gender relations, which in turn is leading to an increase in the demand for the services of unskilled and semi-skilled women. Although Datta's concern does not specifically align with employment issues for women employed in the unorganized sector, her explication of the McDonaldization principles in urban India, support the above claim. In an insightful article titled "MacDonaldization[2] of Gender in Urban India," Datta (2005) posits that just as society is getting McDonaldized as a result of traditional lifestyles giving way to the four tenets of efficiency, calculability, predictability, and control (Ritzer, 2004), gender relations are being renegotiated, making room for more "'efficient,' modern and MacDonaldized roles" (Datta, 2005, p. 126). Acquisition of power, prestige, and status in high-level corporate jobs is only available to women with specific skill sets, and so as they compete to stay ahead in the corporate world, fighting the glass ceiling along the way, women, along with men, are becoming "increasingly sterile, dehumanized, technology driven and demanding" (p. 130). As a result of their need to be in public spaces, there is a growing need to hire the services of housemaids, cooks, caregivers and so on to take care of the domestic realm, thereby McDonaldizing household tasks. The argument has been made that the lives of upper-class urban women are possible because of the services of lower-class women (Qayum & Ray, 2003; Uberoi, 2005;) and even though there is no other research to back it up, not many Indians will deny this fact. Through McDonaldization then, Datta (2005) shows how globalization may just have helped the lower class of women as well.

It is evident that there is a distinct lower class of poor, uneducated women working in unskilled or semi-skilled jobs, most likely to also belong to lower-castes, and a dominant middle-class that has now begun to send its daughters to work in public spaces. There also exists a class of women who are either employed at senior-level positions in organizations or are entrepreneurs running their own businesses. It is quite possible that women employed in these positions hail from the middle-class but have proactively risen a few levels above their class at birth due to their position in high-income occupations.

In order to streamline the process of categorizing the participants of this study into pre-determined occupational classifications, their inclusion into the categories was based on their income-tax bracket as designated by the Government of India. Although these ranges have changed slightly and will be clarified later in the chapter, during the time the study was conducted, the following levels were applicable. There is no tax levied on those earning[3]

Rs.150,000 or less ($3000). The three categories of income-tax structures in India are meant for those earning between Rs.150,001 and 300,000 (between $3,001 and $6,000), those earning between Rs.300,001 and Rs.500,000 (between $6,001 and $10,000), and finally those earning Rs.500,001 and above ($10,001 and above). People in each of these three categories are taxed at the rate of 10%, 20%, and 30% respectively (Key features, 2008).

Women earning less than $3,000 a year are typically employed in the low-income, marginalized occupations, often collectively known as the informal sector. Those earning between $3,001 and $10,000 are employed in middle-income occupations such as teaching, journalism, and social work, while those earning over $10,001 are employed in professional occupations in corporate India, or as doctors, business owners, IT professionals, and so on. For the project, the specific income of women is only important to the extent of categorizing them into one of the three groups.

Next, I detail the occupational engagement of India's working women, from the informal sector to the formal. It should be noted that in most discussions, only the informal and formal sectors exist. For the purpose of this project, the formal sector is divided into two categories (middle-income and high income), thus classifying the occupational engagement of women as: women in low-income occupations, women in middle-income occupations, and women in high-income occupations.

OCCUPATIONAL ENGAGEMENT OF INDIAN WOMEN

Women in low-income occupations

The International Conference of Labour Statisticians (ICLS) uses three criteria to determine informal sector enterprises; non-registration of the enterprise, its small size, and the non-registration of its employees. Hussmanns and Mehran (n.d.) summarize the ICLS's definition of an informal sector as,

> production units that are owned and operated by single individuals working on own-account as self-employed persons, either alone or with the help of unpaid family members. The activities may be undertaken inside or outside the business owner's home; they may be carried out in identifiable premises or without fixed location. (p. 2)

Hussmanns and Mehran (n. d.) admit that countries have usually used variations in how they choose to define their own informal sector. In general, the informal sector has become a "defining feature of underdevelopment. . . . [It has become] synonymous with the kaleidoscope of unregulated, poor skilled and low-paid workers that the observer encounters when walking through the streets of towns and cities in developing countries" (Mazumdar, 2007, pp.

36-37). Its visibility is in stark contrast to the formal sector "characterized by regular and written contracts and therefore subject to state regulation" (Mazumdar, 2007, p. 37). The informal sector is also characterized by little use of technology, long and grueling hours of work often under unhygienic and hazardous conditions, fairly simple production processes, low need for education or specific skills, ease of entry, flexible work contracts, low capital investment, and almost no scope for upward mobility (Breman, 1999; Kantor, 2002; Mazumdar, 2007; Mitra, 2005; Rao, 1996).

The informal sector in India employs over 90% of all working women in both rural and urban areas. The high number of women is a result of this sector providing flexibility of work hours and location, where women can continue to work while minding social norms and taking care of children. The informal workers do not necessarily work in conventional organizations. According to the International Development Research Centre (IDRC), the occupational locations for workers of the informal sector are: dwellings such as their own homes or those of their employers; open spaces such as streets, construction sites, and door-to-door; and unregistered premises such as workshops and stores ("The changing", n.d.). These quasi-organizational structures and alternative work settings provide unique locations and spatial arrangements within which to understand the world of women's work.

Even though gender differentials in pay are typical across occupations in India, it is particularly evident in the informal sector. Even when extraordinary skills or high levels of education are not required, women continue to get the low end of the pay scale. Kantor (2002) posits that women are unable to avail themselves of all the economic opportunities available to them, even in the informal sector. Kantor bases her argument on differences between women intensive and women exclusive constraints. *Women intensive* constraints refer to their poverty and powerlessness, which affect both sexes but are more pronounced for women due to unequal gender status. Women therefore become constrained by their lack of access to productive resources such as tools, equipment, technology, credit, and information. *Women exclusive* constraints are specific to women since they refer to the macro level, sociocultural norms that affect women because of their gender. Both women inclusive and women exclusive constraints work together to impose restrictions and limits on women's occupations in the informal sector.

Studies conducted on women working in mines, construction sites, traditional crafts production, garment industries, and *beedi* (small cigars) making, have consistently reported how they are exploited by their employers and the middle men in charge of negotiating their wage/item of production (Acharya, 2003; Ahmad & Lahiri-Dutt, 2006; Ghatak, 2006; Kakad, 2002). Most laws, given the contractual or temporary nature of their work, do not protect women working in the informal sector. Even if awareness does exist about the applicability of certain laws, they are neither observed by employers nor demanded by the workers. Because of a surplus of available labor in these occupations, the odds are stacked heavily against the women workers who can easily be replaced by others who do not demand a higher wage, better hours, or safe working conditions (Banerjee, 2002). Sociocultural norms also dictate how women get treated in these occupations. For example, the notion of a woman's "impurity" due to the "monthly pollution" (Lebra et al., 1984, p. 6) or menstruation marginalizes women in the construction industry.

> Constructing a new building is considered auspicious; and under the pretext that women are impure, they are not allowed to work in the main areas; and neither are they allowed to touch the stones, bricks, etc. (building materials), or the tools of the mason. Traditionally, this attitude has had a strong presence. In this day and age it survives as a way to keep women outside the male preserve of skilled work, as women in reality do continue to touch building materials as well as work as helpers in almost all trades in the construction industry. (Kakad, 2002, p. 361)

Women in this sector face the triple burden of "reproductive work, productive work, and managing work" (Mitra, 2005, p. 294), implying the demand on both their private and public realms. Women are aware of the unfair treatment. In a study aimed at understanding the level of social awareness among female construction workers, participants reported doing more work than their husbands as a result of having to work on the construction site as well as at home. However, they continued to believe that it was their primary responsibility to do the household work and justified a gendered division of labor (Mathew, 2005).

In conclusion, women working in India's informal sector, who constitute a majority of the country's female labor force, face a number of economic, physical, emotional, political, and sociocultural constraints not only about their choice of work but also about how they are able to experience that choice. Studies such as those by Mazumdar (2007), Mitra (2005), and Carr, Chen, and Tate (2000) highlight the disadvantages of women in the informal sector.

Women in middle-income occupations

As India opened its markets and welcomed direct foreign investment, jobs for educated, urban women increased and middle-class women did not hesitate to avail of these opportunities. Dasgupta (1998) observes that the participation of women in white collar professions other than teaching, nursing, and medicine, is largely a 20th century phenomenon that arrived at a time when women were no longer satisfied having their economic status defined by that of their fathers, husbands, or sons. Even though respectable occupations such as teaching and social work continue to be dominated by women, the IT-enabled job market of the 21st century, which offered more lucrative options with flexible hours and higher pay, led to an increase in the number of female employees in this industry.

Parikh and Engineer (2002) provide insight into the work lives of middle-class women across generations. Their study involved first generation women who entered the workforce in the 1950s and 1960s, second generation women who entered the workforce in the 1970s and 1980s, and third generation women who entered the workplace in the 1990s and beyond. Their study reveals interesting findings and supports the contextual nature of women's work in India.

According to Parikh and Engineer (2002), born at a time when it was unheard of for women to work, the first generation of working women beat the odds with the support of their encouraging parents or were forced into paid employment by circumstances. Despite no female role models and a constant threat of societal disparage, these women took a courageous decision to step out of their domestic confinements.

Ready to get into the workplace in the 1970s and 1980s, much of the work for women of the second generation was already done by the pioneer women of the first. By this time, it was acceptable for women to work in Indian society. Even though women had not started entering the workforce in as large numbers yet, their numbers were significant and visibility of women in the workplace was clear. While the first generation of women entered the workforce despite societal censure, women of the second generation often dealt with societal paradoxes, which, while slowly opening up to women's new economic status, also made the women feel guilty about their potential neglect on the home front. Of course, this may have been an issue with the first generation of working women as well.

Women working in the 70s and 80s had grown up educated, had seen other women work, were aware of their own aspirations, and were willing to put in the hard work and time required to deliver results. This generation of women had to deal with "male chauvinists, resentful elderly women who had scoffed at the pioneers of their own age, of their own era, [and] the jealous women of the same generation who had not [sic] the opportunity to work" (p. 9). In other words, "the paradigm had been changed forever by the pioneers, but the societal infrastructure and the societal transformation necessary to support the new paradigm was not in place" (Parikh and Engineer, 2002, p. 9). It was also during this time that the image of a woman as someone who should and perhaps could do it all, have a career and be a successful home-maker emerged, imposing additional stressors and expectations on these women. The third generation of women who entered the workforce in the 1990s were "relatively less burdened by the baggage of the past, less steeped in legacy, with less need to rebel and adopt reactionary stances" (p. 10). Given that the generations of working women before them had challenged societal norms and consolidated a position for other women entering into the workforce, this generation of women could afford the luxury of choosing to work for self-expression.

The above taxonomy of generations of India's working women does not apply to all Indian women equally. The generalizations are only applicable to educated, middle, upper-middle, and upper classes of women in urban India.

Empirical studies have found that women in middle-income occupations such as teachers, including professors, and librarians, continue to face discrimination at various levels and of various kinds in the course of their career trajectories. The gendered division of labor in India, with its traditional roots in caste-based occupational segregation, along with limited access to education, as well as other social, cultural, historical, and economic factors, has continued to discriminate against women in terms of the kinds of jobs that are "appropriate" for women (Eapen, 2004). Furthermore, women's hiring, career advancement, and wage structure, argues Eapen (2004) are "couched in terms of the generalised social commitment to women's domesticity, arguing additionally that women are secondary earners with husbands to support them and their children" (p. 8), an argument also made to justify unfair pay practices in the informal sector.

Also, as has been argued before, some women justify such discriminatory behavior toward them as socially understandable. The kinds of justification apparent in such cases are a result of gendered socialization and parental attitudes toward work and careers. For example, sons in Indian families are expected to use their education toward career advancement while daughters are provided an education in order to make them independent (Gupta, 2007). Furthermore, education for women was considered more for the purposes of an "enlightened motherhood" (Chanana, 1994) than for individual learning and growth. Using education to make girls independent often translates into using education as a form of "security" in case of marital issues in the future, helping girls attain personal status, and making successful marriages (Sandhu & Mehta, 2007). The focus is thus on familial relationships, rather than career development, and women may themselves embrace this hierarchy.

A factor that forces women to unwittingly favor family over careers perhaps is the lack of validation available in the workplace. A study on women faculty members (Chanana, 2003) at elite Indian universities found that despite there being no formal gendered division of labor with regard to teaching, research, or administration, female faculty were hired at a lower rank (assistant) than male faculty (associate) even when the women had a considerable number of teaching and research experiences, publications, and uninterrupted careers. Women faculty who were also administrators were often overlooked for promotions because of a lack of their visibility in social networking and professional development programs. Because promotions tended to be based on networking, publications, and professional development (in that order), men who focused more on the first and the last often got promoted ahead of the women because of their visible presence.

While men were free to engage in professional meetings, women's desire to be more visible at such events contradicted with the societal and familial restrictions on mobility and household work expectations. Issues pertaining to the disadvantages faced by women as a result of exclusionary behaviors of certain social networks have also been explored in the United States (e.g., Allen, 2000; Fernandez, 1981; T. Holder, 1996; Shenoy-Packer & Myers, 2013). In India, the problem may not arise so much from the social network itself as much as it may from the patriarchal structure of society that disapproves the mingling of women from respectable households, particularly married women, with other men, including colleagues, without a chaperone. Additionally, traveling for work, taking field trips to job sites, working late at night and such activities that are often pertinent to the job and future prospects in the organization may be difficult for women to fulfill due to the reasons cited above. While men are unrestricted in these behaviors, Chanana found that if a woman does choose to ignore societal norms, idle chat and gossip about her "character" are not uncommon. As a result, the woman's family as well as the woman herself may choose to keep a distance from male colleagues in social settings and avoid travel to maintain their respect and integrity as educated, professional women from good families (see Budhwar, Saini, Bhatnagar, 2005) thereby reinforcing stereotypes, a gendered hierarchy, and perpetuating professionally biased oppression and discrimination.

It is important to note that even though some of the observations and findings from previous studies discussed above appear to be dated and more appropriate to an older generation of female workers, more recent findings continue to assert the significance of familial and socio-cultural barriers to women's advancement (e.g., Budhwar et al., 2005; Gupta & Sharma, 2003). In fact, a recent study by Haq (2013) found that the intersectional and complex layers of life that define an Indian working woman—her gender, color, caste, religion, marital status, class, and ethnicity—continue to pose challenges in "personal and professional development by being undervalued, underemployed, and under-rewarded" (p. 171). The changes noted in the work lives, ambitions, and acceptance of Indian working women in the discussion above, while apparent, are perhaps so gradual that they do not yet make for a generalizable and declarative statement on the current status of these women. Meanwhile, data and findings from almost three decades ago may still ring true for women today. For example, participants in Liddle and Joshi's (1989) study made sense of their restricted mobility in four ways. First, the women could not travel because of the lack of facilities such as sanitary facilities, a safe place to sleep, and other factors. Second, despite their paid employment they could not disregard their household responsibilities, including their responsibilities to maintain traditional gendered relations. These gendered dynamics meant that husbands would not permit them to go on trips with other men. Third, the lack of safety was another issue, where fear of sexual assault, meeting strange men, and being away from one's familiar surroundings was not something the women necessarily wanted to do. Finally, the notion of morality, which women feel responsible to uphold at all times, meant that these women had to preserve women's status as the guardians of morality in Indian society and not perform actions that might besmirch this image. As can be seen below, the findings from the 1989 study above are not far removed from the findings from the more recent study below. In the case of the female faculty members, travel to national and international conferences, professional development workshops, and mingling with male colleagues outside of work was severely restricted, resulting in a combination of societal and systemic barriers to their advancement. The unfortunate state of women's careers in academia is summed up by Chanana (2003) as, "Women's careers thus tend to start at the lowest end, move up slowly, sometimes result in promotions against the odds but ultimately culminate with retirement on very low salaries" (p. 385).

While teaching has traditionally been a preferred occupation for women, it now appears to be making way for IT-related jobs. I have discussed the increasing number of women in IT-enabled service occupations several times before. Employment in the IT and IT-enabled services may be construed as middle/high-income occupations depending on the particular position one holds in the organization, but even this increase in numbers is not without its issues. Surely these services have opened the doors for educated urban women wanting to work, however, even within what appear to be equal opportunity occupations, a new category of "women's work" is created where lower status jobs get relegated to women (Eapen, 2004). This is evidenced in women making up 60% of call services jobs, and only 6% making it as project managers (see D. Nath, 2000; Suriya, 2003). In the more advanced professions such as computer software programming, however, Ilavarasan (2006) found that women's experience of job performance, kinds and quality of jobs assigned, and hours worked did not differ from those of men.

The working of women has undeniably altered their lives, including in positive ways. While in the informal sector, women may tend to hand over all of their meager income to their husbands and continue to have a lower status than the male in the family (Mathew, 2005), the status of women in middle-income occupations has definitely improved. Despite continuing to do a disproportionate amount of household work (which has not changed), women now reported engagement in paid employment as making them assertive, equal partners in decision making in the household, being valued more, and as providing a sense of dignity and accomplishment (see Andrade, Postma, & Abraham, 1999; Bijapurkar, 2007; Dutta, 2000; Liddle & Joshi, 1989; Yadav & Kumar, 2007).

The paradoxes in the discussion above and the review of middle-income Indian women once again presents the contradictory scenario of India's working women. India, with a growing economy, centuries old set of culture and traditional values, has only had a little over 65 years of independence to make a current history. Having opened its markets to liberalization leading to globalization and internationalization less than two decades ago, India still has a lot of challenges in its path as it struggles to maintain the old with the new. Of course, such incessant merging of the old and the new is not novel to India, given its history of invasion by foreign rulers. However, in the current global market place, India has had to grow up sooner than time could afford and that has meant taking the women of this country—who have lagged behind men in most spheres, not by choice, but by societal and cultural dictates—along with it.

Women in high-income occupations

In reviewing the literature on India's female managers, professionals, and corporate honchos, the discussion of caste, an inextricable narrative in the work lives of low-income and middle-income women, was conspicuous by its absence. Is one supposed to assume that this construct no longer plays a role in the lives of high-income women? Perhaps. Scholars like Nijman (2006), Das (2002, 2006), and others have argued that caste has given way to the emergence of class-based social hierarchies. Research on women in high-income managerial, professional, and such other occupations instead, covers issues like workplace attitudes, behaviors, discrimination, superior-subordinate relationships, and stress. Gender bias and stereotypes, barriers to women's advancement to senior-level positions, work-life balance, and exclusion of women from informal networks, are other areas of investigation. Of course, no discussion on Indian women and work can avoid societal, cultural, and familial expectations and norms altogether; and so even though such topics are not the primary concern of researchers, they certainly play a role in providing an overall picture. These normative structures for everyday living often create challenges in the workplace.

The paradoxical status with which Indian women have always had to live (Budhwar, et al., 2005) naturally follows them into the modern workplace. Entry into the workplace is determined by factors such as levels of education, English-speaking abilities, and encouragement (or the lack thereof) of family members. Even though in the past decade girls may have been educated for reasons other than career development, middle-class families, who are most affected by the dynamic changes in Indian society (see Budhwar et al., 2005; Ganguly-Scrase, 2003) now encourage their daughters to seek education and avail themselves of equal employment opportunities (Nath, 2000). Thus, the women entering into the urban workforce belong predominantly to the middle and upper middle-class which gives these women a certain edge.

In addition to the "privilege of class" (Nath, 2000, p. 46) that professional women enjoy, Liddle and Joshi (1989) observe that education and parents'— especially fathers' employment and income—influence women's education and employment. That the new economy's work situation is most suitable for educated, middle- and upper-middle-class women has already been established. Suriya (2003) notes that this point is even more poignant in the IT industry where rural women, even if they are educated, are not particularly favored because of their lack of expertise in English. The English-speaking criterion that consequently favors the upper-classes of socially and economically advantaged women automatically makes such opportunities impossible for women of lower classes and rural areas who have not had the resources or opportunities to study English. In an insightful article titled, "Diagnosing and Remedying Backwardness: English Education Defines the New Brahmins and the New Dalits of India," Madhu Purnima Kishwar (2006), founder and editor of *Manushi*, an Indian journal aimed at bringing about social, economic, and politically informed activism, observes, "There are not many other countries in the world where people suffer such severe deprivation and disability within their own motherland for having failed to acquire education in a foreign language" (p. 6).

In a society where the traditional and modern attempt to operate together at all times, in almost every situation, the affixing of gender stereotypes to women in the workplace is common. This is true of women in most workplaces in India. However, it is more prominent when women are in positions of authority, having to manage and delegate responsibilities to male subordinates. Gupta, et al. (1998) found that men assign stereotypes to their women superiors by perceiving them as emotional, less self-confident, and less objective in evaluating business situations. Participants felt that the women were power grabbers who did not empower their subordinates. Gupta et al., (1998) also found that while employees of both sexes were hired based on merit, when it was time for advancement decisions, salary raises, and promotions, gender invariably played a huge role. Pregnancy and, subsequently, motherhood, also meant that women are perceived as less desirable employees. Examples of these differential treatments of women in the workplace are apparent in most organizations—one such being Air India. Air India, the country's national airline, has mandatory annual/biennial medical tests for its female flight attendants and cabin crew. If they are found to be overweight, women are "grounded" or assigned to ground duty. Men do have to get weighed every six months, but no matter how overweight they are not only *not* put through regular medical tests but are also never grounded solely for that reason (Fat air-hostesses, 2008). Another example comes from the Indian government's new appraisal forms for female civil servants (those employed in the Indian Administrative Services) that required them to provide a detailed menstrual history, a history of their last menstrual period, and the last time they availed of maternity leave (India re-assesses, 2007). Given the heavy criticism this form received, the government finally dropped the requirement.

Discrimination, subtle or explicit, has not discouraged women from continuing to enter the workforce and the private sector is now largely preferred over the job security offered by governmental jobs. Salary, responsibilities, and interesting work continue to motivate women to work despite some obvious barriers (Singh, 2002). India's younger generation of "worldly women" (BusinessWeek, 2005) is not afraid of grabbing the opportunities that a growing India has to offer. More and more women are prioritizing their lives by giving precedence to careers over family, postponing marriage, preferring to stay single to pursue career aspirations, charting unconventional careers, choosing to delay motherhood or only having one child, male or female, to facilitate a better work-life balance, unafraid to move to other cities and live alone or with roommates to pursue careers, and defy traditional roles as submissive daughters, wives, and mothers (Bharadwaj, 2007a, 2007b; *BusinessWeek*, 2005; Butalia, 2007; Datta, Krishnamurthy, David, Sen, & Pai, 2007; Pai, et al., 2007; Singh, 2002; Vasudev, 2005).

Discrimination is prevalent in corporate India and the upper echelons of most professions. However, Indian-based operations of multinational companies such as GE, Pepsi, Coca-Cola, Motorola, and Accenture, are among the few who are taking concerted efforts toward providing inclusive corporate environments for women. For example, GE launched the GE Women's Network in 1997 to provide opportunities for women to interact with GE leaders, and attend seminars, networking dinners, and workshops to exchange views and information, and as a matter of policy, it does not hire from campuses with less than 20% female candidates (Agrawal, 2006). ICICI, an Indian company with a gender-neutral work environment and highly supportive of female employees, currently has Chandra Kocchar, a woman, as its managing director and CEO (David & Alexander, 2011). Merely increasing the number of women in upper management as a solution to gender diversity has been criticized by scholars such as P. Buzzanell (1995). However, in the Indian situation, this increase in the number of females at top corporate positions should be considered as a first generation change toward inclusivity and diversity, the beginning of awareness of gendered organizations and organizational practices, and a change in the right direction.

As was seen in the case of low-income and middle-income earning women, the category of women working in high-income generating occupations is also beset with contradictions. With each level of income, it appears that societal, familial, and cultural norms, though still very much prevalent, become weakened or at least more negotiable. Women in this category have much to celebrate and have certainly come a long way. However, one could still argue that the destination was never that beyond reach in the first place for these women, with the advantage of middle- or upper-middle-class upbringing, supportive families, and education in English, on their side. Lucas (2006) supports this argument by summarizing the work of Perucchi and Wysong (2003) and saying, "members of the privileged class, in addition to financial resources, offer their children the social and cultural capital that will ensure their successful entry into specific occupations and/or organizations" (p. 43). Clearly, those fortunate enough to have been born in the middle or upper-middle classes already have the social, economic, cultural, and even political capital needed to enable their career aspirations.

In concluding this section, I once again reiterate the near impossibility of generalizing the case of any one category of women across all women of that category or even to all Indian working women. Studying the lives of Indian women, be it about their work or any other aspect, is not possible without understanding the myriad contexts from within which their situations emerge. Female lives are contested and paradoxically intertwined between the dialectics of tradition and modern, global and local, rural and urban, social and individual, and unquestioned compliance and individual agency.

THEORETICAL FRAMEWORK

Buzzanell (1995) asserts that "feminist perspectives provide us with epistemological, ontological, and methodological approaches to investigate women's everyday lives" (p. 344) by offering opportunities "to create theory and research which enable us to think about how we recreate gender relations socially, historically, and culturally" (P. Buzzanell, 1994, p. 339). I also believe that gender ideologies—"belief systems of separate spheres and social meanings of masculinity and femininity that are negotiated in families, workplaces, and organizational and social contexts" (P. Buzzanell, 1994, p. 342)—are indeed socially constructed. This assertion makes it all the more imperative that we understand the socio-cultural conditions, historical contexts, and contemporary phenomena that influence women's constructions of their work lives as elaborated in the sections above. Commensurate with the goals of this study, I find Feminist Standpoint Theory ideally suited to channel women's diverse perspectives into collective understandings.

Feminist Standpoint Theory

Feminist standpoint theorists believe that women are capable of producing unique knowledge because their experiences are "systematically and structurally different" (Wood, 2005, p. 61) from those of men. The root of a different knowledge among women is a result of their distinct position and standpoint in a culture, where, as a result of the "sexual division of labor ensconced in capitalist patriarchy, women have been systematically exploited, oppressed, excluded, devalued, and dominated" (O'Brien Hallstein, 2000, p. 5). These experiences enable women to develop significant and hitherto unexplored issues and concerns that may not be obvious to the dominant class. Social locations affect women socially, symbolically, and materially (Wood, 2005). Women's unique positioning and knowledge production capabilities do not mean that women, merely by virtue of being marginalized, share a common knowledge. On the contrary, feminist standpoint theorists believe that there are multiple viewpoints and no single view is any better or "epistemologically privileged" (Sloan & Krone, 2000, p. 112) than the other. Feminist standpoint theorists only agree that "women's vision is a better place to begin knowledge production because the standpoint that can emerge from it is an 'achieved' position" (O'Brien Hallstein, 2000, p. 5). Likewise, feminist standpoint theorists agree that a standpoint cannot be claimed, it has to be achieved (Harding, 1997; Hekman, 1997).

I summarize the key arguments of this theory by paraphrasing the five points about the theory made by Wood (2005). First, the unequal structure of society creates different social locations for women and men. These inequalities shape women's experiences and how they come to learn about and live those realities. Second, women's subordinate social locations caused by the interplay between knowledge and power help them create the kind of knowledge that is *more accurate* or *less false* than the one created by members of privileged groups. Third, because women have an outsider-within status by being outside the dominant groups as well as by being intricately located within those groups, they have a double consciousness that allows them to observe and understand those groups. Fourth, achieving a standpoint does not depend on biology or other essential factors. It requires a critical understanding and awareness of one's larger political and social contexts. Lastly, individuals can have multiple standpoints shaped by their membership into different groups.

Feminist Standpoint Theory is ideally suited for this project. First, this study involves women across socioeconomic status, age, class, caste, and generations. Collectively, they are marginalized in a number of ways. Individually, some enjoy privileges that others cannot ever imagine. As individual participant groups, their lives are dissimilar, and yet collectively as Indian women, they are all recipients of differential practices, albeit to different degrees. Their lives and its realities can neither be circumscribed nor explained within any specific theory. Therefore, macro-level perspectives drawn from feminist theorizing best suit my research and its goals. In Feminist Standpoint Theory, I find an ally. By simultaneously accepting the diversity of women's voices and the commonalities that bind them together, this theory offers me a medium to frame my participants' experiences in a coherent manner.

Second, as a "Third World" feminist studying in the United States, interested in conducting research in India, for consumption by a largely Western audience, I am very conscious of my individual location in multiple spaces. Even as I struggle to make sense of and negotiate my multiple identities—as an Indian, an Asian, an immigrant, a foreigner, the "other," a woman of color, a "Third World" woman, and others that I live with, in addition to "feminist" concurrently (see Hegde, 1995; Shenoy, 2010), I am acutely aware of the arguments made by Indian feminists against Western feminisms (see John, 1998; Menon, 2002; C. T. Mohanty, 1984; Mohanty, 2003). I consider it important to be a part of their scholarship and dialogue. In that, I find validation in some other Third World feminists such as Hegde (2000) and Narayan (1989/2004; 2005) who support Feminist Standpoint Theory.

Third, I look upon feminist standpoint theory as an important starting point from which to understand Indian women's experiences. While there may be theoretical, ideological, and conceptual differences in applying a feminist theory developed in the West to Indian situations, feminist standpoint theory accounts for multiplicity of voices and is therefore applicable to women's situations in any society as long as it is the standpoints of those native women that are being listened.

In conclusion, even though Feminist Standpoint Theory was developed by White feminists in the West, the work of feminists of color (e.g., Hill Collins, 1997) has ensured that the intersectionality of race, class, nationality, ethnicity, and other such factors be considered while developing standpoints. This theory appeals to me and is ideal for my research goals because of its embracing of an "interpretive framework dedicated to explicating how knowledge remains central to maintaining and changing unjust systems of power" (Hill Collins, 1997).

ABOUT THE BOOK

This project began with a humble idea. I wanted to explore how society, childhood socialization, and women's own agency (co)create the career discourses that influence India's working women. I wanted to examine the meanings women assign to their work and how they define a "career." I implicitly knew that talking to any one group of women representing a single income category or social class would only reveal a partial story. I wanted to know how Indian women across socio-economic status, employed in a variety of occupations, across generations, caste, class, and income categories made sense of the meta-narratives of work and careers. Of course, unpacking the implications of caste and class is not the primary focus of this project but their influences can hardly be dismissed and so, wherever relevant, they have been included front and center into the discussion. I ended up talking to 78 Hindu working women from the city of Pune, Maharashtra, in India, in face-to-face interviews conducted in Marathi and English, with a smattering of Hindi thrown in by participants as they saw organically appropriate. Initially, this project began in my home discipline of organizational communication studies but as the ideas and scope of the project expanded, the focus shifted to include interdisciplinary perspectives and literature. Therefore, this study also includes relevant insights from and for feminist, sociological, psychological, family, and career studies.

In *Chapter 2: The Materiality of Social Discourses*, I discuss how caste and class discourses are embroiled in a covert conspiracy to sustain the hierarchical status quo, and how participants accept their current lot as evidence of their fate. I also present the meanings participants draw from these societal discourses. More specifically, I show that participants believe that Indian society discriminates against working women but that they do not care much for that rhetoric. The counter-narratives emerging from the findings show participants' understanding that Indian society is actually quite accepting of working women but only when they embrace the self-imposed "be a superwoman" motto into their work lives.

In *Chapter 3: Family Socialization and Career Discourses,* I emphasize familial influences on discourses that shape Indian women's career decision making and work behaviors. By foregrounding my participants' voices, I present findings that highlight how parents, grandparents, significant others, and friends work as career enablers in the lives of Indian women. These enablers encourage women's career development by uttering positive reinforcements, role modeling, and providing realistic visualizations and practical realities of specific career choices, among other practices. More significantly, memorable messages such as those communicated during casual dinner table conversations and story-telling help socialize Indian women into taking socio-culturally approved, gender-appropriate career paths.

Chapter 4: Constrained Agency and Communion articulates the remarkable agency Indian women show in writing the scripts of their own careers. Particularly relevant to women in their 40s and older, I present findings that pertain to participants' strategic negotiations with parents seeking their right to higher education, the assertive yet respectful ways in which they demand a confident presence in their workplaces, and the hard work with which they establish their careers despite setbacks and some opposition. This section highlights the major finding of this study that Indian working women, despite their contemporary lifestyles and 21st century thinking, are steeped in Indian traditions. They demonstrate agency but ensure the harmony of familial relationships and its delicate structure. Agency to Indian women implies the right to make one's own decisions bearing in mind the macro consequences of those decisions on their families.

In *Chapter 5: Meanings of Work and Careers,* the focus is on Indian women's interpretations of the many meanings that can be drawn from work. For my participants, the depth of meaning embedded in their work depended on the ways in which labor met intrinsic and extrinsic objectives. They found work meaningful if it served Indian society, provided them the ability to stand on their own feet by earning an honest living, fulfilled familial responsibilities and other culturally mandated obligations, allowed them an independent identity, provided intellectual stimulation along with learning opportunities, and fulfilled a higher purpose in life. This section also discusses participants' definition of what constitutes a "career" concluding with a metadefinition that emerged out the participants' grasp of the concept.

Chapter 6: Conclusion, summarizes the key findings, observations, and contributions made by this study.

NOTES

1. On December 16, 2012, a 23-year old woman who was traveling with a male companion was brutally attacked and raped. The victim died of her injuries within days of the incident. This case generated widespread anger, protests, and demonstrations in India and abroad calling for overhauling of rape laws and stronger punishment for perpetrators.

2. Ritzer (2004) uses the spelling McDonaldization (without the "a") while Datta (2005) uses MacDonaldization to refer to the same concept. I use Ritzer's spelling in my text but use Datta's spelling when I write the title of her article and cite a direct quote.

3. Rs. = Indian National Rupees (approximated $1 = Rs. 50)

Chapter Two

The Materiality of Social Discourses

Difficulties are a part of our life so there is nothing really to talk about. Our parents told us what to do based on our circumstances. We lived a life of poverty. Because of our poor circumstances, parents did not educate us a lot. Parents themselves were living in such a bad state! When there is no food to eat, how are they going to afford an education? We led our lives in poverty, grew into adulthood in poverty. We could not imagine a different life. Work, if it is outside work [outside the home], we did it, brought money home and managed the household with that money. *Paristhiti hach amcha jeevanacha mudda ahe mulat*—The bottom line is that our circumstances determine our lives because we grew up in a poor household, then our parents got us married off according to whatever little they could afford, given their circumstances. Naturally, they'll get us married to other poor people since we don't have anything to give them [dowry] so we were in similar circumstances [poverty] after marriage. There is no point in considering or wondering whether the husband is educated or not because he will also end up working as a laborer for wages. We will live according to our circumstances. We learned this right from our parents' house that even if we have only one *bhakri* [bread], we share it with everybody and keep quiet. We don't complain. Now we get a good pay, we have all kinds of comforts but we can't forget our past. If there are left-overs from dinner, then we eat that for breakfast, if we don't finish them at breakfast, we re-heat it and eat it again for lunch because there was a time when we didn't even have this to eat. The circumstances from which we came and the current circumstances we inhabit define our life situation. We continue to live in the same circumstances that we grew up in. —Arati, street sweeper

Narratives like the above colored the material realities and work-life experiences of many of the participants in the low-income category. Circumstances or state of existence or *paristhiti* was a recurring theme in low-income participants' candid life stories. One can also see a reconciled and fateful acceptance of one's lot in life in Arati's narrative summary.

The first objective of this project sought to investigate how India's working women come to understand and develop knowledge about work and career as influenced by societal discourse. This chapter unpacks participants' insightful responses and experiences. However, as one can see in the extended quote above, personal life situations are not far removed from socially lived realities.

Not surprisingly, the findings of this study show that the material consequences of caste and class influence individuals' lives in significant ways. Historic implications of caste-based segregation, disparities in educational opportunities, and poverty have very real consequences on women in the low-income category. This was particularly evident in the case of street sweepers and maids. Findings also show that among those in the middle/high-income occupations, levels of education are better determinants of career choices even though within-career advancement opportunities and access to some educational institutions are stalled in some cases due to the reported and alleged reverse discrimination. In India, access to quality education in English is often the privilege of the upper castes and middle-upper classes of society who can afford to send their children to these schools. Because sending children to private schools is the norm rather than the exception, paying high tuition and/or residency costs are beyond the humble means of poor working class people who send their children to subsidized or free government-funded schools[1] where the quality of education is often debatable and the medium of instruction is the local state language.

Regardless of one's caste or social class, though, if women are educated, they are able to engage in occupations that offer possibilities for advancement. Unfortunately it appears that obstacles to education such as parental poverty, familial obligations, and marital financial conditions are what determine the availability of occupational options for the low-income participants in the study.

While I did not ask participants about their specific caste membership, participants *were* asked if caste had any implications on their current occupation. Interestingly, only participants of the upper caste were vocal in their dissatisfaction of how their privileged caste status had negatively affected them while others dismissed caste status implications. Instances where lower-caste women spoke about their caste status and its implications, if any, on their occupations or occupational choice were rare but these cases have been integrated into the chapters wherever appropriate. Upper-caste women expressed a great deal of resentment about having to face a reported and alleged reverse discrimination in the public sector where the Indian government's quota system meant as an affirmative action[2] safeguard for low-caste people denied them employment opportunities despite being the most qualified candidates.

In the following section, first, I describe and discuss women's interpretation of their work limitations and options evidenced in a life trajectory of unfortunate circumstances derived from their caste *(circumstantial constraints* and *reverse discrimination)* and class *(upwardly mobile and class constraints).* When asked about their perception of societal views on working women, participants acknowledge Indian societal discrimination as well as acceptance of working women. In the second part of this discussion, I present participants' defiant views against a discriminating society as well as their mindful and voluntary negotiations in understanding and accepting more positive societal views.

CIRCUMSTANTIAL CONSTRAINTS—*PARISTHITI*

Societal discourses regarding one's own or someone else's caste, class-based occupational ambiguities, and one's current material circumstances define the work lives of all interviewed women, one way or the other. It is important to explain that participants were categorized on the basis on their income according to the divisions made by the Government of India for tax[3] purposes and therefore not all women earning low-income belong to the low-caste category[4].

Participants believe that their low status occupational engagement is a result of their circumstances brought on by the simultaneous lack of educational opportunities. A common theme resonating with women employed in low-paying occupations, such as domestic work, was their *paristhiti* or circumstances. As was seen in Arati's quote that opened this chapter, *paristhiti* determined women's entire life course from birth through their current adult work lives. This inherited *paristhiti* creates an almost resigned outlook in participants' minds. At the same time, contradictory narratives emerging from the women's own accounts show how despite a somewhat passive acquiescence of their life situations, they are determined to alter their *paristhitis* for their children.

Dhanashree started working as a maid due to a lack of better alternatives. Seated amidst a group of women who also worked as maids in the neighborhood in which she worked and were participants in the study, finding comfort in the security of that space, with tears in her eyes, she summarizes the helplessness that drove her to start working as a maid.

> My parents were poor. We lived in poverty. We worked at the farm from a young age. They [parents] got me married off to a handicapped man with one leg. They got me married when I was very young, 13 years. At that time I didn't know anything about selecting my own husband. I just went with what they decided for me. Father said, 'Don't get her married to him, he is a cripple.' Mother said, 'You [father] don't work, there are three girls to be

married and they are all illiterate. How will we pay for their marriages? He [future husband] has agreed to marry her for free, so I'll give her to him.' Even I didn't realize that I could have said no. Mother said, 'If you are going to get married, you are only going to marry him.' So I obeyed her and got married to him. He gave me happiness for five or six years, then I had two children because of which I then got stuck in the marriage. Then he started drinking so I had to start working. Rented house. Mother thought he lives in Pune, works in a good company, he will keep my daughter happy. She got me married to him with that thought but she didn't know what was going to happen in the future. I had two children, how could I leave them? Who was going to take care of them, their feeding, eating, drinking? So I decided I'll stay, work hard and provide for them. Then I started working at four people's houses, earned money, raised my children, and bought a little house [small dwelling in this case] of my own in Pune. How could I just leave and go to my mother's house?

Disappointed but not defeated, Dhanashree decided to stay resilient through life's changes and started working so she could provide for her children. Dhanashree's multi-layered and complex narrative reflects on Indian society, its cultural norms, and the constraints that limit options. Even though her own life was lived in and pre-determined by poverty, she hopes to better the lives of her children through her work. Societally speaking, she knew she would not get any support from her own parents if she were to return home from her husband's house disenchanted by her marital situation. Culturally, an Indian woman's rightful home is said to be that of her husband's. Haq (2013) has explained further how Indian daughters are taught from a young age that the journey from the "'doli' (departure to the husband's house, after the wedding ceremony) to the 'arthi' (departure to the funeral pyre) . . . [is] the measure of a successful life for the ultimate 'Bharatiya nari' (Indian woman)" (p. 173). Therefore, girls are socialized to not return to their natal homes should their marriages fail. In several parts of India, even today, a daughter's return to her parental home after a failed marriage imposes social sanctions on the family, and in extreme cases, ostracism for the woman and her parents from their particular community. Therefore, Dhanashree decided to take matters in her own hands and find work as a maid, perhaps the only job she could get due to a lack of education.

The theme of poor circumstances emerged over and over again, narratives after narratives among low-income women. The women described their circumstances-bound stories in terms of a continuum. The linearity of their life situation began with them having been born in poverty. Poverty was also the reason their own parents were not educated and who in most cases did not understand the worth and value of educating their children, especially daughters. Even when they did allow their daughters to go to school, their education could be discontinued at any time if they were needed more urgently to stay at home to take care of their younger siblings or work in the farms as an additional earning member of the family. Continuing the process, lack of education led to lack of opportunities, which then left them with low paying occupations such as domestic help. As Reshma, a maid, explains, "Work means getting a job after an education. Those who have education, they can get a job. Those who don't have an education, they have to do the kind of work we do." Similar views are expressed by Savita (21), a receptionist,

> . . . and the thing was that our parents had never saved with the idea of sending their children to school. They just didn't think like that, so we couldn't get an education because of our poverty. People who were able to get educated are in good positions today.

That they *had* to work for their family, especially for their children, was a decision that was circumstantially determined but the fact that these participants chose to work and earn an honest living instead of simply accepting their situation speaks to their resilience and resolve to overcome those circumstances despite the simultaneous calm acceptance of their own personal fate. This was evident in Reshma's case. Even though she had a better lifestyle growing up, her current job as a maid is testament to her grit for making it on her own. She recalls,

> My father worked in the Treasury so in childhood we never worked outside [for pay] like this. Our circumstances were very good. At my mother's, we had other women working for us. Nobody [in her natal family] likes that I am doing this job but my circumstances are different. They tell me we'll help you out as much as we can but I don't want to take their help. I feel that I should work hard myself, for my family. I got married early. I had children early. Now I've began to understand that even I should do something for my children. If I work hard for them, they will get a good education. They should also feel that even though our parents were poor they were determined to have a good family and that they never took any money from relatives. So we should also do something with the same determination. My working hard will help them. If we continue to work like this, at least we are standing on our own feet, even though we don't have education, we are somehow standing on our own feet [financially independent]. We at least have the belief that if we work, we will make enough money to at least fulfill some wishes of our children. Even though we are poor, we don't have to buy biscuits worth Rs. 100, even if we buy a small packet, children are satisfied. That is why we work.

Participants were categorical in the declaration that just because *they* underwent hardships does not mean their children are destined for similar fate. These women work hard so their children can have better lives. Their children's education, therefore, was extremely important to them. Says, Asha, a maid,

See my life is spent like this [in poverty and low-paying jobs] but I feel that my children should study a lot, get a great education. Just like how others' lives are stable, like that my children should get an education and do something with their lives. That is my wish.

Likewise, Veena, a street-sweeper recalls her tough times,

I got married at 20. Had two children and after four years of marriage, my Mister [husband] died. Now I had to take care of two children. I had low education. What could I do? I had to take care of the children. Mister did not have a job. I spent 2–4 years working on the machine [stitching things for other people for pay]. I couldn't afford to think of education. I had to start thinking about my future life. How should I raise my small children? When my husband died, my youngest child was of 10 months, the older one was 2 years old. Now I had to raise them and my in-laws did not give me any support. My father-in-law was in a great job but he didn't support me. Finally I had to take care of everything myself and after marriage, parents don't belong to anyone. Whatever the situation is, we have to deal with it ourselves. Today, my children are studying, getting an education. Because I did not get an education, I definitely get happiness is educating my children and I have to take them forward. Whatever unfulfilled desires I had in my life will be fulfilled through my children.

Veena was determined to rebuild a life for her children and herself after the death of her husband. Now, in hindsight, she is able to evaluate her options and in associating a good education with a life out of poverty and of happiness, she strives to live vicariously through her children. However, even when she encountered harsh life changes, she implicitly knew to not approach her parents for help whether it was due to traditional socialization or just the fact that,

. . . Their [parents'] circumstances were right in front of me. There was no question of asking [for help]. My father had a good job but he was a gambler. So I did not even allow myself to think that he could help me. Ultimately, I created this world from zero (gets tearful).

As seen from the many examples, participants' work and family lives oscillate between an acceptance of their own fate and a simultaneous energy to want and do better by their children. They are resolute through their expressions and actions that the cycle of poverty would not continue on to the next generation. Their children would have better lives than they themselves did, and they would make sure of it. So even though participants' narratives often displayed a matter-of-fact, almost helpless and hopeless awareness of their own life situation, when it came to their children their positive and futuristic outlook was infectious and filled with promise for their children's futures.

When asked if their caste had played any role in them being employed in these low-income occupations, all of the low-income earning women answered that caste had not affected them. This finding is somewhat disconcerting. I have wondered about participants' reasons for this response. Does it emerge from a lack of conscious awareness of how caste affects their lives? Does their dismissive answer represent their unwillingness to share that information with me, an upper-caste and privileged woman (See Appendix B)? Do they not want to accept that caste status may have played a role in their work lives or are they simply denying this as fact because it would then, inadvertently mean accepting caste-based advantages/disadvantages? Accepting or denying caste implications on their occupational choices may have direct consequence on their exertion of agency. After all, if everything that happened or happens to them in the past and potential future is due to their caste status, where does that leave their agency in individual will, determination, and fight against the odds? Perhaps the inevitability of caste consequences and the fact there is not much they can do about it is enough reason to not dwell on it.

One participant who brought up her caste in the context of her occupation was Shanti, who belongs to the low-caste *mahar* community and works as a public school peon[5] which is a prestigious government job for people in her caste community where a majority of the women work as maids. Because she stepped outside of her caste-determined normative work role, her employment is viewed with mixed reactions by her relatives and co-caste members. Shanti considers her job better than that of a maid and feels proud of herself for having gotten out of the stereotypical jobs typically done by women of her caste. This shows how hierarchies of occupational reputation exist even within each caste. She says,

> Since they [people of her caste community] aren't very educated, [Shanti's highest level of education is 9th grade, which is a matter of great pride for her] the women among my relatives and people in my neighborhood from my community and of my caste mostly work as maids. Rather than do a maid's job, it is much better sweeping in a school that is run by the government and full of students. People around my neighborhood and people from my caste wonder how I got this job. They keep wondering how come she is doing this job, where does she go, what does she do? They feel pride, and some feel jealous.

Shanti's perspective as an outsider within her community gives her an important insight into how some members feel pride and others feel jealous of her more prestigious job. She realizes that her education helped her get this job—which only furthers the rhetoric of education and opportunities voiced by participants in previous quotes. Low-caste and poor women in low-income occupations did indeed see education as their gateway out of poverty toward better lives.

The theme of "circumstantial constraints" though broad in interpretation and implication, neatly summed up the material realities of participants in the low-income category. Participants work hard to rewrite the otherwise potentially inevitable futures of their children's lives. They show remarkable resilience, determination, and agency in nurturing an agenda which, although disadvantageous to them personally and to their immediate present, would eventually positively impact their children's futures.

REVERSE CASTE DISCRIMINATION

Women in the middle- and high-income generating occupations were more vocal regarding their views on caste and occupational engagement. The Indian government, has, as a policy toward equal opportunities for all its citizens, provided large quotas to members of the lower castes in education and government jobs. Many consider the quota or reservation system a bane to India's progress and question its ill-served purpose today (e.g., Dalmia, 2010; Harris, 2012). The popular argument, not different from those that opponents of affirmative action policies in the United States put forth, is that, as a result of heavy reservations in education and government jobs, incompetent people may get accepted into institutions of higher education [a majority of which are State run] and State jobs solely based on their castes which would otherwise have gone to more qualified and better educated individuals. Due to these societal realities, women of the upper castes feel disadvantaged by their caste membership.

Sukanya (32), an agricultural consultant, is especially forthcoming with her views regarding reservations and calls the discrimination she faced as "a bitter part of my life."

> Sukanya: Ya caste affected me because after just finishing my job I was looking for the [sic] permanent job [tenure-track position] in the university but the posts which were available, all posts are reserved for the caste and there was [sic] no posts for open purpose so I had to . . . I faced some problems in that because I wanted to be a permanent member of that university but being an open category[6] it was not possible for me.

> The issue is only reservation with the government policies that is it because in other countries the government I thought that the government they don't give much attention on the caste . . . they give attention towards completely towards your academic profile or your intelligence but unfortunately in India it won't happen in the government jobs.

Suchitra: So you're saying that your colleagues who belonged to the lower castes could get permanent positions [tenure-track] but because you belong to the upper caste, you couldn't?

Sukanya: Of course, of course and I remember one issue that . . . I had around 82% in M.Sc. [Master of Science] project but one of my colleague is having only 55% but he got permanent with the best post and is working in XXXXX right now. Even after my having . . . I won't say *ki* [that] my profile is much better than him but being . . . if you look at my academic profile then definitely my profile is much more higher than him but being from an open category it was not possible for me to obtain [that] job.

Even though her caste directly affected Sukanya with regard to employment, her parents had prepared her for exactly such a situation. She explains:

They [parents] always used to advise me that I belong from Brahmin community so in India particularly the problem of reservation is very high. My father and mother always used to tell me that one thing about our community [Brahmin community] that can help you survive in your life is your education. Nothing else. So if you get very much highly educated then only you can do something in your life . . . the main barrier in government service that is the caste. [If] you are less educated then with the caste back up you can step much more [go ahead in your career] but in our community it won't be possible so the topmost education that we are able to give you, we will give you. If you have capacity to accept it then that is the only thing which will help you in your life.

Looking out for their daughter's future, Sukanya's parents tried to shield her against potential caste-based reverse discrimination by encouraging education. They believed that higher education was the only way she could successfully compete against her colleagues who belonged to the lower castes. These competitors might get hired initially but because top supervisory positions needed much higher education, she would eventually surpass them professionally. The importance placed on education spans across socio-economic status although their functional and material approach may be different. Low-income/low-caste women, for example, made it apparent that they saw their children's education as their stepping stone out of poverty and toward better lives. Parents of upper-caste women in middle/high-income occupations, on the other hand, chose to use education as inoculation against any potential upper-caste-related reverse discrimination disadvantage. Continuing to talk about the nature of this discrimination, Meena (57) narrates the challenges she faced in securing a job because of her upper-caste status.

I was trying to get a job with a government-aided school. At the time wherever I got a job as a substitute teacher filling in for leave vacancies, I was told that because I am a Brahmin I could not be hired. They were more interested in filling in the quota of low caste people for those jobs. They clearly told me that because I am a Brahmin they could not offer me a job and that I would not get a job being from the open category so don't even try. They interviewed me every 2-3 years and the process of interviewing used to last from morning to evening and they would say *we can select you but we can't offer you the job* then why do you keep coming? So I had this reverse shock that I am not going to get a job here so don't even try. I experienced this in some of the colleges I had applied as well. I got the same message, *you may keep applying and getting invited for interviews every year after year but you aren't going to get it so just don't even apply and don't come for the interviews either.* At the time I felt what was this, what kind of a tradition was this, it was wrong that I couldn't even get a job! I was good and the school validated that as well, they accepted the fact that I taught well, that my qualifications were good but they had to fill in those backlogs of hiring people of lower castes.

Meena's current place of employment is a private school where she did not have any problems getting a job because of her caste status. Nutan (39), a railway ticket booking clerk, says that even though caste did not affect her getting a job, she faces challenges in career advancement. She explains,

The people who have joined Railways after me because they belong to SC [Scheduled Castes—a protected category] and all they get promotion fast so person who has joined railways five or six years after me, they are getting the same salary what I am getting and maybe in another few years they will become my boss. So after having so much service [work experience] also there is no point. The person who is coming behind you they are going in front of you. They will be getting promoted before me.

In addition to reported discrimination in employment, participants also talked about the effects of upper-caste membership in the education system.

Avni (27) says she faced discrimination when it came to being accepted into a good medical school.

It happened with my MD [Doctor of Medicine] admission. My rank was 135 and there were a total of 250 seats but because I was from the open category, I couldn't get admitted to a better college. But people with a rank of 500 got accepted at good colleges because of their low-caste status. I realized the disadvantage of being from the open category.

There are many other Sukanyas, Nutans, Meenas, and Avnis who have faced caste-based reverse discrimination due to the Indian government's quota reservation system. Like Sukanya's parents, Manjula (51), a dietician, also fears the consequences reservation in higher education institutions may have on her children. She agrees that the quota system was started with good intentions "to help underprivileged people access opportunities" but she says that now, "60 years after independence, it is no longer a fair system." Instead of basing reservations on caste, she believes these reservations, if any, should be on the basis of financial hardship, which is a fair point, but one that needs significant policy, legal, and political overhaul. It is not the intention of this book to make commentary on the quota/reservation system beyond the views and experiences retold by my participants. However, a national dialogue on caste based preferential admissions and hiring is important despite having proven unsuccessful at all previous avenues. A controversial topic in India, the quota/reservation system is often only discussed in familiar company. Perhaps it was my upper-caste participants' implicit knowledge of my own upper-caste status[7] that allowed them the candid and safe space to reveal their frustrations over caste politics to me.

CAREER ASPIRATIONS AND CLASS CONSTRAINTS

The instances above explain how caste and one's circumstances are inter-twined. I have already discussed caste-based occupational limitations in a previous section. We also saw how caste membership influences the quality of one's work and career in terms of opportunities and access. In addition, one's placement in a particular social class hierarchy greatly affects occupa-tional choices for participants as well.

Women in the middle-income and high-income categories had the privi-lege of class to begin with. However, the framing of their social class as "privilege" is a matter of perspective since this upper status also comes with its own issues. Surely for those in the low-income category, women doing better than them have the advantage of class but for those who already belong to those upper classes, there exist traditional restrictions on their behavior and occupational choice as was explained in detail in chapter 1.

Priyanka (40s) currently works as a teacher. She says she does not like her job and is bored of it. She says she realized a long time ago that, that was "not the profession for me." Her true career objective was to become an actor, an artiste, something her father refused to let her pursue because of the negative connotations associated with women in the entertainment industry at the time. She explains,

> There in first year [of college], I had watched a play . . . *Himalaychi savli* [Himalaya's Shadow]. There I felt that I should become an artiste. When we were returning from the play, I told him [father] I feel that I should get into this field. He was totally against it and explained to me that I was a girl from a good family, no matter how it appears from the outside, it's not really nice on the inside [the entertainment industry]. I wouldn't have gotten permission from people at home anyway so that ambition got nipped right there.

She says she regrets not becoming a full-time actor even though it was a decision she did not have control over—first because her father did not allow her to pursue that interest and later on because her husband wanted her to have a steady job (as a teacher) so he could quit his job and undertake the risk of starting his own business. Patriarchy and traditional Indian values evident in society strongly influenced Priyanka's options. As seen in the quote above, Priyanka's father relied on patriarchal constructs and forced normative values to make the case for him in reminding her how girls from "good families" behave. These arguably quasi-rules compelled Priyanka to obey her father's instructions. This obedience also shows how important parental approval is to Indian women. Priyanka's occupational woes did not end with being denied permission to pursue acting as a career. She says,

> I am a teacher with XX XXXX [school] but this has been imposed upon me. I absolutely don't like my job. Never liked it but when I started working, there was a need, my husband wanted to start a business, he had left his job and because we needed some income at home, I started working. I got bored of it in 10 years—realized this wasn't my field, not for me. I kept feeling that I should have been an artiste—that bug was constantly attacking me and that bug kept bugging me, still does. Just the other day I completed some work in a documentary film but when I did work [as a teacher], I worked very sincerely. I feel that maybe I will become an artiste if I quit my job but what kinds of roles will I get now? [that I am older]—mother-in-law, older woman roles? I am not really interested in playing those roles.

At a young age, having been forced to accept that she would not be allowed to become an actress and later having to sacrifice this desire again for the sake of a steady paying job for her husband's own career, Priyanka buried her ambitions in deference to her family's interests. Just when she had started performing in plays and begun to do well, it was time to press pause.

> When I worked in plays in 1991, I was even offered a film but then my husband said that if you are going to work in films, I'll close the shutters on my business [sarcastically implying that since she will be the breadwinner, he will no longer need to work, symbolizing a bruised ego]. So once again I had to take a back seat. His career was more important than mine.

It was only much later in life after his entrepreneurial venture had started doing well did Priyanka's husband encourage her to pursue acting but only as long as they were "short inconsequential parts in plays." Priyanka's husband, like her father, was mindful of societal reputation of women in films. He was also of the opinion that a husband should provide for his wife and family. While he initially supported her acting pursuits as a hobby, he emotionally (and sarcastically) attacked her sense of propriety and gender role by making the comment about shutting down his business. This indicates how to him, his reputation in society as well as his own career were unquestionably more important than his wife's career interests. Priyanka's own statement about her husband's career being more important than hers also indicates how women may be socialized into believing that their work is secondary to their husbands'. Some women may implicitly be socialized into accepting that in matters of careers, if anyone has to compromise, it is the woman. Her answer also represents societally influenced parental views about married daughters.

> Suchitra: Why did you feel that his career was more important than yours?

> Priyanka: Family values. That husband, husband's house—that has always been imposed on our minds that our destiny—in short that once we are married, they [parents] told us at that time that now that you are going to your husband's house, you are not to return to this [parental] home. You can only leave your husband's home on four shoulders [in death—refers to four men holding a plank upon which the deceased body on its way to the crematorium, rests—held at four corners]. They actually told us this. Do not return to your parents' house again. So every time I would rationalize it as, instead of creating any issues, let the husband do it, let me do this for my husband, kept doing this and so I pretty much kept my desire to become an artiste bundled up but whenever I get an opportunity, I still do it. Like hosting an event as an anchor, acting in plays, anchoring a show on television a while back, so wherever I can, I make the most of the opportunity.

Priyanka's story represents several aspects of Indian society. First, at a time in her life where she was choosing a career, her father opposed her choice of becoming an actor, citing societal censure, only he framed it in the context of girls from good families not choosing acting as a career—thus appealing to her sense of familial responsibility, reputation, and pride. As an adult when she could have chosen to pursue her acting interests, she was restricted because her husband wanted to gamble with his own career at the cost of his wife's long-term ambition. While the husband could take risks, quit a job, and start a new business, the wife's only role was to mitigate the risks of his career experiments by supporting the family financially. Priyanka, therefore, has always had to make compromises that privileged the interests of the men in her life. Social influences strongly affect familial discourses regarding what work women can and cannot do and some women, like Priyanka, are simply expected to accept these decisions made for them without complaint.

Bindiya (40s), however, was not the kind to accept others' decisions for her, at least not forever. As a college student, she acted in plays and won several awards. When she told her mother that she wanted to become a full time actor, her mother rejected the idea saying, "You aren't doing anything of that sort. Instead, you get a high score [in academic pursuits]." Upon marriage, Bindiya's in-laws opposed her desire for a career in acting. "After marriage, I kept getting offers because people knew I act but since I didn't have permission from home, I had to keep quiet." Bindiya rationalizes that the reason for this lack of permission was the reputation of the profession at the time,

> Basically 20 years ago, the attitude was the character of actors, actresses, what we see around in the industry, the reputation wasn't good, you never know when someone's going to cheat you. So in families like ours [middle/upper class-upper caste], people just opposed . . . so that was it.

In later years, Bindiya did embark on an acting career, which speaks for her resistance and agency and will be discussed in chapter 4. Bindiya's experience shows that family members are easily influenced by larger Indian societal discourses surrounding particular professions. Sandhya's (45) story below represents the strength of conviction some participants showed in going against their spouses to pursue a career.

Sandhya works as an accountant in a government office. Even though her husband was opposed to her paid employment, she continued to work with the backing of her parents.

> When I started working, before marriage, I was with my parents. My father tried hard for me to get a job so I could have steady paid work. He really wanted me to work and was proud of the fact that his daughter was employed because the environment at the time wasn't the kind where a lot of women worked outside their home for pay. At that time, my grandfather—my mother's father, he was like, 'wow you have started working'—in our entire family, a distant aunt was a teacher in Bombay and then me, we were the only two who stepped out of the house to work—so he felt really good that I was working. After marriage, my husband who was a businessman from a traditional household with a conservative family did not want me to work. He asked me to leave my job because he felt it below his dignity to let his wife work. He kept pressuring me to leave my job but my parents were insistent that one does not get a job easily and you have this permanent job, do not leave it, it can be helpful at any time.

Sandhya's story will be discussed in more detail in an upcoming chapter. She was born in a middle-class family while Bindiya and Priyanka are both from the upper class. All three women faced class complexities in their desire to work. Even though they had an education and therefore theoretically had many more options available to them, the people in their lives were strongly influenced by societal opinion, the repercussions of which were felt in varying degrees by the women in the pursuit of their own careers.

People of lower social classes share the belief that women's employment is a reflection on the man's inability to support his family. Seema (20) a live-in nanny, talked about how people in her village still think there is something wrong with the man if his wife works outside the home for pay.

If she is married, then people wonder, why is she working? Isn't the husband capable enough to take care of her that she has to work? Mostly that is what they say. One of my friends started working recently. She made tiffin [lunch] boxes for four people. She has four brothers-in-law. So she has to do all the work at home before leaving for work. I had just visited her in May. I heard people talking, what is this? Isn't the husband earning enough to take care of her? Why did he get married then? Mostly in my village, that's what people say but I don't feel that just because a woman is working, it means her husband cannot provide for her. Now if there are only two people, they have to manage everything themselves. That is what I think but in the village that's what they say, that the husband cannot provide for her, that is why she is being sent to work.

In both the sections above, caste and class implications lay bare the fact that these twin concepts individually and collaboratively influence women's career options. Whether it is the form of inherited poverty and circumstantial constraints or value constructs imposed as a result of class status, women always end up becoming the bearers of societal burdens. These societal burdens need to be borne by the women for whom the consequences of these societal expectations are their everyday material realities.

In the next sections, I continue the discussion on how participants perceive and interpret the societal preponderance on working women.

SOCIETY DISCRIMINATES. WE DON'T CARE.

A number of participants believe that Indian society continues to be discriminatory toward working women despite the major strides the country has made economically. People differ in their opinions about working women in urban and rural India, across the different strata of society, across generations, and according to one participant, between "thinking and non-thinking people."

Aparna (55), a leprosy detection technician, believes that "in urban areas, there has been a lot of change in people's perspectives and thinking. In rural areas however, I don't think people's opinions or viewpoints have changed much." Aparna recalls how even until a few years ago, nurses, women who worked in shift jobs, and in private companies [because government jobs were considered more prestigious and permanent] did not get marriage proposals.

Marriage proposals to girls who worked in companies [private sector] were not easily accepted. There were a lot of women working as sisters [nurses] and in the telephone exchange [government telephone company operators] but they had shifts. People used to think that a woman's first priority should be her home and because her husband isn't going to help with that, [they assumed] girls who worked in shifts must be opposed to having [raising] families. The specific jobs were good but people didn't think they were good because with shift-work, women had to step out of the house to work at odd hours. Security was a concern. With nurses, the profession involved coming in contact with way too many people, especially men, than women were typically allowed to and this was an issue with traditional Indian mind-sets.

Even as society was beginning to accept working women, the expectation continued to remain that women first fulfill familial responsibilities and then, work obligations. Because women who worked in shifts may have to work at hours when they would typically be needed at home, some people believed that girls who were engaged in shift work would not prioritize nor desire to have their own families. As a result, Aparna reasoned that marriage proposals for these women were not forthcoming. Maya, a high-ranking police officer agrees. She says,

> Society isn't that open to women working. Even now, women joining police, it's not easily accepted. Today I was talking to a constable—she's in the job for four years. She was saying it's difficult to find a boy [groom]. Men are not accepting—even now.

Discourses of marriage remain significant in women's narratives. Meena (57), a school teacher, believes that even though she notices changes in some sections of society, in general, Indian society treats working women unfairly. She says,

> In a major way [society discriminates against working women]. No matter what, men feel that the power is in their hands. Women may be earning money but the final decision making at home lies in his hands. But this is changing a lot. Perhaps from now onwards, both sexes will get equal respect.

Listening to Meena, it appears that women's ability to earn equality and respect in society depends upon if and when men "give" it to them.

> Whatever you say, unless men give women respect, she *will* not get it. This fact cannot be denied. If she gets security and protection, she can live safely and happily otherwise the question of her protection itself is a big issue. So women cannot equal men in every respect. Only when men respect women having accepted these limitations or her shortcomings will society become equal, otherwise it is difficult. Attitudes of men should change.

Meena's reference to "limitations" connotes the lack of safety working women may face in their work lives outside of their homes. She essentializes women as dependent upon men for their very survival and happiness, which she constructs as a "shortcoming." She assumes that an equal society between the sexes is possible but only with the cooperation of men. In other words, women's working is not as simple as it sounds. The process of women stepping out of their homes to work is complicated by concern over their safety and security in Indian society, which is given to public sexual teasing, inappropriate touching, and harassment of women in public. It is as if women have to depend on men to live a life of personal freedoms and liberties and a passionate pursuit of career aspirations. According to Meena, women may have become financially independent but do not have much decision-making authority in family matters. This view runs contradictory to what popular media depicts as the new and contemporary Indian woman (see chapter 1).

More participants believe that public reaction to working women depends upon the particular social strata to which people belong. According to Bindiya (40s), attitudes differ based on the particular layer of society. She explains,

> The very high class, rich families where they consider women just as a show piece in the house, is the very rich class; next to that is the higher middle class, I think I am in that strata, where a woman really has her identity now; and even in the family they support her accordingly. In the lower middle class, they don't think of women in the same way, the girl grows up, she should get married and their responsibility is over, that's what they think. In the low class, the slum areas, there is again a difference, their women are working even though they are house maids but still the situation is that the husband is a drunkard and these women work for their families and so even though they don't get proper status in the house, still they are the breadwinners of the house. They may not have much of an identity in that but the family is dependent on them. That is the major difference.

Ujwala (29) believes that society's reaction to working women depends on whether one is a "thinking or a not-thinking person."

> You can think whether you are educated or not it's how you let your personality grow. Thinking people learn to live with changes. Thinking people learn to accept changes. Thinking people like or dislike the way things are going but they see that they have no other options or that they have options so whether it is a man or woman, the fact is that women are going to be working and the earlier people accept it and learn to live with it, the better.

Women continue to believe that there are "pockets of society," "sections of society," "categories of people," and "levels of society," that discriminate against working women. Here, discrimination is not in terms of wages or advancement. The term "discriminate" here implies that working women are discriminated against in terms of the expectations and demands on their traditional roles versus professional roles.

Regardless of how society views working women, the participants themselves were dismissive about societal opinions and this includes women in low-income occupations. Says Sulekha (24), who rolls incense sticks for a living in addition to doing odd jobs around her employer's house,

> Society mocks working women saying that 'there she goes off to work again' but we know that only by working will our living conditions change. It is to our advantage and satisfaction to work. They don't understand that and I am not going to answer everybody or defend my going to work all the time.

For Sulekha, working is an economic need and so even though her conservative community does not appreciate her working, she does not let that interfere with her objectives for working. She makes the distinction between educated and uneducated people.

> Because of old traditions, previously it was the case that men earned money and women managed their houses. It was beneficial for men and that is why they made that rule. They trapped women at home. *Chuul ani muul* [kitchen and the kid], that was all women could do. Those who are educated can understand that it is a need of the times for women to work, those who are uneducated, don't get it.

Sulekha presents an uncomplicated opinion about people's perspectives on working women, one that she does not concern herself with much. She reasons that cultural (patriarchal) traditions and men's desire to retain their advantageous status quo is what led to the creation of the arbitrary rules of a gendered division of labor. In making a distinction between educated and uneducated people, she rests her case matter-of-factly.

Seema (20), a live-in nanny, also supports Sulekha's views.

> People will talk. Some people don't like that I am working like this. No matter who says what about my work, they aren't going to give me money if my circumstances change and I need money. I have to provide for myself so I work. Whatever job it is, it is honest work and I earn my own living. I don't care about what others say. So if they [people of her village community, society in general] want to talk, let them talk, it doesn't affect me. My work is what it is. I work, I get money, and I manage within those means.

Seema finds pride in being financially independent in fulfilling her needs. She believes that since people from her community will not help her if she were to need financial help, their opinion about her working does not matter. She is proud to be self-reliant and capable of handling her responsibilities.

Pooja (50), principal of an international school, and an upper-caste, high-income earning professional, also does not care about what people think about her being gainfully employed. "I couldn't be bothered. Basically I am only worried about what my immediate family feels." Then, she implicates impositions on women's freedom to work with cultural attitudes of an older generation. She says,

> They [older generation] feel that you [women] are rejecting your home and like I remember his [husband's] *mama* [uncle] saying no you shouldn't work and I said, my husband doesn't mind it, my in-laws don't mind, I don't care what others think. Some men do that, some men feel that you should sit at home and look after the children or my home, my parents, or whatever and there are a lot of people like that. Today what is happening is that the present or even my generation, many people are feeling that there is extra income coming, so what is there [what is the big deal] if a woman works?

Even though Pooja does not personally care what others think about her working, she does need validation and support from her husband and in-laws. Pooja is 50 years old. That she will want to comply with what her husband and in-laws want for her is culturally understandable. It is interesting to note, however, that even women in their 20s and 30s who say that they do not bother with societal opinion, care deeply for the approval of their parents.

Tanushree (22) plays multiple career roles. She is a model, a make-up artist, an interior designer, and hosts live community shows whenever invited to do so. When she first decided to move to Pune to pursue a career in modeling, her supportive parents decided to relocate with her in order to provide Tanushree with a home and to encourage her ambitions. As a make-up artist, a profession not considered a particularly high-class occupation in India, depending on whether you are self-employed or working for a big-name organization or brand, among other things, she believes that society may not easily understand her work. However, because she has the support of her parents, she does not bother herself with others' opinions. Just like acting, a modeling career is not always considered appropriate for girls from good families. Tanushree is from the middle class (and by definition, a "good family") and the first in her family to be associated with the fashion industry, much to the chagrin of her relatives, she says. Because this industry demands unpredictable and late hours, a model's name can often fall into disrepute. Here, Tanushree discusses how easy it is for rumors to spread and how grateful she is to her parents for trusting her.

> I feel *ki* [that] it is a plus point of my family or touchwood that my parents are like this [understanding of their daughter's career demands and challenges] but if some girl's parents were not like that it is such stupidity that one statement could spoil her image without any of the reason like you know, and a lot of these things keep happening. Even my relatives, forget about the outside people, they do talk, but even my own relatives and the reason is because my entire family . . . neither from my mamma's side nor my dad's side is into glamour and fashion and all the stuff. So generally they will also talk 'oh she has so many friends and is mostly seen with guys and all and has few girl-

friends so it will all be dangerous for you' [relatives warn her parents] . . . they will keep telling my mom and dad there have been so many clashes [between relatives and her parents] that my . . . but my parents as I said they are so supportive that my mom stopped going to my relatives' place and all that. 'I know what my daughter is doing and all and her career is important, not your gossip and your statements and all, so this is better, you don't approve of it so I will stop coming.' Whenever my mom visited relatives, they will take out [raise] the topics [about her work, the company she keeps, her reputation] and they will start talking and all the stuff. So if you want to be bold, if you want to survive in this field, your family support is a very big . . . means it is a power kind of a thing inside you like you know, leave it, whatever you want to talk, you talk, my family is with me or like my people know me, even my friends and all, they also hear like you know, someone will always say something about you through someone—fashion is a field like you know, you can pass a rumor or gossip like easily, it hardly takes a second and it doesn't take too long for such things to spread.

Tanushree feels empowered by her parents' support of her career and confidence in being able to deal with gossip and rumors. Her parents support her so unconditionally that her mother even cut off ties with relatives who indulged in gossip about her daughter.

Meha (27) works as a supervisor at a multinational company's operation in Pune. When she started working in shifts, often having to work nights, people were ambiguous about her job profile. They assumed she worked at a call center that telephoned people in the U.S. and elsewhere harassing them about credit cards and unsolicited sales. Meha's job profile at her multinational software organization, however, deals only with in-bound callers from English-speaking countries who call in to get their specific software related computer problems fixed. When she first got the job, she accepted it without hesitation because she knew her parents would not object to her working night shifts. "I don't really care what [other] people think. Right from the start, they've [parents] always been supportive [of] whatever I did or even what my sisters did so I just assumed that perhaps they would be okay with it," and they were.

Like the participants above, Jaya (48), a social worker, also only values the views of her family.

> I don't care what anybody thinks. I only give importance to the views of my husband, my children, and because they live with us, my in-laws. Beyond them, I don't care what anybody else thinks. 'Why are you doing this?' I like it that is why I am doing it.

Assurance of such parental support or acceptance from close family was important for women in order to deal with societal opinions. Even women who did not care about others' opinions cared about their family's approval.

Anita (31) is the chief finance officer at an information technology company. She agrees that Indian society discriminates against working women. However, she believes that individuals always have the freedom to decide how much they let what society thinks or says about them affect them.

> Society does discriminate but how that will affect the individual woman or whether she will accept it or not is something the woman should decide for herself. It may not be possible to change society but the individual can decide whether to allow that dogmatism of society to affect her or not. Individuals should avail of available opportunities. People will react to the working woman depending on how she allows them to react to her but society is recognizing women's potential. If you show the capability, the capability is recognized.

Anita's response places women at the center of discursive sense making and sense giving. In other words, by allowing women the space to craft their work stories and experiences in ways that *they* want represented to the outside world, women have the power to structure a positive message about their potential and capabilities.

For some participants like Mohini (63), the do-not-care attitude is more a personality trait than an environmentally determined characteristic. Mohini, is a judge who completed her law degree at 60 years of age, says she has always gone against tradition and whether in her personal or professional life, never cared about societal sanction. She says,

> They [society] never liked [me] because people like tradition and people always like girls and women who are mellow by nature, and I am sorry to say I am not very submissive. If you convince me [about something] then I will honor your wishes, but if you cannot convince me, then I will not be a party to it.

For others, maintaining a do-not-care attitude regarding others' opinions about their careers is only possible after they have successfully accomplished their career objectives. Having worked extraordinarily hard to achieve their current status in the professional hierarchy, these women have detracted naysayers with their work ethic, performance, and other professional aspects that otherwise undergo more scrutiny by virtue of being female. This is true for Maya (51), a high-ranking police officer in the Indian Police Services who believes that because she has earned her rite of passage in the Services, she is now in a position to dismiss any societal disapproval.

> You are seeing me after putting in twenty-seven years of service. So initially it used to bother me what others are thinking. Not about my job necessarily but having accepted the job, whether I am doing well or not. You know I have to prove myself. Now I can sit back and relax—see I have done two districts as an independent police chief. I have done uh . . . two zones in Mumbai and one

of the zones is the toughest possible zone in Mumbai. I have done a stint in
CBI—the Central Bureau of Investigation. I have done a foreign fellowship.
Now this kind, this is considered to be the best profile of a police officer.

As indicated in the examples above, participants strongly perceive Indian
society as being discriminatory and judgmental toward women who work.
These differences arise from individuals' spatial divisions, as well as educational attainment, their social class, and age. Even while women recognize
the negative attitudes toward working women and resist the same with a "so
what, I do not care" defense, that attitude itself is made possible largely due
to family support. Then, as indicated, some women may simply be resistant
to external impositions of dos and don'ts by nature or may now be in a
position to dismiss such attitudes, having nothing left to prove to anyone
anymore professionally.

SOCIETY ACCEPTS. BE A SUPERWOMAN. BE HUMBLE.

Indian society has largely accepted the fact that women now work outside
their homes as members of the paid workforce. Regardless of societal opinion, women have learned to negotiate, resist, and demand their rightful
places. Despite these strides, the current theme underscores the expectation
for and by women to continue to fulfill familial obligations while pursuing
careers. In other words, certain societal members, including some participants, believe that they may have careers as long as their first priority continues to remain with their families/homes. Ironically, perhaps in a case of
internalized normative codes, women also perpetuate societally held role
expectations by attributing them to Indian culture and traditions.
    Avni (27), a doctor of Ayurvedic medicine, believes that women should
seek employment if their working fulfills a financial need in the family. If
that need is already met, then she believes women may consider working
only if they have their family's approval. Avni's statement seems to imply
that to her, working for self-actualization and personal/professional growth is
not as important and especially so if it causes women to neglect their families.

> For those who do have a career (in other words, work) as a hobby, they should
> not do it without considering their family's wishes. They shouldn't go against
> their family members if they say we don't need another income and end up
> neglecting their household responsibilities. I don't agree with women doing a
> career opposing their family's views that she shouldn't and at the expense of
> her household responsibilities.

So, in Avni's view, when women work to fulfill a financial need, their
working is acceptable. However, if women want to pursue careers for its own

sake, because it is something they want to do, and because it interests them, then women may as well not work. After imposing all these conditions, Avni partially contradicts herself but still maintains her perspective on the need for women to fulfill household responsibilities when she says,

> Career is important so you can be independent. I do not approve of our male-dominated society where you have to do everything as the man says but the woman should accept her household duties, her parents' well-being, her in-laws,' take care of her children, her home.

Bhavana (38) is the controller of finance at a multinational company in Pune. Even as a high level executive at the top of her career, she believes that women need to be humble if they want their status as working women to be accepted by their families. "I think people react very well if you are very honest and sincere in what you do. People just need to see that sincerity and you have to be humble, obviously." Bhavana's views imply that society will accept a woman working if she plays down her working status and expresses humility about her work. Sure women can work, but they should be modest about their work, their accomplishments, and their occupational status, in her opinion. The way society reacts to a working woman depends on her inter-personal behaviors and interactions with others. Therefore, as Bhavana sees it, if a woman is vocal about her achievements and makes work the primary focus of her life, her working status is not accepted but if she displays humility by underplaying her successes, she is more easily accepted because then, she no longer threatens the socially constructed delicate male-female, work-family balance.

It is revelatory that even in the 21st century, educated, and extremely qualified women in top leadership positions continue to defer to family and an essentialized femininity that privileges humility and mindfulness. It is simply not enough that a woman is good at what she does and lets her accomplishments speak for itself. She also has to be mindful of others' attitudes and reactions toward her and tiptoe around her family's feelings toward working women. Perhaps this narrative is culturally motivated or perhaps socialization into Indian values and expected norms of behaviors for women are so ingrained into the psyche that women are unable to differen-tiate where individual thought ends and cultural indoctrination begins. Quite possibly, "indoctrination" is a strong word. It is also possible that cultural influences are important to women and they choose to believe in a value system of social and relational hierarchy that places their own worth, accom-plishments, and careers slightly below those of men.

Vijaya (48) is the editor of a newspaper. She nonchalantly opines that women have to be superwomen if they want to have it all. Her quote below represents Indian working women on multiple levels.

Certainly if you are a woman you have to be a superwoman if you are pursuing your career. Whatever career that may be. You may be a clerk in a garment department. Or you may be an earth journalist but the fact is that the burden falls on the woman and the woman has to work that extra hard. But if she realizes—I say that women give an excuse—my family doesn't allow—my husband doesn't allow. But if you can find your space within that you can achieve the skies—for example when I started working full time I used to get up at 4 a.m. and first do the entire cooking for all the seven members of the family because I was staying with my in-laws. I packed all children's *dabbas* [lunch boxes] everything—It's another matter that my you know mother-in-law used to again for lunch change the *dabbas* and make it hot and change the *sabjis*[8] and send it and all that you know that's different. But the point is that I had decided that nobody should put a question that oh this is being left out—that was one aspect from my side.

Family back up is utmost important and then the woman's attitude—both have to really match. Otherwise definitely the whole burden is on the woman. And she has to be a superwoman. I mean I remember that I used to go back you know I used to go back to a village, do that story and come back and write it and then when I used to go back home I never wanted to feel like I'm all dead and gone—although inside I was all dead and gone. You know that's what—that's the price—like I said because I had the passion I didn't want to compromise on anything—like no one should say that—Look because of this you know your children are getting neglected or anything.

Vijaya believes that women have a choice. If they want to have it all, including a career, then they must be ready to put in all the extra work. Vijaya does not confront society. She is not resentful toward the expectations or burdens society places on working women. She has simply found a way to navigate through that situation. Because she was able to do it, she is unsympathetic toward women who are unable to balance the multiple demands of their lives by embodying a "superwoman" identity. She recalls how she woke up early, cooked for everyone, and packed her children's lunch boxes before heading to work so she did not give anybody the chance to accuse her of neglecting her children for her career or family responsibilities. Recall how Maya (51), the high-ranking police officer quoted earlier, mentioned that having accomplished a great deal in her career, she was now able to ignore what others thought of her status as a working woman. Just as Maya had to go above and beyond what was expected of her in her career in the police services, just to prove that she was equally good an officer even as a female, Vijaya had to do the same in her role as a mother and go above and beyond what might have been reasonably expected of her at home so she did not invite criticism for neglecting her family's needs. It appears that no matter what path women choose, they have to continually exert additional energies toward worrying, managing, and re-writing the scripts and lenses with which others may view the negotiation of their work and family lives. Vijaya believes that if women are truly passionate about their work, they will *have* to compromise (because nobody else is going to). Vijaya's views, albeit harsh sounding, shed light on the realities working women have to deal with every day. Being a superwoman is indeed an option, perhaps even a strategy, for a working woman treading the tightrope of work and family. Being a superwoman requires a tremendous amount of energy and time management if a woman has to satisfy everyone's needs and not burn out in so doing. By adhering to the idealized stereotypes of a superwoman, women are imposing significant expectations and stress upon themselves, validating the double standards of a patriarchal society that privileges men's work, and unconsciously shaping the meta-discourses of work that might prove detrimental to future generations of working women.

CONCLUDING THOUGHTS

This section has discussed how Indian women process and respond to the societal knowledge and experiences they acquire over the course of their lives. The following points summarize this section. First, caste and social class continue to play a role in determining the realities of women's occupations. However, unlike in the past when one's caste was a disadvantage to those belonging to the lower category, in modern India, based only on the stories narrated by upper-caste women in middle- and high-income occupations, caste appears to be a disadvantage in accessing educational and employment opportunities due to quotas reserved for low-caste people. Of course, only looking at instances of reverse discrimination oversimplifies the larger social dialog surrounding caste discrimination that continues to plague Indian society today. The points about caste and class made in this book and in this discussion are strictly limited to participants' narratives and the study's findings. The findings from this study are not expected to be generalized across India or all caste groups. Therefore, just because caste did not emerge as a topic of conversation with lower-caste women does not mean that these participants do not suffer its consequences.

Second, educating their children and providing them opportunities for a better future is the preferred route taken by women in the low-income category who desire upward mobility. Their circumstances, including a lack of education, architected by poverty, parental illiteracy, and marital problems, are the main reasons participants cite for their limited occupational choice.

Third, social class affects women across income categories to varying degrees. The outlook for low-income women is positive since their social class can only rise. Class mobility is not a concern for women in middle- and high-income occupations. In fact because these women already belong to a higher class, they are denied permission to pursue certain occupational choices if it reflects poorly on their family's reputation.

Fourt, women strongly believed that even though Indian society continues to harbor negative attitudes toward working women, they did not care much for those sentiments and as long as they had parental and family approval, they would continue to work.

Finally, participants agreed that despite opposition in some sections of society, India has come around to accepting working women. In making sense of these societal contradictions, participants imposed upon themselves an essentialized femininity that required humility in accomplishments and superwoman-like capabilities in meeting the responsibilities of work-life balance. By reproducing societal notions that a woman needs to first meet family responsibilities and then if *permitted* by her family, pursue other interests; a number of these participants have completely bought into patriarchal ideologies relegating women to the primary domestic space. Perhaps this is where the success of a patriarchal social structure lies—when "victims" of patriarchy internalize their "oppression" and start believing that the treatment they get is deserved or right and start perpetuating these ideologies by reinforcing them in their own thoughts and actions, patriarchy has succeeded in reifying itself in being panculturally accepted as *the* social norms for behavior. The word "oppression" above is in quotes because even as some women might consider themselves as targets of an unjust patriarchal order, others might feel empowered in embodying their cultural expectations and becoming the epitome of traditionally and socially desired roles of daughters, wives, daughters-in-law, and mothers. The multilayered aspects of women's working lives, seeped in internally juxtaposed discourses are a new normal for India's working women. Women's work and engagement with their societies, however, is not a linear process where one validates the other through opposition. It is a multidirectional process that includes active involvement, reciprocation, and as will be noted in upcoming chapters, one of continuous renegotiation.

NOTES

1. In 2009, the Indian parliament approved the Right to Free and Compulsory Education Act which guarantees free education to children between 6 and 14 years of age and assures that 25% of places in private schools are reserved for underprivileged children (Department of School Education & Literacy, 2011). Despite the many challenges that the successful implementation of this act faces such as a dearth of qualified teachers, inconsistency in teaching salaries a lack of motivated faculty, questions about the medium of instruction, and others, this landmark decision is a step in the right direction. When the act came into effect in 2010, India became one of 135 countries to provide education as a fundamental right to its children (India joins, 2010). Of course, a lot still needs to be done as India is reported to only spend 3% of its GDP on education (India passes, 2009).

2. With roots that can be traced back to British colonial rule, according to Combs and Nadkarni (2005), affirmative action in India "seeks to remedy the effects of a 3000-year-old rigid hierarchal caste system of power, privilege and socio-economic status . . . and attempts to provide equal opportunities to recognize past and present injustices that impact the social and economic well-being of Indians" (p. 160). Implemented through a numerically designated system of quotas and reservations, the benefiting castes primarily include Scheduled Castes, Scheduled Tribes, and Other Backward Classes, constitutionally termed as being socially and economically depressed classes (Combs & Nadkarni, 2005). With regard to employment, affirmative action programs (quotas and reservations) are only applicable to federal and state government-owned public services and businesses (Jain, Ratnam, & Venkata, 1994). For a detailed discussion, including the benefits and disadvantages of Indian affirmative action policies and programs, please read Jain et al., 1994. For a comparison of affirmative action policy in the United States and India, read Combs and Nadkarni (2005).

3. At the time this study was conducted, the Government of India's tax categorizations were as follows: There is no tax levied on those earning Rs. 150,000 or less ($3,000). The three categories of income-tax structures in India are meant for those earning between Rs. 150,001 and 300,000 (between $3,001 and $6,000); those earning between Rs. 300,001 and `500,000 (between $6,001 and $10,000); and finally those earning Rs. 500,001 and above ($10,001 and above). People in each of these three categories are taxed at the rate of 10%, 20%, and 30% respectively (Key features, 2008). At this time (Budget 2013-2014, 2013), the Indian National Rupee or Rs. was typically holding steady at $1 = Rs.50. At current time, according to the revised 2013-2014 tax rate, for all general tax payers and women (excluding senior citizens between 60-80 years, and 80 years and older), the tax division is as follows: No tax on those earning Rs.200,000 or less ($3,333); 10% tax to those earning between Rs.200,001 to 500,000 ($3,334 to $8,333); 20% tax to those earning between Rs.500,001 to $10,00000 ($8334 to $16,666); and 30% tax to those earning above Rs.10,00001 ($1 = Rs.60)

4. It is important to explain that participants were categorized on the basis on their income according to the divisions made by the Government of India for tax purposes and therefore not all women earning low-income belong to the low-caste category. For those women in this category who were the primary breadwinners for their family, the tax bracket and such a division indeed makes sense. I have also included within this category, four women (two priests, a *masala* [Masala refers to the mix of spices that flavors the dough used to make *papads* or crisp, round-shaped mealtime snack that is eaten with traditional Indian lunches and dinners] maker, and an accountant at a small non-governmental organization) who because of their low individual income are also appropriate candidates for this low income category but did not belong to the lower castes. As part of a family, their earnings, along with those of their husbands, may make them fall into a higher tax bracket.

5. Peon is a socially and culturally accepted occupational title for those working as assistants to personnel in higher positions. It is not considered offensive or derogatory. It represents a person responsible for running errands and doing odd jobs in an organization.

6. Open category refers to those people who belong to upper castes and therefore, by definition, do not belong to any of the Scheduled Castes, Scheduled Tribes, and Other Backward Classes caste-based division made by the Government of India.

7. Some Indians are able to expressly identify caste membership based on an individual's last name. Otherwise, I was directly asked about my caste by only two of the participants.

8. Dry curried vegetables eaten with Indian bread such as *naans, rotis,* and *chapattis.*

Chapter Three

Family Socialization and Career Discourses

FAMILIES, WOMEN, AND WORK IN INDIA

Historically, one's family has been the strongest and primary source of support and coping mechanism for Indians (Prasad, 2006; Sonawat 2001). Budhwar and Baruch (2003) observe that from birth, "Indians are socialized in an environment that values strong family ties and extended family relationships" (p. 702). Therefore what one's family thinks, their opinions and views regarding work and careers, the experiences family members share with each other, and the stories and anecdotes they narrate have long-lasting impressions and implications for children growing up in that environment. Sonawat (2001) explains that despite being a culturally and religiously diverse country where families "have plurality of forms that vary with class, ethnicity, and individual choices" (p. 177), among Indians,

> The family is the first line of defence, especially for children and a major factor in their survival, health, education, development, and protection. It is also a major source of nurturance, emotional bonding and socialization, and a link between continuity and change. (p. 177)

These socialization efforts are pervasive in nuclear as well as traditional joint families where parents, grandparents, and perhaps even some uncles and aunts cohabit under the same roof. Sinha (1984) argues that in Indian families, children are not consciously separated from adult spaces, rather, "the child was free to witness adults interacting with one another in varying moods and tempers, thereby learning a great deal about the elders and their own roles just by observing and listening" (p. 283). Thus it is not hard to imagine that growing up, individuals are influenced by the unconscious as well as the sometimes purposeful and strategic socialization they receive. This socialization has the potential to permeate into individuals' active meaning making processes and interpretations of what work and careers signify and is generally derived from one's cultural, familial, and social contexts. Embedded within this environment is a unique kind of socialization that pertains specifically to work and careers. Known in the disciplines of communication and management as anticipatory socialization, the nature of this socialization has to do with individuals' experiences of the discourses, observations, memories, recollections, and receipt of direct, indirect, and even ambivalent communication acquired during their formative years that then has consequences on their future career choices, development of work ethic, and learning of certain work values, among others. This will be discussed next.

Anticipatory Socialization

According to Van Maanen (1976), anticipatory socialization refers to the preparation individuals undergo prior to taking on organizational positions. The learning that occurs at this stage happens prior to officially entering into an organization (Feldman, 1981). One must note here that this privileging of organization-specific career socialization has been severely criticized by scholars like Clair (1996). Essentially, the argument holds that this privilege afforded to organizational roles and careers is to the detriment of other non-organizational and alternative choices including part-time, seasonal, or temporary work, work done as students, non-traditional careers in the performing arts and such other fields that do not circumscribe neatly within popular definitions of organizational careers (see Clair, 1996 for a discussion on "real" jobs vis-à-vis "unreal" jobs).

The concept of anticipatory socialization is important to this discussion to the extent that it explains the work and career-related communication received, understood, and interpreted by participants and their individual role in affecting its pervasiveness in their own career decisions. In formulating their thoughts and opinions about a particular occupation or organization, individuals are strongly influenced by their immediate environment such as family, peers, institutions of higher education, and cultural influences such as the media (Jablin, 1985, 2001). Merton (1957) believes that this process involves acquiring values of groups or organizations that individuals aspire to belong to, but either do not or cannot, immediately. The activities engaged in at this stage are "forming expectations about jobs—transmitting, receiving, and evaluating information with prospective employers—and making decisions about employment" (Feldman, 1976, p. 434). Thus, the anticipatory phase "focuses on the process by which individuals form expectations about careers, jobs, and organizations prior to entering them" (Jablin, 1985, p. 262).

The first place individuals get introduced to culturally and socially accepted norms and expectations for behaviors, values, traditions, and roles is their home (Chaffee, McLeod, & Wackman, 1973). Thus, the training and preparation to become socialized into work and occupational roles begins in early childhood (Crites, 1969). Jablin (1985) proposed that this stage of anticipatory socialization comprised two related phases: the process of vocational choice or vocational anticipatory socialization (VAS), and the process of organizational choice or organizational anticipatory socialization. The first phase or VAS includes family, educational institutions, part-time employment, peers and friends, and media as primary sources influencing vocational choice. The second phase includes recruiting source effects, realism of job or organizational expectations, and the selection interview (Jablin, 1987). The anticipatory phase has been used to explore multiple pre-organizational contexts. For example, Lucas (2006) has examined the role of communication in the transition of children of blue-collar parents into postindustrial careers, as well as how socializing discourses influence pathways to social mobility (Lucas, 2011). Gibson and Papa (2000) explored how this phase contributed to the process of organizational assimilation for blue-collar employees at a manufacturing plant. Shenoy, Williams, and Linvill (2008) looked at how career messages communicated during the anticipatory socialization phase results in successors of family businesses *choosing* to work in their family's enterprise.

Being raised and socialized into an environment that values strong family ties and familial relationships (Budhwar, 2003; Devi, 2004; Prasad & Baruch, 2004), one can safely assume that Indian families play a significant role in shaping ideas about work and careers in women's lives.

Chaffee, et al. (1973) observe, a family's home is "the only social institution in which almost every child has been involved since birth" (Chaffee et al., 1973, p. 349) which is why Berger and Luckmann (1967) refer to the experiential learning acquired at this stage as primary socialization. Referring to parents as some of the "significant others" (p. 131) in a child's life, they posit that even though the child is not a passive recipient of socialization, the rules of the game are set by adults such that children internalize adults' realities. The training and preparation to become socialized into work and occupational roles begins in early childhood (Crites, 1969). According to Jablin (1985), the anticipatory stage of organizational socialization "focuses on the process by which individuals form expectations about careers, jobs, and organizations prior to entering them" (p. 262). Jablin (2001) argues that individuals develop a set of expectations and beliefs regarding work that are formed out of the verbal or nonverbal communicative actions occurring in their environment. Likewise, Bandura's (2001) social cognitive theory explains that when learning through observation, individuals imitate and adopt the behaviors, attitudes, and values being observed. Individuals also intentionally or unintentionally collect occupational information from the environment and compare this against their self-concept (Jablin, 2001) as they consider "their personal interests and capabilities, weigh the issues and alternatives involved in choosing a particular job or occupation, and finally make a series of choices that influence the direction of their future careers" (Hoffner, Levine, & Toohey, 2008, p. 284).

Goodnow and Lawrence (2001) found that through learning from and negotiating household chores, children learn values such as respect, fairness, and decision making, applicable in the world of paid employment. Thus, long before individuals enter the world of paid employment, their conceptions about what it means to work and earn a living as well as their career aspirations and expectations have already started to shape their work/identity socialization (Lair, 2007). Lair (2007) argues that people start picking up on the various interpretations and meanings associated with work available to them in their environment and in addition to being influenced by socializing agents, proactively participate in growing their subjective sense of what it means to be a professional in contemporary organizational society. This socialization is not limited by activities specific to any one organization, rather individuals learn about their self, social, and worker identity through this process. The nature of this socialization is influenced by society, culture, and class status. For example, in her study of socializing messages communicated between members of blue-collar families, Lucas (2011) explained how her participants' working-class backgrounds affected not only the nature of socializing messages to which they were exposed but also the significance and centrality of work in their lives. In the Indian context, Kapoor (1997) found that the socioeconomic status of one's family determined the work values of girls and that parental involvement in developing work attitudes and ethic in their daughters continued over a prolonged period of time. An important component of anticipatory socialization is memorable interpersonal messages communicated between family members that may play the role of powerful linguistic tools and provide frameworks for individuals to recall and utilize during specific sense making processes (Medved, Brogan, McClanahan, Morris, & Shepherd, 2006). This will be discussed next.

Memorable Messages

In his book, *The Last Lecture*, which Professor Randy Pausch wrote just before losing his battle to pancreatic cancer, he credits his father as being a master at storytelling. He cites several pieces of advice that his father passed on to him at different phases of his life. For example, writes Pausch (2008), "My dad gave me advice on how to negotiate my way through life. He'd say things like: 'Never make a decision until you have to.' He'd also warn me that even if I was in a position of strength, whether at work or in relationships, I had to play fair. 'Just because you're in the driver's seat,' he'd say, 'doesn't mean you have to run people over'" (p. 23). Even though Pausch does not refer to them as such, these little pieces of advice are *memorable messages*. Memorable messages have been defined in several ways as being contingent upon myriad characteristics. In general however, these messages are fragments of everyday discourses that are specific to an individual and that are retained and recollected by that individual at crucial periods in her or his life. Messages such as the ones described above are often internalized and may have lasting influences on how individuals process important decisions.

According to Knapp, Stohl, and Reardon (1981), interpersonal messages are "remembered for a long time and . . . have a profound influence on a person's life" (p. 27). However, not all interpersonal messages are created equal and therefore not all of them are memorable. In order for messages to be forever etched in one's memory, they have to follow certain prescriptions. First, messages that are easily recalled are the ones that have been sent by those older than the recipient. These senders not only have a higher social status but are also respected, loved, and admired by recipients. Memorable messages may be communicated in the form of a rule or a code of conduct. Knapp et al. (1981) observe that the brevity of a message is what makes it of memorable quality. Therefore, they note that such a message may range from a single utterance to a short sentence. Second, memorable messages are personal in focus. They are directed toward a single individual or in our case, toward members of one's family only. It is this individually customized and personally meaningful nature of the message that makes them memorable. Third, such messages are uncomplicated in sentence structure and form. Often meant as rules of behavior, the simpler the structure, the easier they are to remember and recall when required. Memorable messages, thus, are highly communicative endeavors by which "requisite orientations are transferred to . . . participants" (Stohl, 1986, p. 234).

Stories have similar implications on human beings. The extant literature on storytelling in families has significantly contributed to our understanding of communicative processes such as discursively formed ideologies regarding gender (e.g., Knudson-Martin, 1995; Medved et al., 2006; Mize, 1995). The literature reviewed in these essays relate to stories told by members of a family to one another and passed down from one generation to the next in some instances. These stories have to do with family rituals and legacies, and health and healing, among others. There have been no studies done, to the best of my knowledge and research, that have explored the role of memorable messages and/or stories told about work and careers on Indian women. In exploring how women come to understand their worlds of work through anticipatory socialization, this project also investigates the role of memorable messages in Indian women's lives.

This part of the study is constructed on the premise that due to the strong family ties and structures that most Indians come from, one's family unequivocally influences women in all aspects of life including how they come to understand work and careers. Just how family members exert that influence communicatively and how the recipients interpret those discourses is not adequately known. This study assumes that family members or parents in this case, often become career enablers or *individuals who positively, directly, or indirectly, through verbal or practical encouragement and assistance, enable others' careers.* These career enablers are instrumental in providing the anticipatory socialization women experience growing up. Although similar in influence to related terms like mentor and sponsor, career enablers essentially incorporate an empowerment-by-enabling component. These enablers, especially parents and in-laws, enable women to have careers by positive words, actions, role modeling, and primary and secondary professional and personal family balance assistance either through tangible or intangible means, among others. Often the daughters may not even be aware of the impact enablers have on them until actively asked to recall those early career-enabling influences.

KNOWLEDGES OF SOCIALIZATION

Vocational anticipatory socialization (VAS) is understood as work/career-related learning and teachings prior to organizational entry. This research project was interested in exploring the many facets of pre-career entry socialization, or VAS, for Indian women. Specifically, this study was interested in knowing how Indian women are informed about work and careers by the people around them, growing up. In others words, socialization here is defined more broadly as those pieces of work/career-related information communicated to women, subtle or obvious, that ultimately influence their career choices and behaviors. It must be noted that a majority of the findings reported here relate to most of the women but not all of them. Generalizations discussed here should therefore be read as representing, more typically, women in the middle- and high-income occupations, unless otherwise stated.

Findings indicate the powerful role of fathers in influencing their daughters' careers. As a result of parentally allowed freedom, daughters feel encouraged to pursue a career of personal choice. Mothers play a more secondary role to fathers but their significance, especially those of educated and working mothers, is tremendous. In the Indian context, one's extended family also plays an influential role in the growth and development of individuals, which is also the case with women's careers. Sisters, brothers, uncles, aunts, grandparents, husbands, in-laws, and close friends also play a constructive role in enabling women's careers. Participants recalled several messages and stories narrated to them by family members, especially fathers, that helped them at crucial stages in their work and personal lives. As with most things in the Indian context, however, every freedom is conditional upon cultural norms that dutiful daughters and daughters-in-law are expected to follow. These women's stories were no different.

Career Enablers: Fathers and Freedom

Devi's (2004) study on employed and unemployed single and married Indian women found that fathers of both employed groups had higher education levels, had motivated their daughters toward seeking employment, had given equal importance to marriage and career, and held positive views of working women. Likewise, findings from this study reveal the pivotal role fathers play in influencing their daughters' perspectives toward careers and in developing their professional identities. Daughters are encouraged to pursue a career of personal choice albeit within some constraints.

As has been found in studies conducted with women in other cultures, here too, fathers are the single biggest career influencers in the lives of Indian women. Dominantly seen in the cases of middle- and high-income/higher classes of women but also evident in some instances with low-income women, fathers enable their daughters' careers in multiple ways. Categorically, fathers socialize their daughters, with direct and indirect influences. Additionally, some influences were perceptively inherited by the daughters enabling them to choose careers like their fathers. Fathers also influence their daughters by directly, indirectly, or through osmosis (see Gibson & Papa, 2000) teaching them about work ethic and work-life management.

First, I will discuss how direct communication by fathers influences their daughters' career choices. Participants report how their parents did not always give them career advice per se but allowed them the freedom to pick a career of their choice. This was particularly true in case of women in their 20s and 30s.

Direct Influences

Jagruti (34), a radiologist, always assumed that she would have a career and because she knew her father wanted her to become a doctor, she enthusiastically accepted his aspiration for her. She recalls how going by the popular career wisdom of her time, she could have either become a doctor or an engineer.

Jagruti: I had a choice of going either to chemical engineering or medical and my father always wanted me to go into medical although he never enforced it upon me but I knew that he wanted me to go into medical.

Suchitra: How did you know that?

Jagruti: Oh he had been quite vocal about his expectations but since I did not get into I.I.T. [Indian Institute of Technology] I thought that I might as well do medical so I got into K.E.M. [King Edward Memorial Hospital with affiliated medical college]. I had very high marks so there was no problem with the admissions at any time.

Her father was of the opinion that the profession of medicine afforded many additional advantages to women.

My father, as I said, always told me you must get into the medical profession because he felt that it is good for a woman to be in the medical profession because she can do a lot for her family, immediate family as well as extended family by being in the medical profession. He made it very clear to me always he would like me to be a doctor but he never ever forced me or forced anything on me.

Thus for Jagruti, her father's support of a medical career was important in the decision making. Jagruti's father's opinion is externally focused. He wants his daughter to become a doctor so she can help others in the family with her medical knowledge. With such a relational objective, one wonders if her father really wanted her to become a doctor because he thought it was a good choice for *her* or only because it would help others—a selfless nurturing task that is a significant trait of an essentialized femininity. Jagruti is not conflicted about her father's words though. She says that it did not matter to her whether she became an engineer or doctor. She had enough marks to go into either profession but because her father felt strongly about medicine, it just made her decision easier. Furthermore, while Jagruti appears to frame her career decision as her own, interestingly, this decision is rendered complex by the dialectical nature of that choice. On one hand she says that her father was very clear about his wanting her to become a doctor but at the same time she insists that he never forced that decision upon her. Jagruti continues to believe that the decision to become a doctor was hers to make but clearly having her father's approval made that decision even more appropriate. By asserting that the medical field was a gender-appropriate profession for women, and one that would enable her to advise her own family on health matters (thereby privileging a career that contributes toward family welfare), he was also appealing to her sense of gendered, cultural, and familial propriety. Therefore, while Jagruti claims she chose to become a doctor, one cannot deny the direct influence her father had on that choice. In this case, one can see how the father not only communicated his expectations of his daughter but also provided a gender appropriate and culturally and socially approved career path for her. This observation supports Medved and colleagues' (2006) findings in the United States that highlight the gendered nature of socializing messages women receive or as seen here, messages that speak to the appropriateness of a certain profession as being good or bad for women.

Rakhi's (27) father also wanted her to become a doctor. When she was finally able to convince him that she simply did not have the heart to be a doctor and that she wanted to study business administration instead, he supported her decision by seeking out information about different universities and accompanying her to campus interviews. Even though Nutan's (39) father did not give her any specific career advice as such, he equipped her with skills that could qualify her for any number of professions.

> Suchitra: Did your parents ever give you career advice as you were growing up?
>
> Nutan: Ya, my dad never used to allow me to sit at home. He never used to allow me . . . when I was in 7th standard itself, during my vacation he used to take me to the institute. He used to ask me to learn typing.
>
> Suchitra: What institute?
>
> Nutan: Typing institute. He used to ask me to learn typing then once I reached the speed of 40 words then he told me to join for shorthand. Then after that he asked me to join this computer class, traveling tourism course, learning German language. So one or the other, he never let me sit at home. He always used to ask me to do some or other studies. He was never in favor . . . even when I am sitting at home he never allowed me to sit at home. He used to get Competition Success[1] regularly and he used to ask me to read all the books and he used to ask me questions. So these activities he always used to be behind me asking me to do things.

Nutan also says that having learned basic computer skills at a time when Indians were only being introduced to the machine, when her employer, Indian Railways, decided to become computerized, she was already a step ahead of her colleagues and would often help them with their computer problems.

Shanti (35), a school peon, also recalls how her illiterate parents encouraged her to further her education even though they lived in a village with limited resources. The primary objective of educating their daughter and developing her vocational skills was to enable her to have a stable and financially secure future life in case of potential marital problems.

My father always said you should be able to do any kind of job because you never know what situations you'll face in your life. So our father gave us very good values, that if you get a husband who does not look after you, and that is exactly what happened, or if he doesn't work, rather than go to the village and work in the fields, you can sit at home, take care of your family, your children and husband. So he let me learn stitching and that is exactly what happened. For many days, we could keep our family going because I stitched. I even looked after my husband on my income. So from a young age, I could do all kinds of work and jobs, right from working in the fields. I feel proud that no matter what task you give me, I can do it with joy and pleasure and live up to your trust.

Shanti's experience supports previous findings that indicate Indian parents often educate their daughters so they can build educational capital and live independent lives in case of marital breakdown or death of a spouse.

Vijaya (48), editor of a community newspaper, remembers how her father wanted her to either work for the Indian Administrative Services or become a journalist. In order to facilitate the latter, he even contacted some journalist friends of his and told Vijaya to write to them. Vijaya says her father always talked about work, "but more importantly, he would always have a dream for me."

Vedha (49), general manager at a multinational corporation, explains how her father influenced her.

I remember the number of times he had to come with me to the universities you know, to actually fight out my case for getting admission for B. Ed [Bachelor of Education]. So, he also is a very aggressive achiever and does not give up easily. If he is convinced about something, then he just goes ahead and I think that is exactly what has come in us [her and her siblings], that if you believe you want to do it very aggressively, then you achieve it and then you do not bother about what is the consequence and things like that.

Vedha considers herself a risk taker who often jumps into things without fully considering the consequences of her actions, a trait that she says has fortunately, helped her in her career. She attributes this trait to her father being an aggressive achiever himself.

Indirect Influences

Twenty-six years ago when Anjana (48), who is currently the CEO and co-owner of a manufacturing company, decided to become an engineer, engineering was considered a non-traditional career choice for women and this was especially true with mechanical engineering. In fact, just ten years ago when Vidisha (29), who currently works as an information technology risk management analyst, wanted to study mechanical engineering, relatives and friends warned her against it saying that that field of engineering was a boy's world. Anjana's father did no such thing. He merely alerted her to what she could expect if she decided to pursue that career path.

> They [parents] never objected to my decision. He [father] had sat me down and explained to me that it is a very hectic discipline and you are choosing mechanical. First year engineering is common for everybody, specializations begin from the second year. He informed me that I would have to do a lot of physically taxing work from my second year onwards. I said I'll do it. I don't feel anything about it. They never asked me or questioned my decision about why I wanted to do engineering. You are studying, study. There was never a why do you want to do this, just do a B.Sc and M.Sc, they never objected.

Mechanical engineering is considered a very male-dominated field and by making her aware of the physicality involved in the profession, her father encouraged yet prepared her for the realities that came with that profession. Anjana's saying her father " sat me down" should not be interpreted to mean that he disapproved of her choice and wanted to convince her otherwise. Given the tone of voice and the context surrounding Anjana's reply, it was obvious that her father was looking out for her out of concern but not with the intention of changing her mind.

Women's careers have been well supported by their parents, and especially fathers. Parents of women in middle- and high-income occupations have encouraged their daughters to *choose* their careers. It is important to note that even having the freedom to choose or women's intuitive understanding that they could indeed choose their own career paths was enabled through childhood socializing, growing up in families that nurtured that spirit of independence. Anjana recalls,

> He [father] was of the opinion that even though we were girls we had to stand on our feet [be financial independent; see chapter 5]. He always encouraged us to study whatever we wanted. He was even ready to send me out of the house. As in, when I was in Engineering, in 1978–79, there weren't too many women going out, especially in engineering but he had said, if you want to go, my uncle stays in Hubli, and they have a college there, and he had said if I don't get admission in Pune, he would send me there. He never said I couldn't do anything. My older sister did her B.Com. (Bachelor of Commerce) and she was a basketball player. After graduation, she got a government job and he said yes you have to take it. At that time women didn't really work, they didn't have jobs so that way he was a very forward type of a person. He told us that we had to learn how to drive. Basically he would tell us to read a lot, study whatever you want to, just don't quit anything. Really we realize it now. He would tell us to learn typing and we'd feel does he want to make us clerks that we have to learn typing. But now I realize that had I learned it at that time, I would have become much faster on the computer keyboard. Now I do it by practice but his objective was whatever you can possibly study, you should. That was his nature.

Having been raised with many personal freedoms and a father that encouraged and supported his daughters' many endeavors, Anjana felt confident to pursue a non-traditional career.

Most people enjoy watching a classical Indian dance performance representing traditional dance forms. However, few consider taking up dancing as a full-time profession. Sachi (28) completed her undergraduate degree in physics but has been dancing since she was six years old. There came a point in her life when she had to choose between becoming a physicist or a dancer. After evaluating the advantages and disadvantages of both career options, Sachi decided to go with her gut and chose to become a dancer. Her parents supported her decision, but her father also explained the practical consequences of her decision.

> About my dance, my career as a dancer . . . he had told me right in the beginning that if I have to choose this, I have to keep in mind that probably this will not be lucrative enough since funding is also not much like other countries. Learning dance in India, if I represent India somewhere else, yes, but in India itself, not much. We have to really tap the proper channels to get the funding or else it is very difficult to get it. So that is one thing he told me that this is probably one thing I'll always have to deal with but I must not bother myself with it if I am ready to take that step, then go ahead.

Her father identified the drawbacks of a career in dancing but also urged her to pursue it if that was what she really wanted to do, having understood the reality of that career choice.

Thus, fathers have influenced their daughters' career decisions directly or indirectly. Either they have wanted them to opt for a certain career path and then provided all the resources for the same or having allowed them the freedom of choice, ensured their daughters were aware of potential outcomes of their choices by giving them realistic pictures.

Fathers have also influenced their daughters' careers indirectly by modeling their own behaviors through subtle non-verbal but action-oriented messages representing their own careers, or by engaging in career-related interactions with others that their daughters picked up on. These influences were more of an inherited nature.

Inherited Influences

Mukta (25) is a fashion designer who at interview time had just embarked on building her design business. She considers her father her role model since he is also a small-business owner. Her parents support her choice of career but she is particularly observant of her father's work habits. She has seen all the hard work her father puts in at his business working long hours. Having seen her father build his business from the ground up and make personal sacrifices, she says she feels prepared to do what it takes to manage her own entrepreneurial activities.

Padmini (36) is a physicist who, along with her father, a scientist, owns her business. Padmini comes from an illustrious and famous family whose members were pioneers of women's education in Pune. This fact is important in light of the socialization that she has undergone. Padmini explains that a number of family members, including her great grandfather, wrote their auto-biographies, all of which she has read, and found impressive and influential. Her family has always been known to engage in firsts, that is, if you belong to her family, it is generally expected that you will do something different from the beaten path. As a result, she says, standing out by their work and life decisions is the norm for her family. In fact, she says that cousins who actually chose to lead "normal" lives had a difficult time being accepted by others in the family and community. Despite all the over-achievers in her family, she admits to never feeling pressured into doing anything outside of her interests. She says she was indifferent toward her education as a child, but over the years, like the overwhelming number of scientists in her family, she found herself drawn to that career path.

> Padmini: I mean in school I didn't like much studies. Anyway I was indifferent. I knew it was necessary to study so I studied. It was not like I loved a particular subject or anything like that. Because in my family there is a predominance of scientists so it was decided sort of in my own mind that I will also become a scientist.

> Suchitra: Had you decided to go a different route, would that have been encouraged?

> Padmini: Yes. When I did 10th standard, 12th standard [high school] that time this craze of engineering and medical had already started but I had decided that I wanted to become a scientist. I didn't want to go that route [of engineering or medicine]. The only question to be decided was which science stream to specialize in. It was around 11th [grade, high school/junior college] that I started liking physics a lot which surprised my father because he is a botanist and he is not that good in mathematics so jokingly I said that, that [physics] was the only subject my family had left alone for me because in all other fields there in some XXXXX [last name] or the other who has done some good work. So I went on to become a physicist.

Thus, in Padmini's case, not only her father, but other relatives who were scientists, influenced her career path indirectly.

In Maya's (51) case, her father's professional life invaded her personal life too. Maya is a high-ranking police officer just like her father was once. She says,

My father was in police and in police you have—there is no clear-cut division at home or at office. So it was so much a part of our life—police life—it was so—I mean it wasn't discussed as an episode but the culture was very much there that we belonged to police family.

Suchitra: What kind of a culture was that?

Maya: See there'll be constables at home. There'll be sentries outside. In school everyone knew that we are police officer's children, senior officers came home for dinner, for lunch . . . what happens in a police department we didn't know except that these night rounds are there, some operations are being carried out, what are these operations we didn't know . . . that my father can disappear for two days, three days, he can be called at odd hours, he's investigating crime, but what exactly is that crime we didn't know.

Suchitra: Were you ever afraid or worried about what your father did?

Maya: Only when my father went on deputation to BSF [Border Security Force] and he was on the [war] front during 1971 [India-Pakistan] war.

Her father's work experiences did not dissuade her from wanting to join the police force. In fact, she says she knew from a young age that as an "outdoorsy person," joining the Indian Police Services would be an ideal career for her.

Like in Maya's case, Shalini (32) too was influenced by her father's career and became a labor and employment attorney like him.

I used to see that you know, my dad used to sit on a chair and you know, people very senior to him would come and talk to him and you know, seek his advice. So and I was like a kid like I used to be playing all over his office you know and I used to always wonder what is happening like why are these people so like you know they come and they . . . they are waiting for hours together and like you know I used to come and sit on his lap and I used to see the people talking to him and like you know. I used to wonder I was just small, like at the age of five or something and you are not able to understand. So I would sit and see the files and everything and I was somewhere deep down that had an impact you know, that maybe one day I will be sitting in a similar chair and you know, people would come to me and seek advice and that time I used to really feel that oh! Is it like . . . is he so clever that you know people from outstation come and they wait for a long time and it is a different experience so that was an impact that I had in my mind.

Because her father worked from home during his early days in the practice, when clients came to visit him, they were effectively visiting him at home. When she was older, she remembers how excitedly her father talked about his work and court matters.

I used to wonder oh, how boring! . . . but we did not have the heart to say that because he was so excited about it and I would always remember the amount of happiness that he had in telling us you know the entire situation or the case or whatever the narration that he usually told and he still does, like that is one of his nature. I am more quieter like I do not carry back my work at all but like when there is something like, he keeps on talking about it you know, so there were many things and I used to wonder that oh my God! Like you know, like even after completing so many years, he is like you know so happy about telling a particular episode or you know, like this happened in the court and that happened in the court.

With an informed awareness of the profession, Shalini's socialization itself was direct but it was not consciously done in her opinion. That she allowed it to positively inspire her speaks to her individual career interest.

Finally, fathers also taught their daughters about working with integrity and managing work and life.

Work Ethic and Work-Life Management

Chaitali (62), a priest, says she learned a valuable lesson from the example her father set. She says her father was a brilliant man who had graduated with a bachelor's degree from Pune but was forced to work as a legal bonds writer to continue his father's, her grandfather's, legacy.

Frankly speaking he did not like that job. He considered it a very low level job. He had a B.A. from Pune's Deccan College. Had known Guruji Ranade [social activist/reformer], very cultured but because my father was the only child, my grandfather wanted that his profession should be carried forward by his son, my father. So he wasn't too keen on it but he worked hard and did it with integrity. He earned a lot of name in it. All the stamp paper that he worked on was approved all the way up the courts. He tried to do his LLB [Law] in his later years but he met with an accident and so couldn't complete it.

Chaitali noticed that even though her father did not like his job, he did it with the utmost sincerity, which taught her that just because you do not like what you do, professionally, does not mean you should do a bad job of it and that with true dedication and commitment toward that work, one can really be the best at it. Such appreciation for one's father's profession is obvious in the narratives of many participants. Anjana (48), CEO/co-owner of a manufacturing company, remembers her observations of her father:

Basically there wasn't much of a communication between us. Unless there was some kind of an achievement we had got or got some very low marks, we didn't have much conversation. Of course we could tell from his voice or whatever little he spoke that he knows his subject very well. If there was a complicated situation or a problem arose in his field, he would solve it. He had specialized in heat treatment. So he would be reading about that even at home. He was a studious person. He would always be invited by other companies for resolving special problems. We knew that. Now that I am older I know what he did at that time.

Even though Anjana's father was not a talkative person, his actions, incessant desire for learning, and intelligence were noted by her as she was growing up, which came in handy when she had to study for her own engineering degree and eventually run a manufacturing company.

Meha (27), a supervisor at a multinational information technology company, believes that by observing her father, she has learned how to separate work worries from her family life. She considers herself quite adept at balancing (and separating) her work and life because, growing up, she remembers how her father never brought any work tensions home, "My dad, I mean he used to keep his personal and professional lives apart. He always maintained that line." This attitude of her father became a lesson in how to manage her personal and professional lives.

Shraddha (27), however remembers how her father's behavior at home would change depending upon what had transpired at work. Even though she found it difficult to deal with it at the time, she realizes that that experience has taught her not to let her decisions negatively impact anybody else.

Suchitra: What kind of stories do you remember your parents telling you about their work?

Shraddha: *Haan* [Yes], at times you know, what happens is you spend so much time at work, so whatever happens *vahan p*e [over there], you know, you tend to carry it back home, so if it has been a good day at work you know, your parents would be very happy and your dad would be *ekdam* [very] nice but at times if he has had a bad day, then it would reflect in his behavior you know, *thoda aise chidchidapan* [some irritation] and all that and that is pretty natural, I guess for any human being and apart from that, anything specific as such I do not remember much.

Suchitra: How did his behavior influence you?

Shraddha: Ahh . . . you know, when I was very little I used to think *arey kya problem hai, maine kuch kiya nahi hai mujhe kyo daant rahe hai* [What is the problem? I haven't done anything wrong. Why is he scolding me?] you know, but over a period of time, you do realize you know, once you . . . after you have grown up after certain age, you do realize ya, this is just because he has some other baggage and because of that is . . . that is how he is acting so . . . I think . . .

Suchitra: What did that teach you?

> Shraddha: I actually myself, I am very short tempered . . . yea, I am and I get irritated or I get angry pretty quickly you know, I tend to say a lot of things which I would probably I would not mean no harm on that but I overreact at times and that is how my dad is, so I think I have got . . . got that from him, so I think over a period of time that is what I learned that you know, you have to just face your problems and make sure that someone else is not getting affected because of . . . unnecessarily because of all those things.

Even though Shraddha's father may not necessarily have intended for her to extract a lesson from his behavior, observing his behavior provided a useful resource in how not to behave similarly in situations that lend themselves to work-related annoyances and frustration.

As seen in the examples above, fathers have had a strong impact on their daughters' careers. Whether it was through direct involvement, indirect behavior modeling, inherited influences including representing a strong work ethic and lessons on work-life management, providing reality checks, simplifying career expectations, or allowing the space for daughters to learn from careers similar to theirs, fathers enable their daughters to make informed career decisions, manage work situations, and work with integrity.

Career Enablers: Mothers

Relative to fathers' influences on daughters' work and career socialization, mothers did not enable careers in an obvious pattern. While daughters' recollection of fathers' socialization efforts predominantly occurred early in their lives—before their actual career decision-making took place, mothers' advice and enabling of daughters' careers occurred at different phases of their lives including before and during their actual career engagement. For ease of explanation, this section is divided into themes but they all overlap and emerge salient at different times in participants' lives.

Emotional Support and Resilience

Mothers' anticipatory socialization of their daughters' careers was represented in more stereotypically encouraging and nurturing ways. Harsha's (29) mother, a housewife, provided emotional support to her daughter, now a physiotherapist.

> She was very supportive. Whenever I get depressed I am dependent on her. She does not know that but that is true . . . I was a bright child but not an academically perfect child so I was not getting exact marks whatever was needed for that course. Somehow, I was getting lack of confidence which was showing in my writing of my papers. Even if I knew the stuff I would not write. So I was like "I am not going to do this. I don't think I can pursue this career forever." I think there was some time when I felt that I am really going

to quit it. But my mother was like, "no you can do it." She was with me all the time. It is not that she has taken my studies [helped with studies] and stuff like that. She was always confirmative, reassuring that no you can do it and I think that is a strong pillar if somebody has faith in you then you can go ahead. Once I passed that phase I think I did better afterwards. So she was really good help for me.

Like Harsha, participants discussed the instrumental support and encouragement their mothers provided them throughout their lives.

Just like fathers who encourage daughters to acquire skills in typing, computers, and others, mothers too push their daughters toward learning new skills. The mother of Manisha (49), a priest, was a housewife who was illiterate but wanted her children to be educated, and not just academically.

My mother was a housewife but hadn't gotten an education so she had always wanted that we should study a lot. I wasn't very studious. I was a more creative person. I was so-so. I would study as much as I could remember so she would get behind me to study. She never let me sit idle. Do something. You don't like this, do something else. Learn knitting, learn embroidery, do this, do that, she made me learn all that. So today, because of that I am so qualified today. There is nothing that I cannot learn if I want to. I know everything that I need to know for my job. That was her encouragement and motivation that made me do it. Even if my father refused permission for something, she would say, it's okay and encouraged me.

These mothers encouraged their daughters at crucial years of their young lives as they were only just developing their thoughts about work and careers. Mothers provided instrumental and emotional help by setting life examples that daughters recognized and put to use when life circumstances so demanded.

Manjushree (59), a businesswoman, remembers falling on hard times when her father was cheated out of large sums of money by a work partner. He worked hard to get them out of the situation but soon became an alcoholic and passed away, leaving her stay-at-home and newly widowed mother with the responsibility of raising three young daughters. Manjushree remembers,

He [father] would shout a lot. People in the neighborhood, friends would hear him shout but no one made us feel that my father was an alcoholic. They ignored it but we sisters felt quite embarrassed about it. After returning from school, my friends and I would stand outside the house and chat and we could hear him shout. It feels bad to say but once he expired, I felt this great hollowness inside me but I also felt relieved because everything became quiet, like there was no more tension around. I would always stay panicky. What if someone comes home and my father starts shouting? Relatives would be sitting around or us friends laughing and suddenly he would enter the room with a drink in his hand. I loved him but we got over it.

My mother really came through as this very strong person. She was very good looking. After my father died, there was some estate left, some close relatives said that since the girls are so small, let's make a trust because they worried about what would happen to us if my mother re-married. Then a family friend stepped in and said, no the mother is educated and no trustee will feel as much for these children as the mother will and she will have to approach the trustees for her own money every time she needed anything. She would have to show that indeed she needed the money for us. So he didn't want my mother to go through that. He said she was capable of handling this. My mother felt very strongly about that and so she raised us in a very nice manner. She was hurt. She never remarried even though she had many proposals come her way. People were ready to accept her with three daughters but she had been so hurt by the whole thing that she never accepted or even thought about it. She raised us very well. After I got married, I was undergoing a rough patch since my husband wasn't earning anything. So she would give me all the new things she bought and take my old things and use them herself. She was the branch manager, but her car was always in front of my house if I ever needed to use it. After she passed away, I got her car. We got those same values.

Manjushree's mother was a housewife but after her husband died and the responsibility of raising three daughters fell on her shoulders, she trained to become an insurance agent and started working for the government insurance company, soon becoming a branch manager. Manjushree was inspired by her mother and when she fell on hard times after her husband walked out on her and their son, she slowly and steadily created an institute for the performing arts with her son's support. Manjushree was particularly affected by her mother's resilience in the face of sudden hardship and change of circumstances, which was exactly what happened to her after her husband left unexpectedly.

Pooja (50), the principal of an international school, remembers being inspired by her mother's reaction to the sudden death of her father.

This was in the year '69. In fact my father died when I was pretty young. I was only 11. He passed away when we were in Delhi and we shifted to Pune because my mother's side of the family lived in Pune so that's why we shifted here. Then she invested her money in a petrol pump [gas station] on Tilak Road and so between her brother and she, she had that petrol pump. My mother owned it as a partner. Then she also subsequently started a school, a Montessori for which she had trained in the UK several years back before she was married. It came in use you know after so many years.

Amidst her mother's resilience and sustained efforts to provide for her children after the death of her husband, she also perhaps indirectly imparted to Pooja the love for education. It is quite possible that Pooja's own career in education is the result of an inherited career. After all, her mother did pass on some helpful tips. She recalls,

> In fact she [mother] was a pioneer in Poona for you know one of those Montessori methods. I am talking about 1971 when she started the school. She would tell us never think that a child is innocent. They are really smart. They play against their father and mother and come and tell tales in school which are not necessarily true at all so I think that is coming in use now.
>
> Suchitra: How has it come in use?
>
> Pooja: In the sense that now when I am working in a school with children, you can't take them at face value. When they tell you things, you've got to reconfirm if that's really true or they're just saying it. They do, do that sometimes you know just to get a little bit of a sympathy.

Jaya (48) is a social worker who remembers how, upon her grandfather's encouragement, her mother used to "donate" her abilities. Her grandfather (her mother's father-in-law) always believed that if a person had some skill, she or he should donate those skills to people who need them. Therefore, Jaya's mother, who was skillful at embroidery and stitching, designed a large number of clothes and donated them to poor people in their village. Seeing her mother put in her efforts for the betterment of society may have been one of the reasons that attracted Jaya to social work.

Encouraging Daughters to Have Careers

Many mothers who had quit their jobs after marriage or childbirth urged their daughters to have careers of their own. This encouragement can be seen as the mothers' ways of living careers vicariously through their daughters. Cultural norms that existed at the time of their youth socialized these mothers to think of marriage as the ultimate goal of life. Even when women desired their own and independent careers, as a generation, they sometimes had to begrudgingly abandon any such thought in order to privilege their marriages and raise families.

Maya's (51) mother quit her job after she got married but always told her how the time in her life when she worked [paid employment] was the best part of her life. Maya believes that having educated mothers is a strong advantage to the career development of women. She says,

> That time my friends did not have educated mothers. Educated fathers were common in our times. We [she and her siblings] were different—that much I felt but why, how—that didn't strike me . . . and I would say having an educated mother was a big big . . . [deal]

Yamini (31) is an architect who was strongly encouraged by her mother to *have* a career.

> My mother she wanted to be like, I think she wanted to work a lot and she wanted to have her own career and she could not do it so she always encouraged me you know you have to have your own career, you study and you work and be on your own feet and not be in the house working all the time. I think she instigated that a lot in me. I mean she could not do it so she thought my daughter should be able to do it. So me and my sister were always encouraged. My sister is a slow learner, she has Down's Syndrome and so for her, with her she had to be careful but with me, she always pushed me, you have to try doing something.

Tanushree (22) is a make-up artist whose mother worked from home as a beautician. As a result, she got to see the different clients who visited her mother for beauty treatments. This may have influenced her decision to become a make-up artist.

In case of women in low-income occupations, almost all mothers were illiterate but worked as agricultural laborers in farms or as maids. Women recollected how their parents worked extremely hard and long hours. Women in low-income occupations started engaging in paid employment at a young age to help their parents. Says Shobana, a maid,

> Yes I remember seeing my parents work very hard. I wanted to help them in their work so they can be relieved at least a little bit. They got me educated at least a little and because of their work, at least I am able to do this work. If they had got us into idling away time at home just sitting and eating, I would have said I won't work.

For women in low-income occupations, "career" based conversations with their parents were nonexistent. Since many of them were not educated, they did not frame their work in terms of a career. Work was a way of life for them, something they needed to do, and something they had grown up seeing their parents do. Work was essential to survival and to make ends meet. They could not afford to "glamorize" their hard labor as a career. Bharati (45), also a maid, explains quite matter-of-factly,

> Suchitra: Did your mother work?
>
> Bharati: She did.
>
> Suchitra: What kinds of conversations did your parents have with you and your siblings regarding their work?

> Bharati: No. They never talked about it. We worked with them. Like when they make roads, they need to dig old roads, collect the dust and debris, pick it up, we did that. And after coming here, I worked at people's houses.
>
> Suchitra: To help your parents out?
>
> Bharati: As help to parents, yes. Our living conditions were very poor. Our household could only run if all of us worked. It wouldn't run if we didn't work. So we had to work.

As explained through the examples above, mothers had a significant impact on their daughters' lives. However unlike specific career-based influences that fathers provided, participants received more general and supportive lessons from their mothers. Mothers also inspired their daughters by example and staying resilient through harsh life circumstances. While fathers provide practical directions for their careers, mothers provide an all-encompassing support system, motivation, and cushioning that their daughters would need while pursuing those paths envisioned and enabled by fathers.

Work-Life Balance

While fathers provide lessons on work-life management often by indirectly teaching daughters about the separation of the two areas, working mothers are role models for work-life *balance*. Ramya's (47) mother worked for the police and the manner in which she balanced her household and work-related responsibilities taught Ramya to choose a career that allowed her to give her family as much time as she would to her career.

> I think as a woman you should work and you should help. [this] Means you should be career oriented but besides that you have to take care of your house because she [mother] used to get up early in the morning at 3 o'clock. She used to cook food and everything, get ready and she used to go for parade [police marching parade] with very a heavy rifle. So that kind of thing is actually is in our mind that we have to do something and as well as we have to take care of our family.

Whether it was societal or familial expectations, Ramya's mother, like we saw in Vijaya's case in the last chapter, wanted to make sure her family was taken care of before she left for work. Having seen her mother model such balanced behavior, Ramya, who understood the value of a woman's career, chose one that allowed her to comfortably navigate that work-life space.

Mothers of some women like Shalini (32), an attorney; Bindiya (40s), an actor/director; and Manjula (51), a dietician, worked with their husbands (the participants' fathers). While Bindiya's and Manjula's mothers assisted their doctor husbands in their hospitals, Shalini's mother who was a teacher prior to quitting her job after childbirth, handled all the accounts for her husband's legal practice that now includes two of her attorney daughters. It was common for educated and skilled women of a previous generation to be employed in their husband's business. Working outside the home in unrelated public work spaces was only beginning to get accepted but rather than challenge the dominant societal restrictions against their working, a number of women simply preferred working alongside their husbands. All three women are extremely proud of their mothers. Says Shalini,

> She [mother] is very strong and she is very disciplined. I told you she is a teacher by profession, so she has been more disciplined. She like she wants everything very perfect, everything should be perfect like you know, everything like on the table, in your files, in the court, everything has to be perfect. So I guess that helps you and that there . . . somewhere in your subconscious mind the impact is there, so that goes a long way.

Says Manjula,

> She [mother] is a housewife but she was a graduate from that . . . umm . . . *tya kalatali* graduate *ahet* [had a college degree in those days] and she helped my father a lot. When he started his practice [medical practice] . . . own practice, she used to assist him. She learned everything, like the role of a sister [nurse], role of an administrator, role of an assistant . . . she did everything.

Seeing their mothers so proactively involved in working and learning new skills, these women were naturally encouraged to fulfill their own career goals. When it comes to prioritizing life/family over work, Sonal (24), regional head of visual merchandizing for a retail operation, wants to follow in her mother's footsteps. Given that she was newly engaged (at interview time), she mentioned how she had no struggles managing a balanced life especially since she lived at home and only had to manage her own life. However, when asked how that might change after she got married, she said,

> I would do something like how my mother has done . . . she works in the morning and then evening for some time, so she is there when we need her like when we used to come back, I mean not me . . . I used to come back in the evening from the school but my brother and sister used to come back in the afternoon, so she was there at that time. She never used to work in the evenings when we were young. Now she has started. So, she used to work when we were in school. So, something like that you know, so . . . which is flexible.

Sonal's mother, a nutritionist, set her own hours and worked around her children's schedules but now that all the kids are grown up and have their own careers, she is back to working full time. Her mother's flexibility with her career clearly is a model Sonal would like to emulate in the future.

Just like participants were intuitively encouraged to follow in their mothers' footsteps, at least one mother distracted her daughter from taking up an occupation similar to hers. Sakshi (29), a radio host, recalls how her mother, a nurse, always talked about work at home.

> I remember my mom talking about different cases in the hospital since she was staff nurse. She was in the pregnancy unit, she used to speak about how you know, different kinds of cases and diseases and ya, since it was all a medical background . . . a kind of a medical background, they always wanted . . . they kind of enforced this on me and my brother that it is always good that you become . . . do not become a nurse like me, get . . . grow up and become a doctor, so you know, like in typical Indian families, they always . . . they always want their children to do a step higher than what they have been doing, so that is exactly what my mom portrayed to us that okay, you have to become a doctor or something of those kinds but do not get into the profession that we are into right now.

Sakshi's career, of course, is nothing like that of her mother or anybody in her family and she had to struggle to convince them of the legitimacy of a radio host's job especially given the fact that private radio stations were only an emerging market in India in the mid-2000s when she first got into it. The evidence for dissuading children from doing the same job they did was more apparent in the narratives of low-income occupations, particularly the maids.

As already explained in chapter 2, women in the low-income category unequivocally considered education as a panacea—a gateway to better lives; not for them personally as they considered their own situation as pre-destined and likely without hope, but for their children. Participants, like mothers of the women above, encouraged their children to go to school, stay in school, and pursue an education that would help them out of their poverty. Bharati (45), a maid, says, "I don't have a husband. I only have a daughter. I have put her in an English school. I decided that my life was led like this—working in people's houses, she [daughter] shouldn't have to do it. I am working in people's houses, washing dishes, so that she doesn't have to do it." Because of their limited knowledge of career fields and available opportunities for their children, the best women in low-income occupations could do to enable their daughters to have better lives was educate them. In a focus group with street sweepers, the following conversation ensued.

> Veena: If our children are educated, we naturally want that they should work in an office. We won't feel like just because we are doing this dirty job [street sweeping], our children should do it too. Everyone has some expectations.
>
> Suchitra: So even though you take a lot of pride in your work [following up from previous conversations], you don't want your children to take up this job [street sweeping]?

Veena: That's right.

Ganga: We also feel that they should study.

Veena: They should get an education and get an even better job than ours. Work in an office. Everybody has such expectations.

Ganga: They should go further, work in an office, do something, work hard. People should always work hard.

Alka: I feel happy when women speak English. My own daughter, she failed in her 10th standard [10th grade] so I removed her [from school] and made her a nurse [she did not go into details how she did this]. Told her to do social service as well [Alka considers her own work as a street sweeper as social service to the community]. So women should do something different. I feel happy that even though I continued to stay in dirt, the future generation is living well, alongside men. The more progress the future generation does, the better.

In addition to the direct significance given to education, a number of other issues are apparent in the women's responses. First, these participants' ambiguous relationship to their own work is noteworthy. Even though it is not obvious here, as will be seen in chapter 5, these women take great pride in their work as street sweepers. However, here, in expressing their desire for a better life for their children, they acknowledge the "dirty" aspects of their low-status jobs. Second, the emphasis on "office work" and expectations indicate the reverence for white-collar, better-status jobs that do not involve working with dirt. Veena's reiteration of "Everyone has expectations" strengthens the narrative interpretation of the expectations these participants have of their children. While they undergo many hardships as a result of their circumstances (see chapter 2), they are relentless in their efforts to ensure their own children have lives that are differently enabled.

Along with parents who enable their daughters' careers directly or indirectly, there are others who individually or collectively encourage women's workplace participation.

Familial Others and Friends as Career Enablers

India continues to remain a culture steeped in strong family bonds. As a result, one's extended family is often as important to individuals as is their immediate family.

Ujwala (30), a journalist, remembers how her grandfather furthered her decision to become a journalist.

My grandfather was the one who took an interest in this [her career interests].
He had a friend who was HoD [Head of the Department] of the department of
journalism and communication, very senior man. He [grandfather] took me to
him and said, "*tila he karaycha ahe, tar tila hey karu de ka nako?*" [she wants
to do this [journalism], should she do it or not?] so I was like *baba* [here,
grandfather] is taking so much interest. It was really nice for me. So we went
all the way by rickshaw and all. That time *baba* was 78 or something and I was
like really thrilled. So we went to his friend and for me, the trip was more
about seeing his friend and then *baba* said she's going to give this exam so
how should she prepare and all that. Current affairs, okay I read the newspaper. I know what's happening so I went and luckily I was in the top 5. Then
interview, *baba* called him up to say interview *ahe* (her interview is coming
up) and he said she has done well in the exams so don't worry. Lots of
encouragement and mummy was *maha-kicked* [super-excited]. She is going to
do interesting stuff, meet so many nice people, she'll get to learn about so
many topics.

Her grandfather's encouragement, seeking out mentors, and his excitement at
her career prospects were clearly an incentive for Ujwala to pursue journalism. In case of Meena (57), a school teacher, it was her *in-laws*, especially
her father-in-law, who encouraged her career pursuits. A number of working
women who are now nearing retirement grew up in a time when it was not
considered important to educate girls. Even if some broad-minded parents of
that time did allow their daughters an education, they were married off at a
young age and so the remainder of their young adult lives were spent in their
in-laws' houses living by the in-laws' rules. Fortunately for Meena, her marital home had a culture of education and her in-laws encouraged her to work.
Meena remembers just how supportive her in-laws were of her education:

In fact more than my mother's house, it was my in-laws' house that had more
of an academic environment. They never expected that just because I am the
daughter-in-law I should sit at home and cook. In fact, my father-in-law really
wanted me to study further and do something. At the time I was married, I was
doing my M.A. One day when I was cooking, he approached me and said,
"Why are you wasting your time cooking when you should be studying? Get a
packed meal from outside from tomorrow onwards." And he actually made me
do it saying I should be studying and when I am studying, I shouldn't have to
worry about cooking. He was really keen that I study and every facility was
made available to the person who was studying.

Suchitra: For example?

Meena: Like when I was doing my B.Ed. [Bachelor of Education] I was
pregnant at the time. My mother-in-law had to do everything [chores around
the house]. Father-in-law didn't allow me to do anything. So here I was a
pregnant woman, studying for my B.Ed. and getting a lot of importance. Moth-

er-in-law used to take care of everything and tell me to study. Whatever happens, you don't do anything, you study, she told me.

The collective encouragement and support of her in-laws alleviated any cultural stress Meena might have had of not being able to fulfill her duties as a daughter-in-law. In traditional households, especially during the time that Meena was a newlywed, once a son is married, his wife, the daughter-in-law, is responsible for most of the cooking and cleaning, household up-keep, and other tasks, including looking after the husband's parents and any other older relatives living at home as part of the joint family system. By allowing her to pursue academic interests, Meena's in-laws were indeed unconventional for their time.

More recently, Vanaja (33), who is an interior designer, was also encouraged by her father-in-law to pursue her career. He helped her find a job since she was moving to a new city, Pune, after marrying his son.

> My father-in-law helped me a lot. He didn't directly give me contacts but he showed me the way. He said, "What will you do sitting at home? This city was so new to me, new in-laws, we live in a joint family, my husband's older brother, his wife, we all stay together." It was adjusting to too many new things at one time but they were all very supportive so he said you can start working as soon as you wish. First I did one or two projects here, he said, "What'll you do after that?" I said, "I'll be searching for other projects." "So? Between projects what'll you do?" I said, "Nothing, I'll be sitting at home." He said, "Why, why will you sit at home? Join some institute, do some teaching work," I said okay. So he searched for me, he said, "Okay give me all your papers," I gave him my binder. He wrote a cover letter for me and he sent to two colleges, I was accepted at both. The one I currently work at was one of them.

Like fathers, fathers-in-law also helped women in their careers by direct involvement. Mothers-in-law, as seen in Meena's case, often played the silent supportive role in the background. Bhavana (38), controller of finance at a multinational company, believes that her life is in balance only because her parents-in-law, especially her mother-in-law, looks after Bhavana's son. Having their support has also enabled her to pursue advancement opportunities that are demanding on her time. She says,

> My father-in-law has been a Class I Officer in the government and my mother-in-law is also a very intelligent lady actually. She never had a career of her own because they kept shifting [father-in-law's job-related relocations] and so she at that time told me that, "I am very happy that you are having a career of your own and from my side you will never ever face a problem. You don't worry about the house front at all. I will be there to take care of everything. If you feel you are getting a good opportunity then you go ahead" and it has been actually very fortunate that both of them have really stuck to their word. I

mean all these years it has been amazing the amount of support my parents-in-law gave me.

There have been times when I have come to office in the morning at 8 o' clock being there through the day, through the night, and gone home the next day at 10 o' clock in the morning because there were some issues and all. When he [son] was very small, they used to take him in their bedroom, like you do need sleep we will take care of him and he has absolutely been with them throughout. So that was like when she said that and my father-in-law also said, "when this proposal [her marriage proposal for their son] also came and when we saw that you have studied and you are a career woman we have deliberately said yes [in arranged marriages, accepting a marriage proposal has as much to do with familial acceptance as it has to do with the potential spouses agreeing to marry each other]. We know what comes with having a daughter-in-law with her own career and ya it is quite okay with us. It is actually good that you are getting a good opportunity, you should go." So I had that assurance and my husband was always very supportive right from the beginning.

Bhavana is also grateful that her mother-in-law communicates her son's daily activities to her so she continues to feel she has her pulse on her son's daily activities.

My mother-in-law always used to understand this anxiety of mine as a mother. So she used to make it a point to communicate everything about him [son] to me. She still does that. Like when he was a very small child, after I went home, without my asking, she would tell me he did this and he did this, and I did this. She was like, she made a very conscious effort to keep me in touch with what happened with him.

Bhavana believes she has a convenient arrangement with her mother-in-law where unlike other daughters-in-law who want to control the kitchen in a joint family system, she does not interfere with her mother-in-law's kitchen management. In return, Bhavana appreciates the fact that her son gets well taken care of in her absence. The above childcare arrangement may be misinterpreted when viewed through a Western lens. In the Indian context, being a grandmother and fulfilling those duties is considered an ideal transition of life and a culturally expected norm. In fact, mothers-in-law who may not want to look after their grandchildren may be criticized by society.

Relatives such as *uncles and aunts* also provide a supportive environment and valuable work and life lessons. Mohini (63), a judge, was sent to live with her uncle and aunt so she could go to a college in the town where they lived. From her doctor uncle who often treated patients without charging a fee and allowed patients who had traveled long distances to see him stay at his home for the night, she learned compassion and care for others. She also developed a desire for lifelong learning.

I was brought up by him and I learnt all my skills, later on skill which I have developed in my youth with him because I used to play badminton. I used to go out and writing was my hobby, he developed. I used to read a number of books because he was having beautiful library. He was a doctor but he also had M.A., L.L.B. [law degree], B. Ed., at that time. So all that and he always used to say that age has nothing to do with your qualifications and age has nothing to do for gaining the knowledge.

Perhaps this was the reason Mohini continued learning and attaining new degrees throughout her life, including a law degree at age 60.

When Harsha (29) decided she wanted to be a physiotherapist, because no one in her family had much information about this emerging field of allied health, her aunt made an appointment with a practicing physiotherapist and made arrangements for Harsha to job shadow her so she can get a realistic preview of her future career. Yamini (31), an architect, lives in a joint family with her parents, sister, grandparents, uncle, and aunt. She remembers how her uncle and aunt stayed up with her on nights she had to work late on homework and architectural design assignments just so she does not feel alone. Yamini also remembers that being from a famous family, she would often feel the pressures to have to live up to a reputation, but her grandmother told her that she did not have to "see things through her family's eyes" and should be her own person.

Husbands have also encouraged their wives in their careers by playing a supportive role when needed. When Vidisha (29) was pursuing an evening MBA program while working full time during the day, she recalls how her husband would often pick her up from work so he could drop her to her classes. He also cooked and kept her meals ready when she returned home after her classes at 10:00 p.m., behaviors not typically expected of men in patriarchal Indian society. When Sakshi (29) decided to become a radio host, a new generation profession in India, her parents had no clue what that profession entailed and were therefore reluctant to support her, but her husband (who was her friend at the time) stood by her and supported her choice of career and also convinced her parents about the merits of the profession. Meeta (40) works as an accountant at a non-governmental organization. She grew up in an orphanage and was married to a man who was forced to discontinue his education after the 10th grade due to his family's financial circumstances. After marriage, he encouraged Meeta to continue her education so that at least one of them is better qualified and able to help raise their family's collective standard of living.

Like these examples above, there are several others where husbands have supported their wives in their careers and encouraged career growth and advancement. Societally charged class-based mindsets that considered women working a reflection on the husband's inability to provide for their families, discussed in the Introduction section, are non-existent in the discourses of the younger generation of working women. When husbands did object to their wives' working or taking up a specific profession, for example, as was the case with Priyanka (chapter 2), the cases were prominently among a "middle"/sandwich generation of women and men in their 40s and 50s.

Friends have also been instrumental in influencing women's careers by either pushing them into majoring in certain academic programs that proved pivotal in future career decisions or by informing the women about potential professional opportunities. Vanaja (33), an interior designer and teacher, and Bhavana (38), controller of finance at a multinational company, both expressed gratitude to their friends for directing them toward what ended up becoming their careers. In Vanaja's case, her friend brought her information about their town's new architecture college's interior design program. When her friend told her she had looked at the course syllabus and found it interesting, it piqued Vanaja's interest enough to apply to the program and later pursue it as a profession. Bhavana (38), Meha (27), and Shraddha (27) all found their careers through their friends. Bhavana explains,

> Actually one of my friends had appeared for the interview where she was rejected for some reason. I don't know [why] and she was told there itself that you are not selected. Then she there itself told [them] that I have one of my friends who I think you would like and is it okay if she comes for the interview. So on my behalf she herself asked and then she came back and told me you go for the interview. It is a very nice opportunity and my mother said okay just go and see and I went there and things just got moving and they just immediately gave me an offer and said you can join.

Like Bhavana, Meha owes her current profession to a friend. Meha's friend had been offered a position at an information technology multinational company but had turned it down because it required some occasional night shifts. Since Meha had no problems with working night shifts and knew that her parents would support her decision, when her friend told her of this opportunity, she applied, got the offer, and accepted the position. Shraddha had moved away to a southern Indian city for a job but would visit home during religious holidays. It was right before one such holiday visit that a friend arranged an interview for her. She narrates,

> He scheduled my interview at XXXXX and he calls up and my cell is not reachable. He calls up home, and tells my mom, *aise aise maine interview arrange kiya hai, accha job hai, toh kal bhejna* [I have set up an interview for her, it's a good job, so send her over tomorrow] I come home, my mom says you have an interview tomorrow, I said what the hell!

Shraddha went for the interview anyway and got the job. Even though she really liked her previous job, because her parents, especially her mother, said she really missed Shraddha and would like to have her back in town, she decided to return home and accept the new position.

For all the career guidance parents give participants, there were many others who said they were given no specific advice on how to pursue work and career aspirations. What worked to their advantage, however, was that even when parents did not directly give them advice, they allowed their daughters the freedom to pursue a career of their choice. Secure in the unconditional backing of their parents, daughters were encouraged to give wings to their ambitions. This is evident in Anita's case. Anita (31), who is a corporate secretary in charge of managing all administrative and legal compliances for her organization, says her parents never gave her career advice.

> They were very nice. They did not push me in any direction. [They said] You are free to decide what you wanted to do. So parents were quite open to all options. I could do whatever I chose to do which helped. They never gave me career advice. No, but they gave me a free hand. They supported me everywhere I wanted to go. They said that whatever you want to do is okay with us. They gave the financial backing. They gave the commitment. They gave the time required. What more can you ask?

A number of other participants like Anita mentioned how their parents did not give them career advice because they did not want to limit their daughters' options, wanted their daughters to figure out an appropriate career path on their own, or because either being uneducated or unaware of available career opportunities, did not know how and what to advise them. In any case, participants then proactively sought outside resources such as friends, friends' parents or relatives, or books for directions, which speaks to their individual initiative, and agency, which will be discussed in the next chapter.

The section above almost makes participants appear as passive recipients of the socialization, support, and interventions made on their behalf by well-meaning friends. It is important to remember that this study was conducted in retrospection. In other words, the findings discussed above rely heavily on participants' own recollection of their socialization and other experiences. For them to recollect these life events, process them, interpret them, live them, and reproduce them to an interested outsider (author) requires self-determination to want to do something with those recollections. Therefore, one can argue that participants received their socialization and other messages but used their own discretion, interests, and ambitions in pursuing personally significant work/career interests.

Even though all of the above narratives are recollections based on memory and therefore, clearly memorable, the next section includes findings from participants' responses to specific memories about work/career-related incidents or stories that had special significance in their professional lives.

Memorable Work-Life Messages

Right from their childhood, participants recalled receiving several different kinds of messages or stories from their parents and close family regarding life, work, and careers that influenced them in various ways. Such recollections almost always preceed with "father/grandfather/mother . . . always told me . . ." "would always say . . ." and such indications of repeated utterances. Some of these messages are obvious in the discussion above. Some more specific messages pertain to negotiating social class, work situations, priorities, a work-life course of being, and gender.

Negotiating Social Class

Jaya (48), a social worker, is from a humble family from a village. She says, growing up, she had friends who were richer than her but that she never compared herself to them because of her father's advice.

> Because my father would tell us from a young age—if I rarely ever said she has something and I don't have it—he would say, when we are walking, we should not look at the man on the horse and think that he has a horse and we don't. We are walking, we have *chappals* [a type of footwear] and boots on our feet, we got this, we should look at someone who doesn't even have shoes to wear and think about how fortunate we are to have it. Think about that and that thought was so firmly ingrained in our minds that now I only compare myself positively to others if I ever do compare myself with anybody. In my job I meet so many people who at times can't even afford one meal a day. I feel so fortunate.

Similarly Manisha (49), a priest, recalls how because of her mother's advice, she learned to be content with her life circumstances.

> My childhood friend was a very rich girl and I was from a teacher's family. The size of this room was about the size of our house and that was also made from tin roof. If you sat on a stool, you could touch the tin roof. We lived in such a small house but our mother had told us, we should walk by looking at the road below us, not by looking up. If we walk by looking up, we'll stumble upon something and fall. So I never felt that I wanted anything that my friend had.

By "looking up," Manisha's mother referred to a nose-in-the-air attitude that reflected a lack of humility. By looking at the road ahead, Manisha knew where she was and where she was heading—enough to keep a person grounded.

Seema (20), a live-in nanny, learned the value of work and money from the message she received from her father.

Papa used to talk about how he would eat *pao* [bread] when he was younger and spent days like that in poverty. At that time the situation was really bad. They didn't have enough to eat.

Suchitra: How did what he say influence you?

Seema: Influence in the sense we learned how to spend money wisely. We learned to work hard . . . everybody at home work, including my little brother. It was never that just because they were boys they just sat around doing nothing. Everybody did his or her share of work. Mother used to do everything but then she was sick all the time.

Negotiating Work Situations

In addition to negotiating class status, parents conditioned their daughters against potential obstacles that may await them in their future work by advising them about managing challenges. Tanushree (22) recalls dinnertime conversations that taught her about work ethic.

My dad, he is very time punctual kind of like you know, very much, so he is like he used to tell us I had gone today but boss came very late and all, one hour late, this and all, so he would get very pissed if somebody comes late and all the stuff, so . . . that he used to tell. So I used to always feel that like you know, means these are the things which you should learn like if you are going somewhere or somebody is coming to meet you, this, that and all, so you should be aware about the time, or how you should speak, what you should do.

Dinner time conversations from her father-in-law helped Vanaja learn about managing workplace situations.

He had a business and he used to constantly tell us what happened in the business. We always used to sit together, have dinner together. Whatever happened at work, in his pharmaceutical business, people said this or that, they had to constantly keep in touch with doctors, all the big institutes, he had a habit of telling us everything—that was the best. I don't remember my father telling me every time, coming back from work and telling me this, this, this happened but my father-in-law used to say, come sit, everyone come and let's talk—this happened today, that happened today and that way he used to tell us about all the problems,

Suchitra: How did that affect you?

Vanaja: He used to tell us about some typical problems, how he solved it or how he could have solved it in a different way so the problem solving techniques or the lack of solving because he always used to say, however big or small, you can tackle any problem so the problem won't look like a problem. So every time I have a problem, I think how can I solve it, just start thinking, I don't go, oh my god, this is a problem what to do because if you do this you start creating a bigger monster out of it and your brain stops working. You have to overpower the problem and problems are there everywhere, every time. If you think it is a problem it is a problem, if you don't look at it as a problem, it's not so that thing really taught me. Whatever you say, do it, if you say something, follow through with it. You have to take the brickbats as well as compliments, take responsibilities of your actions.

Bindiya (40s), an actor/director, learned about managing workplace and life problems from her doctor father.

Father used to always tell don't retreat in the face of hardships. You will have hardships when you want to achieve something. Don't avoid doing anything because that path has hardships. If you start doing that, you will never achieve anything in life. You don't have to go fill pots with water like us or don't have to study in candle light but you will have problems that your time throws at you and you have to face them. So face the world. Face your problems as they come and don't avoid them.

These words have helped Bindiya deal with work issues at her own production company. She learned from her father that, "there are so many problems that if you start avoiding them, they start piling up. Resolve them right there. Stitch in time."

Negotiating Priorities

By communicating stories and drawing on mythological incidents, parents taught their daughters how to negotiate priorities. Jagruti (34) narrated a story her father's supervisor once told him that he then came home and told his children. This story, she believes, taught her to better manage work and life priorities.

He [supervisor] used to tell my father that Mr. XXXX, suppose you are traveling in a car and it's a busy road and you are at 60–70 [kilometers] speed as in the sense not a lot of automobile traffic but let's say Senapati Bapat Road on which you have plenty of pedestrians and a dog happens to come in front of your car and there is a car behind you. There are people near you so if a dog just chances to come in front of your car what would you do? Would you brake and try to save the dog or would you not brake and simply go ahead? I don't know what my father answered but his [the supervisor's answer to this question was that you don't brake and you let the dog die because if you brake and stop you are going to kill the man behind you. My father was pretty impressed by this whatever he had said and I somehow remember it all the time.

Suchitra: How do you think it has affected you in your career or work or life? Has it influenced you in any way?

Jagruti: I think I do think that I'm a good person at deciding priorities and I think I have been able to decide my priorities maybe because of this I don't know but somewhere its stuck in my mind that it's better to kill a dog than to kill a man. Although I can get arrested by the PETA for this but somehow it is stuck in my mind.

Sakshi (29), a radio host, remembers a story her grandfather always told her about Chhatrapati Shivaji, a national hero from the state of Maharashtra, that helps her decide on priorities.

My grandpa used to tell me this story about Shivaji's life where he tells his soldiers, "*adhi lagna Kondhanyache, mag lagna Raybache.*" Shivaji is at war, fighting on the front and his son is supposed to get married but he says no, first I will go on the front and fight and then my son Rayba will get married. This was something which I really applied. I remember applying because you know, even in my family when I have to do something, now that you have told me I think I am relating to it. When I have to do something I always prefer my work first and then the rest of the things, not then family, but the rest of the things. For me, work definitely comes first.

Nutan's (39) father's advice taught her better time management and consequently aided prioritization as well.

He used to tell me not to waste time, how you have to utilize your time. Once time gone never comes back. So he always used to tell me that this is the time, this is the date this second if this goes will it come back? That is a question he always used to ask.

Negotiating a Work-Life Course

Parents encouragingly taught their daughters about work values, relationship negotiation, managing hardships in work and life, and work ethic.

Shipta (32), a branch manager at an insurance company, remembers her father telling the family that his factory was going to close down, which may mean that he would be without a job for a while. He told her and her siblings that if that happened, they may not be as financially sound as they were then. Shipta took this message to heart and immediately focused her energies on her education. She realized that if she were to have a future, she would have to be able to afford it on her own terms. Thus, very atypical of Indian girls growing up in the early 90s, Shipta started working part-time while still in school. She started tutoring neighborhood children and eventually started working as a typist at a local organization. She worked all the way through college in different positions and paid for her own education. Her father's words at once made her independent and responsible toward the course of her own career.

Manjula's (51) father and grandfather were both doctors. Her maternal grandfather and uncle were also doctors. She remembers how her father would talk about his everyday work experiences at home but what she recalls most was, "He would always say there are two angles to the medical field, one is the treating part and the other is the personal part, one supports the other." Having heard this from her father, as a dietician, she is always careful about how what she says will affect her patients.

Avni (27), a doctor of Ayurvedic medicine, also recalls a message from her father regarding her responsibility as a doctor.

> My father always said don't look at money. Your success is more important and your treating your patients is important. Don't run behind money. If you run behind money you may end up doing the wrong things, you don't want malpractice. Money you can earn that anytime. As you get successful, you will keep getting money.

As a doctor, her father reminded her that her main career objective should be toward her patients and if she did this, success and money would automatically follow.

Negotiating Gender

Finally, participants also recalled a few gender references in the messages they received. Mohini (61), a judge, remembers her mother telling her that in life it was more important to be a good human being than follow the norms of one's gender. This message is particularly important given the period in which it was communicated. This message was imparted somewhere in the 1950s, when women were expected to strictly adhere to their traditional gender role. To Mohini, this conveyed her mother's openness to non-traditional career options and the fact that she should never restrict herself in her career goals just because she was a woman. Mohini also attributes the successes she has had in life to her uncle with whom she stayed for a number of years, attending college in his village. Here she recalls how her uncle's encouragement to learn new skills kindled in her a love for learning, a lesson she remembers for life. She also talks about how because her doctor uncle cared for patients above and beyond his duties as a physician, she learned about treating everyone as equals, regardless of arbitrary caste, class, or social status hierarchies. She recalls,

> He [uncle] always used to say *ki* [that] age has nothing to do with your qualifications and age has nothing to do with gaining the knowledge. The knowledge is such a thing that till the last breath you should always try to get, acquire, strive for—that he used to say. So all those things I got from him. I rarely remember my father telling me anything because I was all the time in the early school days and he was always out of the house . . . he [uncle] always

used to say *ki* [that] whatever you do in further life but all those things [continuous learning of new skills] will always be with you and you will be happy. If the time comes you can use it. If the time does not permit you then restrict yourself in that way—but he taught me all those things right from there and he never treated that I am not his daughter because my first cousin [uncle's daughter] also was there. So in that period I have developed my sense for library [uncle had a huge collection of books], then doing good gestures for society because we were having doctor [in the] house [uncle was a doctor] so a number of patients coming.

In those days some of the patients used to stay forcibly because they cannot travel back like that and in that way we used to tender their needs. We never felt we were doing some service. It was a part of living with my uncle. Being a doctor he used to feel that we are supposed to serve. If somebody comes at the time of *khana* [meals], we always used to think let's [ask them to] join [us] for lunch or dinner whatever. So I have never had the concept of separatism or individualism in what we call today's life, or private. I am not a private person. Today even if you feel that if you ask with my staff they will say *ki* [that] though she is a judge or she is the president of this particular forum she is of that nature. The moment I leave this chair I am equal to them so I don't have the *malki* [entitlement].

Rajani, a corporate recruiter, remembers overhearing her father tell her mother,

"She [Rajani] won't be like a normal housewife but be definitely like a son so don't worry and don't bother that we don't have a son because she would be like a son," so that was a moral boosting he used to give me till my childhood and that is the reason my confidence level was extremely high because of my father's constant boosting to me. He used to encourage me of course to participate in "n" number of activities but at the same time he has never treated us [her sisters and her] as a daughter. He always treated us as a son. Total independence was there. We were free to go anywhere.

Referring to Rajani as a "son" was a compliment to her that signified her father's trust in her to shoulder responsibilities and see them through successfully. By equating her to a son, he was essentially communicating to Rajani that she enjoyed the privileges of a son such as permission to return home late night and mobility freedom. Rajani felt proud of her father's confidence in her and later in life when she had to single handedly set up her company without the support of her husband and in a new city, she recalled her father's words and faith in her abilities. One can see how a socio-culturally influenced preference for sons makes Rajani construe her father's comments as a compliment. In several parts of India, a daughter is seen as a parental responsibility that concludes once they marry her away in mutually agreed-to marital arrangements. A son, on the other hand, brings the new wife home to live with his family and together, with his wife, is expected to look after his aging parents. Rajani's father's comments saying that she would be like a son to them implied that he was supportive of her having a career and becoming financially equipped to look after them in old age without having to depend on a son.

Participants lovingly recalled messages their family members gave them over the years that came in useful in negotiating the many turns of life and work.

CONCLUDING THOUGHTS

The findings discussed above contribute to the literature on (anticipatory) socialization in several ways. First, it builds on our current knowledge of the anticipatory phase of organizational socialization theory by presenting unique findings from India's working women. More specifically, the findings from this study enable a comparison with the factors of vocational anticipatory socialization that Jablin (1985, 2001) proposed, thereby helping Western audiences understand how this phase may be similar to, or different from, socialization as documented in current organizational literature. Second, by exploring the role of memorable messages or anticipatory messages (Lucas, 2006, 2011), the study sheds light on how Indian women are influenced by day-to-day conversations about work and careers, how these influences affect their career choices and decisions, and teach them strategies to deal with workplace issues.

First, I discuss the contributions made to anticipatory socialization. I need to clarify that the findings and discussion here represent women of the middle- and high-income occupations more than women in low-income occupations. According to Jablin (2001), individuals develop a set of expectations and beliefs prior to starting work at any organization. These ideas are formed out of the communicative actions occurring in the individual's environment. These vocational anticipatory factors are: family, educational institutions, part-time employment, peers and friends, and media. According to Jablin's model, families, especially parents, influence children by teaching them values about work through everyday discourses such as dinner-time conversations regarding their own work, stories parents and other family members narrate with work as a central theme, and family-related organizing activities such as doing household chores, among others. Educational institution, or one's school and school-related activities, as the first formal organization of which individuals are part, explicitly teach individuals core competencies and strategies to deal with future places of employment, introduce individuals to information about different occupations, and various communicative behaviors needed to fulfill future organizational roles. Part-time employment influences adolescents by providing them opportunities to develop relational communication skills. Peers and friends teach individuals about communicating in organizational situations by instructing them appropriate on expression of emotions when working with others, ways to problem-solve, and maintain relationships. Finally, media, especially television, persuasively influence individuals in the way that they present occupational roles and images of different professions.

In the Hindu Indian context, factors of vocational anticipatory socialization that influenced women's career choices, work ethic, and work values are parents and extended family members, especially in-laws and friends. Not surprisingly, one's family emerged as the single most influencing factor in the lives of India's working women. Not only was family *the* primary source for anticipatory socialization, it was also directly responsible for women's career choices and how those choices came to be realized. Of course this does not always imply a direct influence on any specific career path, although that *was* seen in some instances but it does mean that familial influences and enabling allowed women to make informed career choices, stay resilient through their choices and the challenges faced along the way, created in them a strong work ethic, and variously taught them appropriate workplace behaviors.

Parents provide exceptional support to their daughters during their formative years. Parents, especially fathers, either collected information about different occupational opportunities and careers for their daughters or encouraged their daughters to engage in activities that enhanced future employment opportunities. Fathers provided direct and indirect socialization by talking about their own work and careers. They also socialized daughters into a certain work ethic and work-life management. The daughters who inherited their fathers' careers and career traits by following in their footsteps or by imbibing the same strong hard work ethic and values absorbed these lessons. Mothers were especially influential in the lives of working women by providing emotional support and exemplifying resilience during challenging times, by encouraging daughters to have careers, and imparting lessons of work-life balance. Younger women in their 20s and early 30s have also been influenced by their mothers' careers. Seeing their mothers engage in what appeared to be seamless transitions between their home lives and work lives has inspired women of this generation to do the same.

Extended family members like in-laws, especially fathers-in-law, are an important source of anticipatory socialization for Indian women. This finding was understandably more apparent among the older generation of working women in their late 40s to the 60s. This goes back to when girls were married at a young age and in some families, as soon as they completed their undergraduate studies. Once married, in-laws had significant influences on women's lives. Fathers-in-law provided information similar to fathers and encouraged women to have careers. They encouraged their daughters-in-law to further their education and engage in paid employment for its own sake and not because the family needed their earnings. Other relatives like uncles and aunts provided supportive environments by answering questions about specific career options, by collecting prospective career information for the women to review, looking out for potential problems they may run into with different occupations, and by providing comforting words and encouragement during the women's pre-organizational entry days.

Friends were the boundary spanners who sought specific career-based information for themselves and shared them with the participants. Friends were also responsible for pushing women into certain career paths. They either came to know of a career opportunity in some organization and then contacted the women to interview at that place, or brought in application forms to professional schools and made the hitherto undecided women apply to those academic programs. This finding is different from the one highlighted in Jablin's review. The latter discusses peers and friends as influencing emotion management, problem-solving, and relationship development, important skills in a future workplace. Surely Indian friends also influence women in similar manners but in terms of being career enablers, the contributions of friends was more instrumental in women's career choices and the fields they chose to pursue.

Part-time employment is only now becoming popular in India. If conducted a decade later, the findings of this study may show this factor as a stronger influencing enabler. Educational institutions, and media, were not cited by participants as sources of VAS.

This study contends that factors of anticipatory socialization are socio-culturally constructed. Indian culture values the bonds of familial relationships as the foundation for any individual achievement. One's family is the single biggest factor influencing women's socialization toward work and careers. This study supports the arguments against the organizational focus of anticipatory socialization in the literature. Given the finding that this construct is socio-culturally determined, individuals of a given culture, while being directly socialized into worlds of work and careers, may also be socialized into these worlds by being simultaneously instructed to follow the tenets important to the people of that culture. In the context of Indian women, this study concludes that anticipatory socialization is a vital tool by which parents and others exert influence on women's work attitudes, behaviors, and values, while teaching them the importance of familial relationships. Either by role modeling or direct transmission, individuals significant to the women highlight the importance of a work-life-family balance while pursuing career interests. It is this socialization that enables women to make compromises in their careers willingly, something that will be further explored in the next chapter.

The current study further contributes to our understanding of anticipatory socialization in the following ways; first, vocational anticipatory socialization not only includes learning during individuals' pre-organizational entry, but in the Indian context, it is also the time when women's careers are enabled by their parents and other significant people in their lives. It is during this stage that women exercise agency in pushing for their education, and developing an understanding of what it takes to be successful in their chosen future careers. Second, vocational anticipatory socialization is not a one-way linear path, from sources of socialization to individuals or women in this case; it is not even a two-way street as proposed by Jablin (2001), where individuals and organizations influence one another; it is a highly interactive and cyclical path where knowledge about work such as work values, workplace do's and don'ts, and strategies for work, and family balance get passed down from one generation to another and new information brought in by the younger generation, in turn, influences parents. Thirdly, it is erroneous to assume vocational anticipatory socialization only teach individuals about vocations; communicative processes and activities during this stage also teaches individuals what is most important and valued in their socio-cultural environment alongside working and having careers. In this study, what was most valued by women was their time with their families. Women learned that they could have any career they wanted but they should also be able to do justice to their family and especially children. Fourth, socialization practices and implications differ across socio-economic classes. Educational levels of self and parents, as well as one's family's financial stability, among other factors, affect how women get socialized into worlds of work.

Finally, the current study also contributes to the literature on memorable messages. Memorable messages are significant during the vocational anticipatory socialization stage (e.g., Gibson & Papa, 2000; Lucas, 2006; Medved et al., 2006). To summarize Knapp et al. (1981), in order to be memorable, messages have to be conveyed by older individuals respected by the recipient, they have to be personal in focus, they need to be communicated as a rule or code of conduct and should be short, and lastly, they should be uncomplicated in form and structure. While the first rule also applies to the findings of this study, the current study found that messages do not have to be personal, be expressed as codes of conduct or short, or be simple in syntactical arrangements. What really helped recall and make these messages indeed "memorable" was the lesson that was inherently embedded in them. Participants in this study recalled long messages rich in metaphors and analogies, either told to or by people they respected. They remembered those messages as mentioned because of the quality of the lesson to be learned from that message, and because of repetition. Due to the findings of this study, I also include memorable stories as important socializing factors. Thus, as long as messages have valuable lessons to impart and are repeatedly communicated (told directly to or overheard) to individuals, their length, sentence structure, and personal focus has little to do with making them memorable.

As discussed in the introduction to this section, these findings more directly represent women in the middle- and high-income occupations. Socialization experiences were similar among women in middle- and high-income occupations but there exist differences between middle- and high-income earning participants and low-income earning participants. While most of the discussion above relates to the socialization of women belonging to the upper categories, for women in low-income occupations, parents typically emphasized the value of hard work, which in turn they passed on to their children. While education for their children was foremost in the minds of low-income women, their own parents did not give education much importance. However, value in honest work, defined in terms of paid employment or in the case of these women, physical labor, and a strong ethic were continually being communicated.

The next chapter will discuss how career and work socialization also enables Indian working women to negotiate agency amidst sociocultural constraints.

Table 3.1. Visual Representation of Jablin's (1985, 2001) sources of Vocational Anticipatory Socialization and Comparable Sources/Career Enablers of Indian Women

Sources of Vocational Anticipatory Socialization (Jablin, 1987, 2001)	Sources of Vocational Anticipatory Socialization/Career Enablers of Indian Women (in order of significance)
Family	Immediate Family - Fathers
Educational Institutions	Immediate Family - Mothers
Part-Time Employment	Extended Family—In-laws, Uncles, Aunts (Immediate Family – Husbands)
Peers and Friends	Friends
Media	Role Models—Family Members, Specific working individuals (e.g., male relatives of friends)

Sources: Jablin, F. M. (1985). An exploratory study of vocational organizational communication socialization. *The Southern Speech Communication Journal, 50*, 261-282. (and) Jablin, F. M. (2001). Organizational entry, assimilation, and disengagement/exit. In F. M. Jablin & L. L. Putnam (Eds.), *The New Handbook of Organizational Communication.* (pp. 732-818). Thousand Oaks, CA: Sage.

NOTE

1. *Competition Success* is a general knowledge and current affairs magazine targeted specifically for those interested in careers in the Civil Services, public-sector undertakings (or government owned corporations) or the Indian Defense Services.

Chapter Four

Constrained Agency and Communion

In Western scholarship, agency and communion[1] are considered the "two basic dimensions for describing and judging persons and groups" (Abele & Wojciszke, 2007, p. 751). Several scholars position these two dimensions as diametrically opposed to each other (e.g., Abele & Wojciszke, 2007; Moskowitz, Suh, & Desaulniers, 1994; Pringle & McCulloch Dixon, 2003). They argue that agency is concerned with the pursuit of individual goals, represents the action of *doing*, and believes in controlling one's environment and expressing independence through self-protection, self-assertion, and autonomous actions (Littleton, Arthur, & Rousseau, 2000; Marshall, 1989; Pringle & McCulloch Dixon, 2003). On the other hand, communion involves a consideration for group goals, a "being" outlook toward life situations wherein individuals strive to work in harmony with their environment (Pringle & McCulloch Dixon, 2003), believes in developing cooperation, integration, connections, and relationships. Despite the inherent differences of approach, Marshall (1989) considers both agency and communion "basic coping strategies for dealing with the uncertainties and anxieties of being alive" (p. 279) and posits that agency is more characteristic of men than women. According to Pringle and McCulloch Dixon (2003), and agency "expresses itself through control over the environment" (p. 294) and represents the action of "doing" (p. 294). It is characterized by autonomy, initiative, and adaptation (Littleton et al., 2000). On the other hand, communion represents a "being" outlook toward life situations wherein individuals strive to be in harmony with their environment (Pringle & McCulloch Dixon, 2003).

This research study wanted to explore the nature of agency embodied and represented by women in receiving, interpreting, and appropriating socialization messages. Arguably, Indian women face competing socialization discourses that simultaneously acculturate them into socially and culturally appropriate behaviors that meet familial and gendered expectations while encouraging them to exert individual initiative, control, and career management within prescribed limitations. Furthermore, given the changing fabric of Indian society (Gupta, 2007; Prasad, 2006), expectedly, there are differences across generations of women in how they display agency or communion. In examining the lives of Indian women, in part, this project has investigated the nature of influences Indian parents have on their daughters' work and careers (not necessarily careers per se, but career-based decisions and decisions made in one's everyday work life) through everyday discourses and communicative behaviors pertaining to work and careers. The influence of socializing messages was examined in chapter 3 in which the onus was on parental/familial communication presented to and recalled by the participants. This chapter categorically discusses how participants (specifically mid- and high-income women) make sense of the choices available to them and navigate the influences of socialization.

The findings of this study indicate that participants exert both agency (constrained) and communion where individuals *choose* to be in communion or as defined here, in harmony with their sociocultural and environmental socialization. Therefore, even though some scholars consider agency and communion as two opposite concepts women struggle to balance, this study found that women exert their self-will in choosing to accept and adapt to their environment, thereby showcasing agency even in communion. Thematically, the first section below will discuss agency, constrained or otherwise broadly; the second section will more categorically unpack the harmonious nature of agency exerted by participants.

Be Someone, Somewhere

Women across income categories exhibited agency. To begin with, some of the women in their late 40s and 50s reported how they had to strategically negotiate with their parents their access to education since the dominant thought of the time was to get daughters married off as soon as they were old enough, which often meant late teenage or very early twenties. Charulata, a 61 year-old co-owner of nurseries, remembers that when she touched her grandmother's feet to seek blessings [a common practice in Hindu Indian culture] before her examination, her grandmother blessed her with the words, "May you find a good husband" instead of wishing her the best toward academic success. Some participants, like Priyanka, had to convince their parents to allow them to get an education.

Priyanka (40s) currently works as a school teacher. (Some aspects of her life were introduced and analyzed in previous chapters.) She says she was only able to get an education because she insisted on it and convinced her father of her desire to further her academics. Priyanka's father, as was customary in the days of her youth, wanted her to get married as soon as she completed high school. He told her that they [parents or relatives, as is typical for arranged marriages] would find her a "nice, rich husband" and get her married. Priyanka insisted that she be allowed to attend college and at least get a bachelor's degree. She believes that because she was the youngest child and her father's favorite, she got her way. Her older sister, who was married by then, also helped convince their father to allow Priyanka a higher education. Priyanka knew she wanted a degree but did not care about the specific field of study. When some relative suggested that she study Ayurveda medicine and become a doctor, she agreed but because the university was three kilometers away from their village, her father refused to send her there. So Priyanka studied at the local college with her father's approval. Once she got her bachelor's degree, her father told her to get married. However, she had other plans.

> That time, I had a teacher who told my father to send me to study Law. "She is a good speaker and she lays out good points," he told my father, "Send Priyanka to study Law, she'll become a great lawyer." But the law college was outside of town and [was in the] evening from 6–9 p.m. so evening classes and outside of the village. Impossible! So I said okay if not law, I'll do an MA. He [father] refused. "We've made you a graduate, now you get married." Again I tried to explain to him that I'll get married as soon as I complete my post-graduation. I had gotten a scholarship after graduating so I told him my education won't cost you anything. Then he agreed. Everybody in our family has gotten married between [the ages of] 16 and 20. I was the only one who had stayed back. He said you are 22 now, another two years means 24, but I convinced him because I was the youngest, I was determined and changes were happening. Then I did MA. The day I gave my final exams, [parents] looked for a husband. On the third proposal, I met my husband and we liked each other and the wedding was decided immediately. Until I got married, to get married and to start a family that was the only thing we knew.

Priyanka exhibited agency in negotiating her education and marriage. As she acknowledges, changes had started to come about in Indian society, meaning that women had started stepping out of their homes to get an education. Work and career wise, society was still conservative toward women, but education itself was slowly becoming acceptable. It is important to note that despite these changes, marriage and family continued to remain the primary objectives of a woman's life. Therefore, during this timeline of Indian women's work history, any real progress had to effectively consider redefining progress as the delicate balance between these traditional mindsets and the individual woman's educational/occupational interests. This did not mean that the two sides were irreconcilable. It simply meant that any negotiation of women's personal and professional interests *had* to actively include a dialogue about marriage and family. More recently, younger women are al-

lowed the freedom to make decisions independent of marriage/family consid-
erations and focus exclusively on education and career.

Rakhi (27), an insurance manager, too took charge of her educational
pursuits. Her father wanted her to become a doctor and even made her take
the Pre-Medical Tests required to qualify to study medicine in India, an
examination at which Rakhi failed. Finally Rakhi told her father that she
would no longer be forced into medicine. She wanted to do an MBA. She
negotiated her choice for business management by discussing Indian leaders
like the Ambani[2] brothers and mentioning that she would like to see these
people, and be like them. At the time she says, growing up in a small town in
north India, she had no real idea who these leaders were except that they
were really big names in business but she used their names to convince her
father to allow her to do an MBA, which her father and family eventually
supported.

Rakhi also narrates what happened when after having finalized two business schools; she visited one of those schools for a selection interview.

> The only thing when it came to the personal interview, the principal asked
> me . . . I used to be very lean and skinny, I mean I am better now, I used to be
> very skinny earlier you know, and I used to hate that. If somebody used to talk
> about it, I used to hate that and that person [principal] talked about that only.
> He did not ask me any academic question, he was like *beta* [here, child], 'Why
> are you like this? Why do you not eat something?' Why . . . I was so bugged
> up with this.

This paternalistic attitude, which was perhaps well-meaning, was completely
irrelevant and inappropriate to the education admissions acceptance process
and being put off by the focus on her physical frame instead of her academic
credentials made Rakhi decide against that school and she chose the other
one in Pune, instead.

A desire to pursue higher education for a better future for themselves is
evident among the younger generation of maids who are getting fewer by the
day. Sonali is a maid who is only 18 years old. After her father died when she
was in the fifth grade, so as not to "burden" her mother with having to look
after her, she lived with her employers and worked in their homes while
continuing to go to school. At interview time, she was doing a diploma
[certificate] program in Fashion Designing while working as a maid so that
she can have money to pay toward the fees. She says she is educated until the
10th grade and she did it by working as a maid and paying for it herself.

Answers that represent agency among women in the high-income category show a strong sense of focus. These women have a strong resolve to do
something with their lives and education. Of course such resolve is evident
among women of the low-income category as well but oftentimes the best of
resolve meant they ended up working as maids because that was the reach of

their resolve limited as they were by circumstantial constraints discussed in previous chapters. In other words, even though women in low-income occupations may have been determined to better their lives, and be someone or do something exceptional, their limited financial means and educational levels prevented them from doing so. In terms of displaying agency regarding their work and careers, there is no significant difference among the middle- and high-income women except the extreme focus that several women in the latter category mentioned they had had from a young age.

Shipta (32), an insurance executive, explains how she was a shy and timid girl compared to her outspoken sister. However, unlike her older sister, "I was very focused what I wanted from life, like my dad was not earning so well financially at that point of time but then I knew what I have to do in my life." Her sense of responsibility developed at a young age when she realized that her family was not well off. To make up for that financial reality, she continued to remain focused on what she needed to do with her life and better her situation. Atypical of middle/upper middle class Indian girls of her generation, she worked part-time all through high school and college to pay for her own education.

Sakshi (29), a radio host, believes the reason she is in a new generation profession[3] working at a radio station is because she always wanted to do something different.

> I love talking, I love connecting to people, I love being on air. I love being in a profession which is definitely *hatke* [different] than anybody else would do . . . I mean if you . . . see, one more thing, I would love to share this with you since you are writing, I was always one of those kinds where I wanted to do something different than what other people did. There are many incidences which I can share like when I was kid, when everybody had red umbrellas; I always preferred buying a blue one, when everybody had those typical compass boxes . . . Camlin compass boxes, I always preferred to have some other color in it, so I never liked to copy anybody. That is exactly what I did in my profession, I never copied anybody.

Sakshi's continued desire to stand apart from the crowd and be unique in her choices inspired her to embrace her career even though the reaction at home was less than enthusiastic. She recalls,

> When I ended up being a R. J. [radio jockey], when I showed the letter [employment offer letter] at home to my parents, my dad got up and said well, "It is good as a time pass [hobby], as a . . . like I mean if you want to earn your pocket money, finally you can do that with my permission but what about teaching?" [She had trained to become a teacher]. My mom was a little surprised and at the same time very insecure about the profession. My grandpa said, "Do it till you feel like doing it, leave it later, and get back to whatever you wanted to do earlier," so I got different kinds of reactions.

My husband was the only person . . . obviously, that time he was my friend, not even a boyfriend, a friend . . . a very good friend. He was the one who said that, "No, Sakshi, I think whatever you are doing will be great. I mean do it, take it up as a complete profession, like a full-time profession," so ya, my friends were very excited. They were excited on the whole fact that a new radio station is coming up in Pune . . . but see, you know, you are in that age when you end up discussing your pay package and suddenly when they come to know that the pay package is much higher than what they are getting [at their other jobs] . . . so some of my friends were very excited, some were jealous, some were again trying to figure out *ki ye kya hai, kya hone wala hai.* [what is this? What is going to happen in this new job?] Nobody knew about it, so . . .

After the initial hesitation, which was only because of their uncertainty regarding the profession, her parents and grandfather supported her career choice and cheered her success. Sakshi mentions how even though her friends were excited at her job, some were indeed jealous of her salary and wondered what this new career avenue would bring with it. Through it all, Sakshi remained steadfast in her resolve to take on an unconventional career path and despite the somewhat mixed reactions, continued on that trajectory and achieved great success.

Shalini (32), a labor attorney, also explains how she had a strong internal drive, a passion about what she wanted to do.

I wanted to do something really nice even if it meant that I had to work hard for it or may have to sacrifice my friends. I chose to do that because I feel that I was very focused. When you are in third standard [third grade], you are hardly eight years old, seven-eight years old, so from that time, I had this passion in me that I wanted to become a lawyer, so I guess when I actually completed my Law, I was very passionate about it. I have always dreamt about it and I had . . . like others would say that no, I never dreamt about doing this or like you know, I would not be . . . I would not have dreamt about coming into this stream but I always dreamt about this. This is what I wanted.

Suchitra: You really wanted to do this!

Shalini: I wanted to do this like, everything like, whenever like, even in school or colleges when someone would ask what would you like to be, someone would say this and that like you know, but I always said I wanted to do this. I took my education in that manner and I was very focused, even in my college, even . . . like there are many girls or students, they do not know what they have to do after their graduation. They may think that I want to do this, I want to do that but I was very focused and I just wanted to be here you know, and I knew that if I was . . . if I completed my graduation, I would be able to give my 100%. I do not know there was something in me that just kept on telling me that you have to be here and I am very passionate about my work . . .

The passion to become a lawyer kept Shalini focused on the career path ahead and as she mentions, she even chose college courses that would count toward her goal of becoming a lawyer.

Vaishali (37), a doctor of gynecology in Ayurvedic medicine, always knew she wanted to become a doctor.

Ujwala (30), a journalist, also stayed focused on her goals throughout the phase of career planning and made her own decisions, but for a different reason.

> The thing is I've always had the habit of doing things on my own since I was a child. I would probably talk to my parents, but I prefer deciding on my own so that way there are less people to kick if you go wrong.

Madhura's (55) story of how her career found her instead of the other way around represents the anguish and frustrations felt by a generation of women who felt trapped between having to follow tradition and stay at home as wives and mothers and wanting to do something for themselves. It also represents agency and a serendipitous calling toward a career. Madhura's story begins at life before marriage when she was turning out to be among one of the few highly educated women of her generation.

> I completed my post-graduation in English literature from the University of Bombay. I did my undergrad in English. I did my post-grad in English, then I had enrolled for Ph.D. and I got married and so I had to leave my Ph.D. and mine was the last batch where we could enroll without doing M. Phil. [directly for a Ph.D. program]. Inspite of all this I had to come to Pune, we had to shift [relocate] due to our business matters and my husband started his business here so I had to shift along with him that is why I had to *leave my dream incomplete* but I don't regret now but there were moments when I was frustrated.

Madhura had already enrolled for a Ph.D. program when she got married. As a dutiful daughter and wife observing familial obligations, after marriage, she quit her program and moved to Pune with her husband to support his new business, leaving her "dream" unfulfilled—a decision that she says she does not regret but which she certainly associates with moments of frustration. She explains why:

> Suchitra: Was it your dream to get a Ph.D.?

> Madhura: Not exactly that. Once I got married and got into the family fold and started sharing and holding the responsibilities here, it wasn't that, *that* dream was very significant for me. But that [getting a Ph.D.] made me feel I was somebody and I should try to find my own self. There was some kind of suffocation because you see my mother's generation, they were happy with

what they had. They were happy rendering services to the people in the house and they were catering to the needs of the members of the family. All such things were happening then but then *think of women belonging to my generation*, we had some basic education, we knew that there was something better we could have done instead of just whiling away time or wasting our life in just doing cooking and looking over the household. There are no regrets now since I found a unique field and I have found a different path which perhaps I wouldn't have done by being on the regular path that is set for women so after the age of 40–42. I started working in this field and this has given me tremendous happiness because now I know that this is a unique field which I am fortunate enough to have.

In the quote above, Madhura explains that getting a Ph.D. in and of itself was not as significant as what it represented to her in terms of an identity. It made her feel like she was "somebody." Madhura articulates the dilemmatic frustrations that women of her generation felt. She explains how women of her mother's generation might have been happy serving their families because their sense of self and identity was assumed to be tied to their homes. However, Madhura's generation of women had gotten an education and knew they could explore alternative possibilities if they so wanted. Since Madhura had to leave her education incomplete and give all her time to her family, she mentions feeling suffocated in that arrangement at times. After moving to Pune, Madhura decided to take on paid employment and after getting a teaching degree taught at a school until her daughter was born. Then for 14 years, she says she did "nothing."

And 14 long years I did nothing. Nothing in the sense it wasn't nothing, actually it was much more than what I am doing now because I think that is a universe in itself when you cater to the needs of the people at home. I don't think I whiled away that time. But as a human being when you have so much to offer to your own self. I don't believe that we offer a lot to the society as such.

Madhura felt content fulfilling her responsibilities as a wife and mother but continued to feel that she was missing something in life by not giving something back to society through her work (outside of the home) especially since she knew she had so much to offer. Finally, when she was old enough, her daughter convinced Madhura to step out of the house and find a job. Madhura's current profession happened, as mentioned above, quite serendipitously. She recalls,

I was at the juncture where I did not know what to do with my life and my daughter had already hinted that I would have the emptiness syndrome (laughter) so I was just wondering as to what to do with my life. There were moments of frustration. Obviously. And I wanted to do something with my own life but it is very difficult to start off on one's career again and anew when you are almost at the end of your family responsibilities. I was just wondering. I was to take up a job actually as a teacher in a college. Then one day I went with my husband to this blind school where my husband used to donate money every year on his birthday. I just accompanied him. I had already okayed [accepted] the teaching job. I was to teach at the junior college level. I saw the plight of the children there [blind school]. There were small children walking on the staircase and they were just helplessly walking on the staircase and toppling. One child came and hugged me and the child was homesick and the child was thinking I was the mother and when I saw the child I was so touched. I just walked out and told my husband I don't think I should take up that teaching job. I'll do something with this [blind school] and he also okayed [agreed] it. He said, "I also wanted to give some time but I couldn't so I donated money all these years. Now you give your time to this cause" and that's how I decided to get into this field.

That episode 12 years ago led to the birth of Madhura's blind school for youth who no longer qualify to remain under government programs once they turn 18. She takes in walk-ins as well, of which she says she has many who come in having heard of her through word of mouth. She teaches almost all general subjects until a bachelor's degree to 100 to 125 students, both males and females, with both English and the state language, Marathi, as the media of instruction. She has built a small library of books in Braille, a computer laboratory, and invites industry experts to teach her students computer hardware skills so they can learn vocational skills. Since Madhura operates her school from her bungalow, the blurring of home and workplace is obvious. On any given day, she has five to ten students staying the night over if classes run late and they are unable to find a bus back to their homes. She says her quest "to be something, somewhere, somebody," has been satisfied.

Madhura's current profession has been enabled by a number of factors, but none of it would have been possible had Madhura herself never felt the urge to do something and contribute her skills and abilities to society. That Madhura's work today meets an acute societal need and gives her satisfaction is merely the consequence of her efforts. The theme of her story continues to be her own passion and resolve to want to excel somewhere by doing something beyond enabling her family and her own daughter in their pursuits.

When it comes to fulfilling one's educational or career goals, women have not hesitated to put in the sweat and tears, as was the case with Rakhi (27), whom we saw earlier negotiating entry into a business school. After completing her MBA, she got a job as an insurance sales agent. Rakhi was new to Pune, having only been here the two years during which she did her MBA. She did not know the local language, Marathi, and did not own a vehicle [a scooter in this context], a necessity for sales agents who travel a lot. She had student loans to pay off and as a normative expectation of an earning member of her family, also needed to send money home to her family, all of which put a heavy strain on her mental and physical health.

> My salary was 9,000 coming in hand [after taxes], out of which 5,000 was going for loan installment. I was having only 4,000 in my hand. Out of that 4,000, I used to pay my 1,000 rupees phone bills, okay, and something I used to send home also. Mama *ko bhej diya ya aise kuchh kar diya, brother ko chahiye to de diya, sister ko chahiye to bhej diy*a, [mama needs some money so send it to her, brother needs some, sister needs some so I kept sending money home] . . . I traveled by buses, autos [auto rickshaws], and all that you know, and which was a very tough task, very, very tough task because traveling by bus to Pimpri and from Pimpri if somebody is called to Nigdi or Chinchwad or M.I.D.C. [suburbs at different ends of Pune], it was very tough you know. I used to catch auto or sometimes if I do not have money, I used to walk down for long, long distances, I used to walk. If somebody asks me to do that today, I cannot do that anymore. I will better leave that job only. It was only . . . I think . . . it was something superpower *jo tha us waqt* [that I had at that time] which could make me do that. Otherwise, it is very difficult. I used to carry my bags, it used to be very, very heavy. We used to walk down long, long distances and then *bus ke liye paise lagte the* [needed money for the bus]. Sometimes I used to skip my meals because I did not have money, sometimes I used to check *ki is mein kaunsa* fit *baithta hai,* 15–20 bucks *mein kaun sa fit baithega,* [what can I eat for the Rs. 15–20 I have left] sometimes I used to skip it. Most of the time, I used to skip it not because of money, money was also one reason but most of the time, I used to skip it because I used to feel alone.

Rakhi went through a lot of struggles before she finally settled into her new city and job. Today Rakhi is an insurance manager at a different company and feels that she is finally at peace with life. The many challenges Rakhi had to face, including not having a scooter to travel between clients' visit sites to not knowing the local language [even though English and the national language Hindi are widely spoken, in sales, knowledge of the local language can give an agent an advantage] to figuring out how to manage her meals in the limited money she had, are all part of an experience that Rakhi accepted as a working woman. She had carefully argued for and convinced her father to allow her a degree in business administration. It was important to her to succeed in her chosen field as well as meet familial responsibilities. As the oldest child, Rakhi remembers growing up in a humble lower/middle-class household. She therefore felt an immense responsibility toward her parents and siblings and wired home part of her salary to make their lives somewhat better even though she had to undergo a tough few years herself.

In addition to taking proactive steps to push for their education and displaying strong resolve and resilience in overcoming the odds, women in middle- and high-income categories are also instrumental in proactively furthering their career ambitions.

Harsha (29), a physiotherapist, mentions how she would actively seek out references on physiotherapy and read them, or access sources from journals available online to further her understanding of this newly emerging field in India. She volunteered to be part of a free medical clinic that traveled to rural areas and administered health check-ups and treatment to villagers. She was the only physiotherapist on the tour and was still a student when she got this opportunity, but she grabbed it for the experience. She also mentions how in addition to starting her own practice, she took up a part-time position at a hospital to get a wider range of cases. While there, she also actively sought out a mentor, an orthopedic surgeon, so that together with their combined knowledge but different approaches, she could learn the best of both fields.

Shalini (32), a labor attorney, could have easily joined her father's successful legal practice upon completing her law degree. Instead, she chose to take up a job in a different city with a different firm so she could get some outside work experience. She explains her decision,

> I got a placement in XXXXX, Bombay, so they were the solicitors and I was working with them though I had a very good set up in . . . of my own but I just chose to you know, just go and learn a little more from outside because once you are in, you know, in your own set up [father's well-established legal practice], you tend not to get the rough things you know. Everything is laid like comfortable. You are placed in a very comfortable situation but when you go out, you work, you have to do all things by yourself, then there you may not have such a you know, what do you say such a smooth sailing like you know. You have to look into everything, you have to do all the things, so I stayed in Bombay. I stayed in a hostel for the first time, so they were the golden years of my life, staying in a hostel and working and it was a nice experience but I gained a lot of experience from there and I should say that I was really fortunate because I got to learn really from them and people in Bombay . . . like they were very particular about a lot of things, about the way the working was, the way they talked with their clients, and they were international clients and huge multinationals coming in and you know, I was just off the college and like, you are not that groomed you know, you are just out of the college and suddenly you are there and sitting in a board room. So it was a little difficult thing that I guess they were very . . . like now when I look back I feel that ya, those days really taught me a lot and like how you look into papers, how you go through the files, how you like, how you just study you know . . .

Shalini's decision to work for someone else to gain experience from the "outside" reflects her agency in taking control of her career. This work experience provided her with important outsider perspectives that she brought with her when she eventually joined her father's law firm.

Before starting her new job as an IT product quality analyst, Shraddha's (27) two previous jobs were in two different cities, away from Pune where her parents lived. When Shraddha's new job took her to Mumbai, a city only

80 miles northwest of Pune, her parents were concerned about her staying away from home on her own for the first time but Shraddha was determined and brought her parents on board by reasoning with them that because Mumbai was not that far away, she would visit every weekend or they could drive in to visit her. Shraddha considers her mother's concern about her going away and living by herself "natural." Finally, the situation was resolved after her mother called some relatives in Mumbai and made arrangements for Shraddha to live with them and have them as her local guardians. Although she agreed to the arrangement, once in Mumbai, Shraddha rejected her mother's idea because she "wanted to be more adventurous." She took the accommodation provided by her organization for the first couple weeks till she knew her colleagues and later on moved to an apartment where she lived with a co-worker as her roommate. Even though her parents allowed her to pursue her career in different cities, within two years of her working, they wanted her to return home because they felt she had lived away far too long. They also wanted her to get married and insisted that she find a job in her hometown. Her parents' behavior is representative of parents from the "middle" generation. They gave their daughter the freedom to pursue her career but also felt she needed to fulfill traditional daughter roles such as living with them and getting married at the "right age." So while girls had the freedom to pursue their career dreams, they needed to do so by being mindful of traditional expectations.

When Rajani started working as a recruiter, after having just moved to Pune, and without the support of her husband who chose to stay back in their native town, her many financial hurdles never weakened her resolve to excel. She took the initiative to meet with company executives, ask for work, delivered on the results, and continued to further her knowledge and skills in the field.

> I started my business on August 15, 1996 and after doing *puja* [offering prayers] and all I went to the Hadapsar Industrial Estate by bus because I was not having two wheeler [scooter], not even bicycle. During my first visit, I just saw one board of the organization [randomly saw the name of a company on the door/building]. I just went in and I met the managing director of that company and I said that today only I have started my company. I have done the *puja* and see this is my visiting card and this is my introduction letter. We had a brochure, well printed brochure and all that. These are the activities. Can you please support us giving your first assignment to us? He said, "Why not? It is my pleasure. These are the assignments. See, why you are talking about one assignment take four assignments, start work on it." Then he took two people from us [recruited candidates she recommended]. So from day one I started to get business and till date I have never faced any problem, you know. Problems were there you know. . . . ups and down were there no doubt about it but I was continuously backed up with the assignments. So plenty of assignments were there. We did a lot many mistakes. We learnt a lot because I was

totally ignorant about corporate culture, so I learnt about corporate culture, mannerism, etiquettes and how to deal with multinational, how to draft the letters, how to present yourself to them so these were all the things I learnt. It was a long process and many people contributed. My clients have contributed in my development. So this is how the journey started on August 15, 1996, and that was the beginning of my profession, my career in the true sense you can say. Initially we used to provide manpower to the very small offices, companies then we got XXXX Group then we started to deal with XXXX Groups. These groups were the initial supporters and lot many learning you know. Continuous learning from newspapers, current affairs, many books on management. Then I took admission for MBA, I did my MBA from XXXXX affiliated with the XXXXXX University, U.S.A. This is my MBA degree [points to the degree on her wall], I did my MBA with specialization of marketing and that completed five years back.

In addition to actively seeking recruitment jobs and not being afraid to learn from her mistakes and from whoever was willing to teach, Rajani continued to hone her skills by completing a degree in business administration.

Bindiya also showed agency in designing the course of her career. The stigma and negative reputation associated with a career in entertainment has been discussed in previous chapters. Understandably for their generation and times, her parents and in-laws encouraged Bindiya to pursue any career of her choice as long as she did not become an actor. Given the lack of permission to do so, Bindiya forced herself to keep her passion for acting buried for years. In the interim, she worked as a teacher, completed a diploma program in business management, and worked as office administrator for her husband's manufacturing company but never gave up on her dream of becoming an actor. She reports being depressed and frustrated with the life she was leading at the time, not being able to do what she really wanted until she finally reached her "boiling point."

In our Indian culture, we are all suppressed from day one. First, the father, then husband, father-in-law. We are pressed under that pressure. Most often we cannot expose our true identity. I was of a rebellious nature from the beginning. I thought I had tolerated enough, so it was about time to move on. So I said I am not going to listen anymore. If they allow me fine, if they don't allow me, still I am going to do it. So even my husband realized, now she is not going to listen (laughter). Finally on Gudi Padva [auspicious Hindu religious day], I started my own production house. My first production was XXXXX. The play had already been staged previously but I brought it back on stage. Everything was new: the music, the set, the cast. It was a very nice experience for me to launch my own production on a professional platform. I was acting, producing. I got a good response from the audience. I didn't have much experience with running a production house like a business, taking care of all the financial aspects so maybe I lacked those skills somewhere. But it still went on for 52 shows, all over Maharashtra and Goa.

Bindiya also mentioned how at one point the frustration of not being allowed to be an actor had gotten so much to her that she had decided to divorce her husband if he did not support her acting career. Of course she says he never did object to it but he also did not want to go against the will of his parents who had refused permission to allow their daughter-in-law to act.

As is evidenced in the narrations above, women have not feared to step up and exert their influence on their own careers when they needed to. Be it asserting their right to education, albeit in the form of peaceful negotiation, or displaying the grit and determination to overcome obstacles to career growth and development or even resisting "permission" to pursue a particular path, women have acted as self-agents and contributed toward their own careers.

In a culture such as India's, interpretations of socio-cultural influences on lifestyle, ways of thinking and behaving, and observing of rites and rituals among other things, often get absorbed into people's everyday realities. With changing societal and professional expectations, this study found that parental controls were slowly relaxing to favor their daughters' individual career choices. Unlike a previous generation that unapologetically privileged marriage and family over women's careers, today's parents of women in their 20s and 30s may even support their daughters' single-minded devotion to careers. Work and family life can never truly be nurtured without one clearly affecting the other. The dichotomy is simultaneously materialized in everyday lives. Also, the two should not be considered as opposite ends of a tightrope where only the brave can venture over to one side or the other. Rather, the messy concepts of work and/or family are very personally experienced and systematically and strategically managed. Quite interestingly, this study found that despite a cultural awareness, openness, and embracing of working women, the participants themselves chose a path of compromise so as to remain in harmony with their perceived socio-cultural/familial responsibilities and expectations.

In this study, participants were asked numerous questions about how they balance work and family/life, the challenges they faced in walking this balancing act, the support system they did or did not have, their own views on privileging work or family, and so on. For all the agency participants displayed in negotiating for their education and pursuing their career aspirations fearlessly, Indian women have their priorities well sorted out when it comes to questions of balance. While they readily admitted to the everyday struggles of finding that elusive work/life balance they had no doubts in their minds about which of the two was more salient to their lives.

IN COMMUNION

As discussed in the sections above, to Indian women, what their families think about their working and having a career is very important. While many women in their 20s and 30s talked about the importance of work in their lives, the support of their families and their own willingness to do what their families expect out of them is beyond negotiation. Prasad (2006) observes that, "The need to be sensitive to everyone's needs means that everyone's individual freedoms are compromised to a greater or lesser degree" but argues that the patriarchal structure of traditional Indian families makes such behaviors essential to peaceful co-existence. During the interviews, I did not hear from or meet a single woman who wanted to have a career exclusively at the cost of family. This led women to voluntarily make a number of compromises in their careers and the fact that *they* chose to do so speaks to their agency. Of course just because they chose to make those compromises does not remove them from occasionally regretting those decisions, compromise related or otherwise, but what they consider more important is the fact that they *chose* to do so and for that, they have no regret. These decisions indicate their desire to stay in communion with their environment—their parents, husband, children, and in-laws.

Marshall (1989) argues that in honoring their own values and heritage, women are "reclaiming the positive aspects" (p. 277) of their socialized worlds of knowledge (including careers) developed through relationships and families. Likewise, rather than consider themselves victims of their circumstances or socialized diktats, women in the study were simultaneously negotiating agency and communion by displaying "constrained agency." O'Brien Hallstein (1999) explains that, "*Constrained agency* simultaneously grants women agency *and* recognizes that that agency occurs within constraints" (p. 37). Such a perspective gives primacy to women's interpretive capabilities but recognizes that our "socially constructed subject position" (p. 38) occurs amidst the constraints that act as conditions upon our lives. Participants in the study are embedded within a socio-cultural-familial tripartite context but accept the constraining effects on their careers as something that needs to be negotiated albeit amidst tensions.

Ujwala (30), a journalist, decided to quit her job after the birth of her son. Her aunt, who had continued to work through her pregnancy and motherhood, advised her not to quit just as her editor who recommended against it. Ultimately, weighing the pros and cons, Ujwala decided to take a break because she did not want to have her son raised by nannies. Once he was old enough, she enrolled him in daycare and started working part-time again, a decision that she admits, has not been easy.

This going back to work now has taken a lot of effort. Everybody [she specifically meant her in-laws] hates the idea that son is in daycare for two days but
c'mon I need to do things now and two days in daycare will do my son a world
of good. So now two days a week I work full day. The other days I free-lance.

Ujwala felt a maternal as well as a professional tug. She quit her job as a
journalist and stayed with her son for a while but as she says, it was time to
get back to work. At the time of making the decision to quit, she made a
conscious decision to do so to be fair to her son and to herself.

In the sense that I have chosen not to be a full-time journalist because life as I
saw it, when I was a full time journalist, it is something that you give yourself
to completely 24/7, 365 days you are thinking of stories if you are not doing
them, otherwise you are reading stuff that other people have done and are
either kicking yourself for not doing it despite knowing about it or kicking
yourself for not realizing that it could be done. So after a point you know that
if this is going to be life then it is not healthy if you are going to have a kid.
After I had the kid I decided to take a break for this reason.

Vidisha (29) was forced to take an extreme step and quit her job when her
organization refused to let her take an extended break from work to be with
her husband when he left for the United States for six months.

Suchitra: What were you going through when you had to leave your job and go
to the US?

Vidisha: That decision was an on the spur of the moment decision where I
decided I had to quit my job and I have to go, something like that. I mean I
hadn't actually planned for it but then those people [employers] were not ready
to give me leave and all so I said like no, I'll leave my job and go, it's okay.

Suchitra: So you didn't fear the repercussions?

Vidisha: No, not really. I was like if I am able, I'll definitely get a job again.

Suchitra: Did you . . . get a job after you returned?

Vidisha: Actually being in the US, I was out of touch, not even using a
computer at home, so I was completely blanked out for six months without any
computer, without any, I mean my mind whatever knowledge I had you know,
had rusted so getting back, I was not very decided on whether to do a job or
not. But then after sitting at home for one month I said no, I can't sit at home
any longer. So I started hunting for jobs. Ya in the beginning it was difficult. I
searched for two three companies and I got rejections so then I approached my
old company again who were ready to take me back so I joined there again for
eight months and then I quit [she switched jobs after quitting].

To Vidisha, being with her husband was more important than having a job. She knew she would get another one because of the confidence she had in her abilities. Despite the fact that she was not able to practice her skills while in the US that led her to having difficulties finding a job upon her return, she showed agency as well as humility in approaching her previous employer again for a job, getting retrained in her previous skills, and then quitting for a better opportunity. Even though her former employer gave her her job back, Vidisha did not think it was necessary to stay loyal to the organization. As is representative of changing work contracts, Vidisha moved on to a better job when she got the chance to do so.

Like Vidisha, Jaya (48) also made compromises in her career, but for a different reason. Even though Jaya had the opportunity to advance in her career as a social worker to a more supervisory role, she says she did not pursue those opportunities because, "If I keep going up in my career, I may lose my bond with my children and husband so I am happy at my level." Jaya deliberately took a backseat in her career because her relationship with her children and husband is more important to her than her career. She believes that if she were to take those advancement opportunities, she might miss out on her time with her family due to professional responsibilities. Therefore, she prefers to be at the position where she is at, having willingly stunted her hierarchical rise in the organization.

Pooja (50), the principal of an international school, always wanted to be ground staff with Air India, India's national airline. During the time she applied, the wait list for applicants was two years. When Pooja finally got an offer from Air India she decided not to take up that job, a decision Pooja regrets today.

> I regret not taking up Air India. I feel I would have been I mean I would have had a different career all together but not regret in that sense. That was really what I wished for but circumstances did not allow. I already had a child and I didn't want to leave him alone. I mean I was sure of that. I would be living in Gujarat, coming to Bombay, staying as a PG [paying guest—temporary accommodation], not what I wanted to do.

So after being on the wait list for two years, when Pooja got the opportunity to work in the career of her dreams, she declined. She went for the final interview because she says she wanted to have the pleasure of being the one to turn them down and not the other way around. In those two years from her having applied for the position and gotten an offer, she had married and had a child. The dream was no longer viable given the changed life situation where she would have to manage different cities between her work and home and a young child. So she declined the job because she wanted to be with her son, this decision in favor of her family at the cost of her dream job, changed the direction of her career entirely. When she first articulates her decision, she talks about regret but her answer is somewhat ambiguous.

> Suchitra: If you did not have a child, would you have pursued this career?
>
> Pooja: I was married by then so no.
>
> Suchitra: And if you hadn't been married?
>
> Pooja: Then yes, definitely.
>
> Suchitra: Do you feel that you were restricted in your career options because you were married?
>
> Pooja: No.

She says she regrets not taking up the Air India job. Then, she says had she not been married she would have taken up that job. So one would assume that her career choices were limited in a way because of marriage—or that marriage foiled her plans of having her ideal career. Her answer, however, is that it did no such thing. Perhaps the meaning is in the word "restricted." She was not restricted per se because she could still work in any career field she wanted to as long as she gave priority to her family. She explains,

> I am not a very ambitious person. I mean I do want to achieve something definitely that drive is there but I am not that I'll do it at any cost, no. I mean okay if I am making somebody unhappy I won't do it. I am basically that kind of person that I don't want to cause unhappiness to anybody because of me . . . That's always been my thing. Even after marriage, my father-in-law said, how will you live in Bombay and even when I went for the [Air India] interview and all, he got a little worried, where will you stay and how are you going to manage with a kid and all so I said okay fine then I won't do it. It was just that way. It was never a personal thing that no I have got it so I am going to do it.

Pooja is very clear that her family comes first but that is mostly because, admittedly, she is not very ambitious. She does not wish to chart her career path leaving unhappy people along the way. She wants to work and have a career but only so long as everybody affected by that career is also happy. She is not the kind of woman who would choose to have a career over everything else. She was not willing to let her son grow up alone or leave him in daycare. She therefore sacrificed that particular career path—Air India ground staff—but she made peace with that situation and decision. One thought could be that perhaps she is representative of the more "typical" Indian woman of her generation who will not go against the wishes of her elders. On the other hand, maybe she is truly *not* that ambitious and being more of a family-oriented person, she merely enjoys the freedom to work. Because work is not a primary contributing factor to her sense of self-worth or identity, it remains in the background; as necessary but not required. The decision to want to respect and observe others' opinions, willingly, even if it means compromising on one's career takes agency. Indian women may *choose* their career decisions but they do so after having listened to their close and immediate family members, which includes parents and in-laws, and after being sure that their decision does not inadvertently inconvenience others. Their own sacrifice and inconvenience, well, that is not considered more important in the grand scheme of family solidarity and relational harmony.

Shraddha (27) currently works as an IT product quality consultant. In her previous job, she worked as a technical team leader at a multinational company. She had to work odd hours that included several night shifts. As a result when she got married to a man who had a similar job profile, she realized that she barely got to see her husband. Before this could start affecting her marriage, Shraddha decided to quit her job and stay home so she could spend more time with her husband. Even though her organization was willing to make alternative work arrangements for her like job sharing, she preferred to take a complete break. Eventually when she decided to re-enter the job market after a year, she found her skills were already outdated and that she needed to develop new skills to get a job. So she did a certification course in product quality assurance and testing and found a job in that field. She explains,

> The first thing that people see is how your experiences have been and the time they see a gap, what you were doing for this one year, whole year and it is very difficult for a person . . . you know, or probably it was difficult for me to convince someone that no, that is something that I wanted, people always thought why is it . . . you know, they always tend to get negative thoughts, why is it that she worked in a company like XXXX and took a break, no, is it something she did not get along with her managers for some reason or was it something else, so it is difficult to convince people that, that is something that I wanted. It is the best reason I used to use, I got married, and I wanted to [take a] break but my marriage was never affected apart from the timings factor, my husband never opposed me working and things like that but that break does affect your prospects in future and even when you are negotiating salary and stuff and then once you have a break, it is difficult to get back to that level. I have experienced that that is how it is.

Although she took that break willingly and because she wanted to, she had to deal with the consequences—first, people did not buy the fact that she merely wanted to take a break to be at home; people presumed she left due to a problem with her employer. This change in societal perception is noteworthy.

Whereas, a previous generation of working women may be expected to quit their jobs for domestic and family reasons and nobody would question or second guess that decision, in Shraddha's case, the fact that she decided to voluntarily "take a break" from having a career so she could spend more time at home and be with her husband appears to have gotten quite the opposite reaction. This is just one of the many examples that reinforces the changing perceptions of Indian society toward working women. Second, she faced problems with negotiating salary due to the gap on her resume; and finally, she also found it difficult to get to the same position/level in her profession as she had prior to the break. She says that despite the initial frustration, she accepted the situation by rationalizing it as a part of any woman's life — compromising for her family. Even though she says she never regretted her decision, she often wonders about what might have happened to her career had she not taken that break. She reasons that the break was necessary. "There was too much mental exhaustion, as well as the stress from traveling and work pressures had become too much to handle," so she accepted the consequences, ". . . so I just accept . . . yea, fine you have to you know step down a little and then again climb up." Shraddha's decision to quit her job was also relationally motivated. Again and again findings indicate that even though a career has its own place in an Indian woman's life, one's relationship with close family certainly takes precedence.

Sandhya's (45) husband did not approve of her working status. Despite his disapproval and the emotional struggles she faced, Sandhya remained steadfast in her decision to continue to stay employed. When she could not manage a colic baby and her work, she went on a leave of absence but never quit. In this extended narrative, she recalls the journey of her experiences.

> After marriage, my husband who was a businessman from a traditional household and had a conservative family did not want me to work. He asked me to leave my job because he felt it below his dignity to let his wife work. He kept forcing me to leave my job but my parents were insistent that one does not get a job easily and you have this permanent job, do not leave it, it can be helpful at any time. So because of that, because of them, I was on leave for two years, and kept pushing the decision ahead. After two years, I said I was going to return to work. I wanted to work and on my insistence, I went back to work. Even then he was against it. Then we had children and once you have children, you need to pay attention to them, so once again he said, now leave your job for them. Then I decided that I will manage everything at home but still continue to work so that he won't have any problems. When relatives visited like I said earlier, if the sister-in-law visits, I was expected to be home with her all the time and you just have to do it. I felt a lot of pulls in numerous directions at that time but I was determined to continue my job.
>
> Then, as our circumstances changed . . . son grew up, I had to pick him up, drop him, I couldn't wait for or attend or take much of an interest in any of his

activities or events because I had a job. So I became inattentive toward my son and family members started complaining that I wasn't taking care of my son because of my job . . . "He behaves like this or that when you go out, his friends tell him your father is so rich, you don't lack anything so then why does your mother work . . ." When they started saying that, it started affecting me. I felt that I am missing out on something and neglecting him so I sent him to a hostel [boarding school]. He studied at a hostel 4th and 5th standard [grade].

I had the same situation with my daughter. She would cry a lot as a child and nobody took care of her. Nobody was even ready to take care of her (tears—cries a little)—"She is your daughter and you—you deal with her." [it is a cultural expectation that in-laws and relatives contribute to raising a child]. Nobody took care of her because she used to cry a lot. My husband started to harass me about leaving my job once again. So then I went back to work only after she started going to school. I took leave when I went in for her delivery and was on leave until she started going to school. I didn't leave my job even then, just went on leave. At the Zilla Parishad [City Government], I was helped by elected officials with their contacts who were kind to me and so I did not have much of a problem with that. So I was able to continue.

I obviously had to make a lot of adjustments in my job. When my daughter was born, we were well settled—we had money, but as our children's education costs increased, my husband's business started going down and education expenses were going up. I had decided that what I couldn't accomplish, I should let my children do and I wasn't going to compromise on that. At that time I didn't think of quitting my job and now I can't even entertain that thought because I really need it now. I cannot leave it now. I will continue in it because both my children are studying well. I need my job a lot now and I will progress as much as I can in it.

Sandhya's candid narrative touches on several key issues, two of which will be discussed. First, consistent throughout her story is the presence of her husband and his insistence that she quit her job whether it was to assert his breadwinning role as the male or to essentialize Sandhya's as the mother who needed to be there for her children. It must have taken a lot of determination and resolve for Sandhya to defy her husband's demand and continue working even when faced with cruel remarks from outsiders as well as family members. Second, the cultural and familial expectations that Sandhya faced are not uncommon. Participants continually channeled societal and societally-influenced personal thoughts about how women should privilege their children and the household over their careers. Sandhya had to fight against these cultural mindsets even as she took on the guilt of not being there for her children while continuing to work. When compelled to do so, instead of quitting, she chose to take temporary leaves of absence thereby maintaining her employment status. Thus, Sandhya showed incredible agency in figuring out the most appropriate action for her and her family at the time having considered the financial, emotional, and familial needs.

A number of narratives retold above reflect on the strong family values that are embedded within the essence of Indian women. Admittedly, a number of the decisions explained above occurred amidst constraints. However, a number of women had no conflict where their priorities lay and happily chose family over career, exerting decisional agency in harmony with their socio-cultural climate.

Anahita (53), a landscape designer who also owns her own landscaping business, has an adult son and continues to hold traditional values about mothers and childrearing. She says,

> Personally, I think woman once she has a child, you need to give that much time to your child you know and especially when a child is a baby until the time girl or boy needs the mother, the mother needs to spend some time with the baby you know. So I do realize it is a little old fashioned of looking at things but once you have the responsibility of giving birth to a child then you need to look at that child's psychological and physical upbringing as well so until the time that the child is completely weaned off her mother even in terms of being able to bathe himself or herself, educate himself, I think the mother should spend a lot more time with the child then the girls are doing right now. But that is my personal view.

Without ambiguity, Anahita, considers a child's early development and formative years as a mother's responsibility. She disapproves of what the "girls are doing right now" alluding to a younger generation of women who may choose alternative work-life arrangements or privilege work/careers over childcare duties even though as seen in this study, younger women are also highly cognizant of their priorities and privilege family over careers whenever possible even though their careers are also of utmost importance. In doing so, these women choose to make flexible work-family arrangements that allow them the space to keep working while giving them the time needed with their children.

Jagruti (34) and Anuja (44), both doctors, a radiologist, and an anesthesiologist respectively, put limitations on their careers so they could devote more time to their children. Says Jagruti,

> I have made the choice of working part time—that is totally personal. I will not say that a woman working 8 hours a day is doing something wrong. Don't get me wrong. I am not of that opinion. Each to his own. In fact, I feel children of woman who are out of the house for 8 or 9 hours are extremely independent. I was extremely independent as a child since my mother was away for a good 8 or 9 hours every day. So I really I don't think that what I am doing is right or what somebody else is doing is wrong. It has its advantages. So each to his own. I think it is a matter of having your priorities right. More importantly, I

had decided long ago that until my second daughter becomes my older daughter's age, another three years, they are going to be top priorities. If they are ill I simply don't go. Luckily my hospital is next door so I tell them that you call me if there is anything urgent or you call me if there is any patient and I will come. Otherwise I just take a break. If I have parent-teacher meetings that always comes first. Everything else comes later.

Anuja too carved out time for her career while privileging her time with her children, especially since her husband had extremely demanding work hours.

I have put limitations on myself. I have not been a totally out and out career minded person. I don't work from morning 7 to 8 o'clock. I have limited work for my own priorities. My husband is a gynecologist and he is not at home for almost 12–14–16 hours in a day so there has to be somebody looking after the other things also so I have restricted myself and I am happy doing it.

Suchitra: So that is by choice?

Anuja: Yes, that is by choice.

Suchitra: How has this affected your career advancement?

Anuja: Yes, it has halted it to a certain extent like possibly I have not been . . . if I were to compare with my husband, he has been able to go ahead a lot but *somebody has to take the back seat.*

Suchitra: And how do you feel about that?

Anuja: I don't mind doing it.

Of course, the balancing act that gives primacy to family over careers takes time to get honed. For Bhavana (38), controller of finance at a multinational company, as a newlywed and new employee, and later a new mom, adapting and accepting the many changes came with a sense of guilt.

I had just gotten married. I joined [started working] in September 1994 and I got married in December of 1994 so it was like a complex period at that time and just newly into the family and just newly into this job. I always used to feel those pressures of having to establish myself at both the places. Though everyone in both the places were like very supportive and caring but still you have this feeling that you are not doing enough here and you are not doing there and wherever you are you feel guilty about the other so that has been, but that has been a part of being in the corporate world so.

Suchitra: Do you think it is more so being a woman?

Bhavana: It is more so. I think so because I never found my husband having that. If both of us got up in the morning and just had our breakfast, he used to walk out without guilt and I used to walk out with guilt.

Developing agency in how one chooses to write or rewrite the rules of a work-life formula that works best for oneself requires experimentation. It requires confronting one's insecurities and battling doubts about how successfully a particular balancing strategy would work or not. These participants face many of the same dilemmas working women all over the world face, yet their struggles are simultaneously compounded by the socio-cultural expectations Indian women encounter in having to meet their traditional duties as daughters, wives, mothers, and daughters-in-law; and alleviated by the assistance provided by extended family members, affordable maids, and other domestic staff like cooks. Yet, the journey is one's own to make and learn from.

Maya, a high-ranking police chief, learned what works best for her by "trial and error."

See it's trial and error. I don't say I'm balancing it. At one time I'm balancing it—the next minute, I'm not so. See I'm not . . . I've realized I've got good common sense and I'm also able to realize that women have biological clock also ticking. I'm fond of kids so I had my first child. Then I'm also ambitious. I did some field postings where I could not afford to have a child especially a young child. Then I gave a gap of—my second child—after seven years. So it's some common sense. Since I didn't have many people to guide me, many women to guide me, I have found that if I give a gap I can bring up my kids. Now also I am learning, now my second child is still in tenth standard. Eighties, nineties we did not have working women model. You know if you remember my mother left the job after she married, so either you get married or you work. Then it was you get married, you work but you don't have children. Now in my case I wanted to have both but I didn't have any model. I have trial and error—I have—now I feel my generation can guide the younger generation—that you can be comfortable—no need to make a big issue out of it. You can do both.

Women like Maya want to lead by example. As members of a generation that was learning to step into the workforce albeit with some trepidation, unsure of expectations on the professional and familial front, devoid of existent work-family balance models, they had to chart their own path, learn from the consequences of their experimental ways, and independently figure out what worked best for them. Having traversed that path, now, participants like Maya are confident that the current and future generations of women workers will avail of and develop alternatives to the work-life conundrum.

Unmarried women also made important career decisions centered on their family. Sukanya (32), an agricultural consultant, explains why she chose not to become an architect,

> Because for each and every woman there are two parts of life, that is before marriage and after marriage. So the maximum part you can spend it with your parents that is the part before marriage. So if I choose to be an architect then I have to leave them in very early years and the time span which will be available to live with them will be very small. So I feel very nice that up to master's degree I lived with them and enjoyed my career and all that.

Had Sukanya chosen to become an architect she would have to move to a different city for education [since the university in her town did not offer that program]. By choosing not to do so, Sukanya is pleased that she got to spend more time living with her parents. She is acutely aware of the temporal demands on her life—her time with her parents is limited, given the custom that upon marriage, a woman leaves her parental home and moves in with her husband's family where the couple then lives with the husband's parents. In order to therefore maximize the amount of time she gets to be with her parents, she chose to study agriculture since the agricultural college was in their city.

Sonal (24), a visual merchandiser for a retail grocery chain and in charge of 31 stores in Pune and surrounding areas, studied in London for a year and later worked for an apparel company in Mumbai for a year and a half. As a result of these stays away from her parents, she now feels she should spend the remainder of her years (before marriage) with her parents. She also turned down an opportunity to be regional manager because that meant moving to Mumbai. "I want to stay with my parents till I get married because I was away for two-and-a-half years." Shipta (32), an insurance executive and branch manager, also refused a promotion for the same reason because it meant she would have to move to Mumbai where the corporate headquarters is located and she did not want to stay away from her parents even though the distance between Mumbai and Pune is only a three hour drive with well-connected buses, airplanes, and trains, running frequently and at convenient times.

As can be seen from the examples above, women, both married and unmarried, were willing to take a break from their careers or even forgo opportunities completely if it interfered with their family priorities.

CONCLUDING THOUGHTS

There are several enabling agents that power agency. Agency does not exist in a vacuum. It is enabled by societal structures and communicative

(re)constructions of direct and indirect socialization messages acquired
through an individual's grasp of cultural knowledge about one's environment
and norms of behavior. Women in the study certainly exerted agency and did
so as defined at the beginning of the section through self-assertion, self-
protection, and self-expansion. They made the choices surrounding their
work lives and careers. Sure some of those decisions may seem skewed
unfavorably against the women to the advantage of their families, but as the
women themselves admitted, their families and relationships are more important to them than single-minded pursuit of professional lives. Whether it is
through the active execution of agency or through making choices that enable
a harmonious coexistence with their environment, *they* make those choices
and therefore accept the consequences of those decisions. Even though some
scholars criticize the action-oriented analysis of agency (see Luck &
d'Inverno, 1995), agency in the Indian context and as uncovered in this
study, continues to remain a highly action-oriented construct. Even in communion, women have turned active agents, enabling the decisions and related
consequences in their own lives.

Parents of the new generation of the female Indian workforce have been
part of the sandwich generation straddling two cultural upheavals. These
parents had their own parents and in-laws telling them what to do and how to
lead their lives. Even though acts of resistance and agency were still evident
in some cases, as a generation that was taught unquestioned obedience, wom-
en in the study in their late 40s, and 50s reported how they did not even
realize that they could demand explanations for certain behavioral expectations. They did as they were told. Many of my older participants grew up in a
time when children of progressive parents were able to get some education
and find regular jobs, not careers. If women worked, it was assumed they
worked to meet the family's financial needs. Therefore, career development
for its own sake was never an idea that entered their minds. "We didn't think
like that," is the answer I commonly got from women of this generation when
asked about their career choices. However, once this generation of women
grew up and had children of their own, they wanted their children, especially
daughters, to get all those freedoms and choices that were denied to them. As
a result, and as was evident from the examples above, parents, especially
mothers of this generation, educated and uneducated, working and not working, low income or middle or high income, all encouraged their daughters to
get an education and have careers. Fathers provided the needed practical
guidance and mothers, the strong solid background support. Women in their
late 40s and beyond recall that in the years they were growing up, women
were neither expected nor encouraged to work outside the house. None of
their mothers engaged in paid employment. Women could be employed in
their husband's family business or medical practice but that employment or
any other for that matter was not supposed to be engaged in from the per-

spective of earning a living. Work was not to be a constraint on their time as familial duties superseded all other roles. Therefore, typical nine-to-five jobs were unimaginable for most women at the time. Because their parents grew up with limited choices (or if any), working women of today in their 20s and 30s could afford the luxury of having options and their parents' permission to pursue a career of personal choice. As has already been discussed, parental "permission" and approval continues to remain important to Indian women.

Another important finding from this section is that very few women can truly claim to have completely self-enabled their work lives and careers. India continues to be a culture strongly intertwined with the old and the new and so even though working women enjoy personal freedoms that their predecessors could not even imagine, these dutiful daughters continue to respect their parents' and other family elders' opinions regarding how they should manage their work and personal lives. This indicates that some Indian families, albeit inadvertently, present a delicate dilemma to their daughters, at once enabling agency but at the same time limiting the scope of agency by appealing to their sense of familial obligations and traditional roles.

Pringle and McCulloch Dixon (2003) view agency and communion as two contrasting ways human beings manage environmental uncertainties. The reason I use both these concepts together under the section of agency is because the findings of this study do not show an obvious division between the two. Of course Indian women struggle for balance between agency and communion as is obvious from their many "I regret (that decision), but I don't regret (that decision)" outlook toward the many decisions they have taken. The important point of diversion is that even when women have made those decisions to be in communion, they have made those decisions willingly, because they wanted to and not because they were told to do so. One may argue that the women would not have taken gaps in their careers in the first place had external circumstances not stimulated them to do so. The point is women themselves consider marriage and children important life-changing events that necessitate a flexible view on careers. While many women of a previous generation chose to completely quit working after pregnancy and childbirth, the younger generation of working women today consider these events as natural and openly negotiate arrangements that enable them to balance work and family and return to work in motherhood. Eventually what emerges stronger from this discussion is the relational focus that defines women's work lives and a *redefinition of personal agency*.

Having understood and made sense of societal expectations and perceptions of working women, deconstructed and (re)interpreted familial and cultural socialization, and negotiated agency amidst constraints and in communion, the next chapter discusses how Indian working women situate the meaning of work in their lives. In other words, the next chapter seeks to address the question, "What is the meaning of work for Indian working women?"

NOTES

1. Even though the word "communion" has origins in the Christian faith, my application of the word in this chapter and elsewhere in this book is based on my personal secular interpretation of it as a concept that allows for harmonious exchanging and blending of myriad, perhaps even contradictory forces to co-exist simultaneously.

2. The Ambani brothers, Mukesh and Anil, are consistently ranked among India's richest billionaires (Mukesh has been ranked India's wealthiest person for three consecutive years from 2011 to 2013 by *Forbes* and was also ranked the world's 12th richest man in 2012). After a bitter feud that emerged after the death of their father, Dhirubhai Ambani, all assets and properties were divided between the two brothers, Mukesh and Anil, who independently ran their own organizations; Reliance Industries and Reliance Communications, respectively. In recent times, the brothers have called an end to the split and developed collaborative business projects (Karmali, 2013).

3. Even though the history of radio broadcasting in India dates back to 1927 (All India Radio, n.d.), it was not until the mid-1990s and especially the early-mid 2000s, that FM radio really took off in India. Up until then, All India Radio monopolized Indian airwaves. With the opening up of private FM channels, radio broadcasting opened up new career options for young jobseekers, one of which was that of a radio announcer or radio jockey. This profession came to be considered a glamorous and hip career by many, the allure of which however remained lost to an older generation in the early days of the private FM boom.

Chapter Five

Meanings of Work and Career

It is no surprise that several of the pieces of literature on women's work begin with the sentence, "Women have always worked" (e.g., Kessler-Harris, 1981; Ostendorf, 1998; Ruddick & Daniels, 1977). And so they have. Holder and Anderson (1989) observe that the reasons, rewards, costs involved, and the circumstances under which women worked may, however, have been varied. An interest in women's work lives and its subsequent implications on other spheres of their lives was seldom deemed worthy of research in the past. Perhaps as a result of the limited number of women in the paid labor force or perhaps because of the ambiguity surrounding their unpaid but required work (due to essentialized expectations that women should naturally do what women are "supposed" to do—cook, clean, run a household, care for the children, and so on), women's employment histories were not well documented and historians of women's work often faced a dearth of reliable sources (Hudson, 2001). In addition to the lack of resources, the ones that were available did not present accurate information due to the fact that there existed "contradictory and inconsistent instructions" on how women's work was to be classified. Hudson (2001, para. 5) also argues that the nature of women's work—often part time or casual—was not considered important enough to declare. After all, women's stories were not of any particular interest to the intellectual community (Laird, 1989) at the time. Similar assumptions can also be made about the value of Indian women's work and how it was perceived in Indian society.

Astin (1984) agrees that women's work expectations are often shaped by their socialization experiences but maintains that this argument alone does not justify having separate theories of career development for men and women. She contends that,

> Women and men share a common human condition and live together in the
> same world of personal obligations and other sociostructural imperatives.
> Therefore, a single theory should be able to account for the work behavior of
> both men and women. (p. 119)

Astin's perspective above is one I disagree with and I am supported in this
perspective by several scholars who have argued the difference in patterns
and phases in women's work and careers vis-à-vis men (e.g., Chang, 2003;
O'Neil & Bilimoria, 2005; Pringle & McCulloch Dixon, 2003; Whitemarsh,
Brown, Cooper, Hawkins-Rodgers, & Wentworth, 2007). O'Neil and Bilimoria (2005) summarize the need to study women's careers (and consequently
work behaviors in their careers) in and of themselves because of the ways in
which family responsibilities, relational dimensions, underrepresentation,
and token status in higher organizational levels impact their careers differently from those of men's. Seen in a different light, however, Astin's arguments
may have had some observational merit since very few studies during the
time of her writing had ventured to find out if and how women's work
behaviors and experiences were different from those of men's. This obvious
lack of research was also apparent six years later in 1990 when Chester and
Grossman lamented the non-attention given to

> the phenomenological experience of work for women: that is studies that focus
> on how women view themselves as workers, how they experience their work,
> and the meaning they make of it in the context of the rest of their lives. (p. 2)

In recent times, the different organizational, professional, managerial, and
general workplace experiences women have from men has been well re-
searched across disciplines (e.g., Ashcraft, 2005; Barrett & Davidson, 2006;
Buzzanell, 2000; Cheney & Ashcraft, 2007; Dow & Wood, 2006). I would
also add that not only are women's workplace experiences different from
men's, the significance they attach to their work and its outcomes are different as well. According to Grossman and Stewart (1990), the common assumptions underlying women's work are that women work for social contact,
to avoid boredom, and to earn supplementary income for their families.
These assumptions, however, may not be accurate portrayals because such
assumptions are complicated by the "different meanings attached to women
and *women's* work by the wider culture" (Stewart, 1990, p. 261, emphasis in
original). Stewart supports feminist theorists like Wollstonecraft (1978) and
Woolf (1974, 1977) who have tied meanings of work for women to the
"position of women in the culture at large, and women's consequent experience of many aspects of the culture and especially of themselves" (p. 262).

    In the next section, I discuss the cross-cultural perspectives that determine
how individuals evaluate and find meaning in their work differently across
cultures.

CROSS-CULTURAL PERSPECTIVES ON THE MEANINGS OF WORK

Pringle and Mallon (2003) observed that, "all careers evolve within a country's unique historical, economic, and socio-political context" (p. 840). One's culture provides mental maps for determining normative behaviors and actions appropriate in different situations (Schwartz, 1999). In particular, individuals' value orientations toward work differ along three dimensions depending upon how culture emphasizes conservatism versus intellectual and affective autonomy, hierarchy versus egalitarianism, and mastery versus harmony (Schwartz, 1999). Naturally, cultures and nations are expected to differ in their construction of the meanings of, or symbolic value in, their work (see Ciulla, 2000). Derr and Laurent (1989) argue that nationality and national culture are significant factors in determining individuals' internal career orientation, which they define as "a person's own subjective idea about work life and his or her role within it" (p. 455). Presumably then, meanings of work differ not only within cultures across social class, job categories, and generational differences (Smyer & Pitt-Catsouphes, 2007; Song, 2006) but also between cultures. Inarguably then, one's culture, traditional expectations, behavioral norms and customs, and society can influence how one defines work. Scholars studying the meaning of work need to pay particular attention to these and other society/community-specific peculiarities when the meanings of work and the meaningfulness in work.

It is possible that groups of people in similar situations, occupations, organizations, and socio-historical, econo-political backgrounds have more or less comparable orientations toward the meaning of work. I do not in any way claim that the meanings of work are similar for all women just by virtue of being women. I do, however, argue that in addition to the economic reasons for which women may work, there are additional variables and meanings in work for women. Women, after all, as Aptheker (1989) reminds us, have a different way of seeing and interpreting the world; a distinct way of experiencing social consciousness from men, one that is also affirmed by a feminist standpoint perspective. For example, Altschuler's (2004) study of ethnically diverse older women found that for these women paid work meant financial independence from men and making up time lost due to decisions taken to live up to societal, cultural, and familial expectations. Among Japanese Okinawan women, Lee (2006) found the meanings of work to range from self-growth and development to dealing with practical issues such as paying for their children's education. Ostendorf's (1998) inquiry into the meaning of work into women's life unearthed that women primarily associate their work meanings with personal development and emotional well-being. In an intergenerational study of Indian women, Parikh and Engineer (2002) found that women who went to work in the 1950s and 1960s defined success at work in terms of contributing to society and social responsibility, those women who went to work in the 1970s and 1980s defined success as the ability to balance multiple roles, while women who went to work in the 1990s defined it in personal terms, as achieving financial independence, happiness, and self-actualization. Other scholars have emphasized relationships, connections, and interpersonal attachments as meanings women associate with their work (Chester & Grossman, 1990; Crosby, 1990; Grossman, 1990; O'Leary & Ickovics, 1990; Rayman, 1987). Indeed as Ostendorf (1998) observes "the meaning of work is multi-dimensional and that psychological, relational, and economic factors are all important and interrelated variables in understanding what makes work meaningful" (p. 155).

Meanings women assign to work are also complicated by the traditional role expectations and the multiplicity of roles women have to deal with every day of their lives. The purpose of this review has merely been to offer an alternative perspective on how women vis-à-vis men may construe meaning in their work and to emphasize that work meanings should be studied as being different for women and men.

Even though the brief review above does not categorically discuss the work lives of Indian women, the purpose of the section was to introduce readers to a snapshot of the broad literature on meanings of work. Invariably, the meanings assigned to work by the women in the three categories used in this study are going to vary depending on their unique circumstances. As Lair, Shenoy, McClellan, and McGuire (2008) argue, an irresolvable tension exists between the narcissistic and socially desirable construction of "meaningful work" and the condescension of the "meaning of work." This politically contested space is complicated further by the intricacies of caste, class, race, ethnicity, and religion.

Participants of this study were asked the following questions in order to develop an understanding of what constitutes as the meaning of work in their lives; (a) What is the meaning of work for you? (b) Why do you work? (c) What is most meaningful about your work? and (d) If you were given all the money in the world that you would ever need and want, would you still continue to work? Why/Why not?

The themes drawn from the study indicate how India's working women construct the meaning(s) of work in their lives. Evidently, the meaning of work for Indian women depends upon the extent to which their labor meets certain intrinsic and extrinsic objectives.

In other words, in order for their work to have meaning, participants say that their work should do at least one or more of the following: (a) serve the larger Indian society, (b) provide the ability to stand on one's own feet by earning an honest day's living, (c) involve active engagement in paid employment, (d) fulfill personal/familial responsibilities, (e) establish individual identity and reputation, (f) provide learning opportunities and intellectual engagement, and (g) fulfill a higher purpose.

Work as Serving the Larger Indian Society

This theme resonated with almost all participants. Regardless of the nature of their occupation, be it a street sweeper, a maid or a journalist, these individuals strongly believe that their work contributes to the betterment of Indian society in some way or the other and this in turn made their work meaningful.

Arati[1] , a street sweeper, believes that by sweeping the streets of Pune city she is cleaning out the filth and providing a cleaner place for people to walk or drive on. When asked what she likes about her job, she says:

> This job is a kind of social work. Even though we work for the Corporation [city government], even though we draw a salary for our job, cleanliness is our profession and is a kind of social work that is why I like this job.

By framing her profession as being that of cleanliness and work for society (rather than a means to draw salary), Arati creates a positive identification with labor that many might label as "dirty" or stigmatized work in Western societies (Kreiner, Ashforth, & Sluss, 2006) or labor befitting lower classes or castes (Kolenda, 1964).

Interviewed street sweepers assert their pride in their occupation as sweepers. When asked if she would prefer to do the same job but in an office building instead of the streets, Ganga replies, "Now this is all I will do. This job involves cleaning the world, which is *punya*."[2] When asked, "Why do you think that is *punya*?" Ganga says, "When we do all the dirty work, people cover their noses but we don't do that. We clean filth [by sweeping the streets of the city]." Explaining further, Priya, who is also a street sweeper, says, "Now these *warkaris*[3] are going to visit. So many *warkaris* visit our Pune. They create so much filth and yet we clean it without complaining. We just think we've found God by doing our job." Arati also commented about the blessed nature of a job that many would consider "dirty." "They [*warkaris*] sit anywhere, eat anywhere and throw things around. We clean it all up. We just assume we found *Pandurang* [native word for a Hindu god] in cleaning up after them. We just assume we actually see Him." For the street sweepers, work is not simply labor that has value but it is the particular form of cleansing the world and of achieving *punya* through work that others find distasteful and disgusting, that is meaningful.

When asked about pride in their jobs, the women explain that street sweeping is a privileged job to have in their lower social class/lower-caste communities. This government job gave them "*waras haq*" or the eligibility of passing on their jobs to their children after their death. Alka also observes how many women, including relatively well educated women from castes higher than theirs, actually aspire to be street sweepers because of its generational job security.

Bharati (45), a maid, who works in four different households, falls into the low-income category of participants. Despite her own meager earnings where every day is a struggle for a better life, she says, "What is the point of earning if you can't help someone else? If we help someone, we'll get blessings in return." Bharati explained how even with her modest income, she always makes it a point to give alms to beggars. After all, she says, "I am better off than they are." Bharati is proud of the fact that even in her role as a maid she is able to serve other people. When asked to elaborate, she says:

> Now for example there is this person who's house I work at who has a neck problem. He was an engineer who worked for 18 hours. Now our necks are straight, can hold strong, but his neck cannot stand steady. Once the doctor gives an injection, it can stay straight for about two hours. I massage him with Ayurvedic Narayan Oil [medicinal herbal oil]. As long as I massage him, all over his back, he can hold his neck straight for about 2 to 2.5 hours. Then again it glides. So this massage that I do, I feel good. Why do I feel good? The wages may be more or less, that is not the question but my work is helping somebody and the work I am doing is *punya* [blessed] work. I feel that if I do this good work, tomorrow God will help me if I am in trouble. That's how I think of it.

In Bharati's quote above, we can see how her desire for *punya* or blessing and credit for the work she does means more to her than the wages she gets. It may be the case that for women in low-income occupations, this internalized aspiration for credit in one's next life (see Footnote 2) makes the low status of their occupations worth the hard work and acceptable for its potential reward in a future life cycle.

Participants' narratives were filled with how they make sense of their work in terms of giving back to Indian society. By framing their work in terms of service to society, these women seem to justify their employment as dirty workers. In doing so, they are actively constructing a positive identity for themselves while promoting their work as being valuable. These participants are thus drawn to the intrinsic value of their labor. They seem to have reframed the Indian proverb, "Work is Worship" into a work mantra. By alluding to the metaphor of 'worship,' these participants literally and figuratively evoked religious aspirations as well (see Shenoy-Packer & Buzzanell, 2013).

While for some like Jaya (48), a social worker, who supervises the teaching of children of migrant workers at construction sites, the service aspect of their work is obvious. Even Rajani (42), a recruiter, finds her job to be meaningful because it allows her to give back, a thought that just seems to be a natural extension of what she does. Says Rajani,

> The society has given so many things to me from my childhood, so whatever knowledge I have knowledge, values, virtues I have if I don't give it back to society then I think there is no meaning in living life.

It is by using her skills and knowledge that she is able to match potential job candidates with the right employers. Rajani says she finds her work meaningful when she helps those feeling hopeless without a job find one. In doing so and bettering her clients'/job seekers' lives, she finds her own work consequential and full of meaning. For Manisha (49), a priest, who performs religious ceremonies at people's houses, the meaning in her work is derived from promoting traditional Indian values and culture among the younger generation as well as building community. She says,

> So by working in this profession I am supporting our traditional Indian values and culture, it is like we are encouraging it, and often kindling it, especially in the younger generation. That is one objective. It is like we are giving a hand to a national cause. Today there is a need to raise nationalistic thoughts among our people today. If values can be guarded and maintained in every house, you'll notice that during festive times and special prayers, a lot of family members get together, and love is automatically created among all family members. So whatever we say helps solidify those feelings among family members. So if there is love among family members, they feel attached to their houses, if they feel attached to their houses, they feel closer to their society, if they feel closer to society, it'll automatically translate into love for the country. So that is the circle, which makes this profession extremely pure.

Women across income levels and age groups framed the meaning of their work in terms of how it contributes to the larger Indian society. Given the fact that since ancient times Indian women have been handed over the responsibilities of keeping and promoting cultural values, traditions, and customs of the country, it is no surprise that over the years, women have proactively internalized this task. So much so, that while at one time, as housewives, women could actually specifically concentrate on propagating the sense of community building, serving one's society and nation, in the 21st century when all of these women work and bring home their share of the earnings, they continue to frame the meanings they derive from their work and professions in terms of how it helps fulfill societal needs.

WORK AS PROVIDING THE ABILITY TO STAND ON ONE'S OWN FEET BY EARNING AN HONEST DAY'S LIVING

Women across income levels agreed that financial independence was of utmost importance for all women regardless of the particular type of work they are involved in or how much money they make. Standing on one's own feet is the literal translation of a phrase in the local language, Marathi. Because the phrase is part of the general parlance in this part of India, it was used either in its original form in interviews conducted in Marathi or it was translated by the women into English as written above when the interviews were conducted in English. Regardless, all participants affirmed that a woman simply had to be financially independent. The reasons for why they should be financially independent differed among women across income levels.

In the case of Manisha (49), a priest, working gives her the financial independence to choose on whom she spends her money. Explains Manisha,

> Human beings should be financially independent, that is my strong opinion. There are a number of things in a woman's life, where she feels, let me not ask for it. At that time she feels I should step back. I know from my mother's experiences. She was a housewife so whenever she needed something, she had to ask father. When does this question arise—when there is a mother's place [a natal home] and an in-laws' place. If you want to give something to your mother's place, how can you ask something from your in-laws? You don't want them to taunt you about it that you are always giving things to your parents. If you have your own money you can give whatever you want to whoever you want, give something to your brother or anybody else in the world, but that's only when you are financially independent.

For Anjana (48), who is the CEO of her own manufacturing company, work has come to mean more than financial independence; it also brings along a heightened respect at home.

> I think your being financial independent helps improve your importance in your house, with your husband, and your other relatives. Even if nobody in the house needs your income or your income is not the primary source for running your household, people respect you more if they know you are a financially independent woman. In our country, no matter what anyone says, women don't have as much financial independence.

For Charulata (61), the co-owner of three nurseries, women's ability to stand on their own feet is security against untoward incidents that might befall the family. She believes that if in such a situation a woman's earnings can help her family pull through the hard times, then that work is meaningful to that woman. Such views were uttered by several other participants who believed that a woman's earnings may very well be supplementary to her husband's, but it *was* her money and would stand her in good stead should one's financial circumstances change.

Despite the understanding that women need to be financially independent, this independence was permitted only if it was earned out of an honest day's living. This sentiment was also strongly felt and uttered by women from the low-income category.

Sulekha (24), who rolls incense sticks for a living in addition to doing odd chores around her employer's home, says that money got from hard work is the only "right" kind of money one can have. She says, "The happiness I can earn from money that I have earned with self-respect and my own hard work, I cannot get that from money that comes easily [through devious means]." Thus, the meaning of work for Sulekha comes from being financially independent—the independence of which is based on earning money through honest means. Reshma, a maid, firmly says she would refuse any money that was simply given to her if she had not worked for it. By putting in her sweat and toil, she says, she will not only have earned that money itself but she will also have passed on that work ethic and values to her children.

While answering the question about whether they would continue to work should they be given all the money they would ever need and want, all participants agreed that they would want to continue to stay employed.

Arati and Ganga, both street sweepers, insist that they would continue to work regardless of how much money was handed to them.

> Arati: Of course I'll work. I don't want the money in the first place [money that was just handed out to her]. I only want money that I can get through my hard work. Any additional money and it comes with a lot of baggage. People become lazy, isn't that so? Then we start expecting a lot of things. We start desiring this or that, right? We are used to spending our paycheck month to month. Whatever money we earn, we have to ensure it lasts us the whole month and it does. The worries of the next month will be thought about next month itself. If we work, we get money.

> Ganga: I don't want any money even if you give it to me because the satisfaction I can get with the money I can get through hard work is not present in money got through *haram* [illegal or prohibited means] and one can never be successful through such wealth. In fact my pains may increase if I am too relaxed. Now I am this fat, I will become this much fat [moves her hands four inches away from her hips on both sides to indicate a growing girth].

Thus, work had meaning because it provided the means for women to stand on their own feet and make them financially independent. However, the meaning was only true to the extent that it allows them to earn money through honest, hard work.

Work as Active Engagement in Paid Employment

Several participants framed their work as having meaning for them because it provided them an alternative to "just sitting at home and doing nothing." Participants are especially harsh toward the idea of "staying at home all day" and not being gainfully employed. Even when monetary gain was not the criteria, the fact that stepping out of the house keeps them occupied and engaged with external (not home-related) tasks is meaningful.

Anahita (53), a landscape designer, says:

> I would start brooding. I will feel wasted. I don't like to sit idle at home, working is a better utilization of my time. What will I do sitting at home? I would find it very difficult to be sitting at home and you know waiting for my husband, waiting for my son that would be very irritating for me.

Similar perspectives are echoed by Bhavana (38), the controller of finance at a multi-national company. She says, "I don't see myself sitting at home and fretting and fuming and waiting for them [husband and son] to come back home. Why are they late and so on. I don't see myself sitting at home in any circumstance." Jagruti (34), a radiologist, confirms, "I definitely knew that I wanted to do something with my life. I was very clear. I did not want to be a housewife and stay at home." For Manjula (51), a dietician, working means a change in attitudes. ". . . the enthusiasm that you need for life comes by working, you don't get it simply by staying at home," she says. Shipta (32), manager of an insurance company, feels a sense of loss when she is not working. She says, "You grow old if you are not working I feel. That is very much required for me in life. If I sit at home also for two days, I feel that I have lost something."

In the women's own words, discourses surrounding their perception of their world of work requires an active engagement in an external work-place—an outside sphere separate from their domestic responsibilities. For those participants in the middle and high-income categories, monetary gain was not a concerning criterion because they had sufficient household income. In other words, if they so choose, they can afford the luxury of "not-working" for pay. They believe that stepping out of the house means leaving the idle private realm, not "living at the cost of others," and engaging in meaningful external (not home) tasks.

Even though participants may not have intended harsh judgment toward non-working women, it became apparent that our working participants often and unapologetically consider themselves better than stay-at-home "non-working" women even though some were quick to acknowledge the contributions made by housewives. By framing their sense of working selves as being externally engaged, they discount the contributions made by housewives to their families and the work that is incessantly being done by women who remain outside of the paid employment space for personal, familial, cultural, societal, or other reasons. This resonates more glaringly in the words of Sakshi (29), a radio host, who says:

> I work because I cannot stay at home *vella* [empty—not doing anything]. I really cannot do that. I work because ya, for pay, definitely. I mean I do not want to deny the fact and I work because I know I will not be able to stand the emptiness of you know, being a housewife. That is the most difficult profession but I do . . . I know that I will not be able to handle that.

While complimenting the role of a housewife as being "most difficult," Sakshi also indicates that this role brings along with it a feeling of "emptiness."

To some participants, this active involvement with work also relates to keeping their bodies in motion. Those in lower income occupations talked about how one of the benefits, given the nature of their work, is their ability to maintain their physical health. Although work itself fulfills other needs and objectives, continuing to stay healthy and physically fit was also a significant reason for working. When asked if she would continue to work even if she was given all the money in the world that she would need and want, Asha, a maid, responded affirmatively and explained that it is only when bodies are in motion that individuals stay healthy and alleviate ailments. Ganga, a street sweeper, noted the finite nature of her earnings and rationalized that wealthy people who are not actively engaged in labor often undergo major medical procedures. By working in a job that requires her to physically labor, Ganga reasons that she has the advantage of a healthier body over wealthier, non-working women. Therefore, in addition to other internal validations, as long as one's physical self engages in paid employment, work is meaningful.

Work as Fulfilling Role-Related Responsibilities

Participants consider work to be meaningful if they are able to fulfill their role-related *kartavya* or responsibility. How they perform what *kartavya* is associated with their station in life and material resources. Women from the low-income category discussed their need to work as having emerged from a lack of better alternatives. These women accept the adversities of their lives—poverty, illiteracy, abusive marriages—and situate their current work situations within the framework of their larger social conditions. There is an acceptance of the inevitability of their work, whether it be sweeping streets or working as maids. This acceptance of one's life situation stems from a theory of fate influenced and justified by the concepts of *karma* and rebirth (Kolenda, 1964). Many Hindus believe that one's actions in a previous birth determine one's fate and social status in present life and because one's current life is pre-determined, these women assume they have no control over their fate. They can, however, exert some level of control over their next birth cycle by fulfilling the righteous duties and responsibilities of their current lives. To these women therefore, the meaning of their work comes from being able to fulfill familial responsibilities such as educating their children and saving for their daughters' marriage ceremonies as is traditionally the custom in India. Even among low-income women, in cases where both the husband and wife work, participants are proud of the fact that along with their husbands, they are able to contribute to the welfare of their families.

Says Bhumika, a maid, "I have three children. I got them educated, got them married, so I have to help in the house. How can I let my husband take on all the burden of the house?" Burden is constructed in terms of contributing to family responsibilities and household duties. For Seema (20), a live-in nanny, who wanted to be a teacher as she was growing up in her village, life had other things in store. Her mother's health started deteriorating and she soon became confined to her bed. Seema now works as a nanny and sends most of her salary home to her parents in the village for her mother's treatment. Her responsibilities also include saving for her own marriage, which in India, as mentioned above, is otherwise typically paid for by parents. She says:

> Now I am working in this job and I am happy. At least I have some money. I have some savings after having sent money to my mother. I don't have to ask anybody. I am saving money for my marriage also. I won't take anything from Papa. I don't like to take anything from them [parents]. I am like that from the beginning. I've always wanted to work and even as I work I have taken care of the household. I always wanted a job, whatever be the pay, whatever be the work. I was ready to do it, even if it is a lot of hard work in the beginning, I will learn it and do a good job.

With women from the middle and high-income occupations, responsibility got defined differently. For these women, who also, not surprisingly, came from upper castes and social classes, working is often an option. Even though a number of women in this category work for self-actualization, financial independence, and constructive engagement of their knowledge and abilities, given their family circumstances, should they choose to do so, they could opt-out of the paid employment space. It was evident in the narratives of low-income women that the choice of working (or not) was never considered. In fact, working, in order to provide sustenance and better lives for their children was non-negotiable. It was not a choice. Despite the compelled nature of work, that this work also enables them to meet their familial and cultural obligations and responsibilities allows these women to draw positive meanings from their work. It can be argued that drawing meaning from work per se may not be an organic thought that women in lower-income occupations consider. The primary reasons for working for pay relate directly to putting food on the table and paying for their children's education. Therefore, I argue that the very idea of extracting meaning from work or constructing work in terms of its meaningfulness is a privilege enjoyed predominantly by the upper classes (see Lair et al., 2009) who indeed have the freedom of occupational choice and more opportunities to make meaning.

Harsha (29), a physiotherapist, derived her meaning of work and responsibility by serving her patients. In doing so, she believes she gets her patients' *dua* (blessings). Nutan (39), a railway ticket booking clerk, finds her sense of responsibility in bettering her children's lives. "My parents gave me a good education; so I am working to make money to give my children a better life," she says.

Women who had more opportunities and resources in life construct their performance of *kartavya* differently. While still channeling the concept of *kartavya*, this idea once again held a privileged dimension for upper classes of women. Because university admissions are extremely competitive in India, when someone gets accepted at an institution of higher education, it necessarily means that several other equally deserving candidates did not get in because of the limited number of seats. As a result, a number of women feel a strong sense of commitment to the education they had gotten and the only way they could make their education matter and thereby justify their having gotten accepted to those universities was by continuing to work in the fields in which they got their degrees. Says Ujwala (30), a journalist, "If I didn't do what I was trained and educated in, I might have done something that wouldn't have required a seat to be taken up." Having gotten a degree in journalism and by working as a journalist, Ujwala finds meaning in her work by having fulfilled her responsibility toward the student community. Likewise, Vanaja (33), an interior designer, also feels fortunate to have gotten an education in the same field as the one in which she works. She explains, "Whatever I studied, I'm putting it back [into the society]. Sometimes people do [study] something and then they end up doing [work] something else but here I have done what I've wanted [education] and I am doing [working] what I want to so I've got both things."

As explained above, for India's working women, responsibility gets redefined depending on the nature of one's work, one's social class, access to alternatives, and the personal objectives that need met. Women derive meaning in their work by fulfilling these responsibilities whether it is toward their family or community.

Work as Establishing Positive and Individual Identity

Understandably, engaging in paid employment helps participants establish their identity and their sense of self in society and among family members and relatives—important criteria for defining meaningful work. As has already been described in previous chapters, Bindiya (40s) struggled with the idea of becoming an actress for a long time. Her parents and in-laws were against her choice of profession given the negative reputation that the entertainment industry has typically had in the past. Finally after working as an administrator in her husband's business and raising her two children, in her 40s, she decided to take the plunge into her desired career. At current time, Bindiya is not only an actress, she is a businesswoman who owns a production company and also directs and produces movies and plays. She says:

> I work to help myself and to have my identity. I don't do it for others. Like I told you when I was going through this stagnating part of my life, I realized that if I didn't do something soon, I would have only been left asking myself questions for the rest of my life, like what have I done in life? If I didn't do anything, why did I live? The purpose of life is to do things that you like, that people like and do something for society for other people and for yourself from which you get satisfaction.

Bindiya describes the phase of her life when she stayed at home looking after her children, in-laws, and her husband's business as a "stagnating part of my life." Even though she was employed in her husband's company, that employment did nothing to establish her personal identity. She had always wanted to be an actress, having won numerous awards for her performance in school and college plays. However, because she did not get permission to pursue acting as a career, she felt stifled and constricted, having lost her true "self."

Sonal (24), a visual merchandiser with a chain of grocery stores, is responsible for designing store layout, branding, and promotions for 31 stores in Pune and surrounding areas. For Sonal, working not only enables an identity, it also helps her have an answer for people's inquiry into her professional life. This is an interesting transition for Indian society as gradually, women's working is becoming the norm and educated and qualified women who do not work are often questioned about their reasons for not engaging in gainful paid employment. Continues Sonal:

> I get a chance to express myself because it is creative and it gives me an identity. I mean I have an identity; I am doing something you know. I mean I do not want to sit at home and you know when people ask what do you do, I do not want to say that I am sitting at home. I want to show that I have studied so much and I am making use of it because otherwise then all of that just goes for a toss so I want to go ahead and you know work, so I mean because first of all I like it and I do not want to sit at home.

Like Bindiya and Sonal, Seema (20), a live-in nanny, also finds meaning in her work by its ability to help have an identity. She says:

We should have our own identity. Life shouldn't be about eating and gaining weight. We should do something with our life, people should know that this person, oh ya, she does this, there should be recognition of me, my identity.

Jaya (48), a social worker, and Meena (57), a middle school teacher, both realized that stepping out of the house to work raised their status within the family. Explains Meena:

Now that I am older I tell my younger friends, do something, stand on your own feet, and along with a career, women should have their own money. One's husband money is always there but the self-confidence one gets when she works, the kind of identity one will have in one's social circles is important. And more importantly, the attitude of your family toward you changes now that you have started working, started earning an income, and have responsibilities at work.

Jaya echoes Meena's sentiments even though money was not a criterion for her:

I was always at home like I don't have my own identity, like I have no work, you take me for granted so I started getting frustrated. It wasn't right. I felt I had to get out of the house. I don't care if I don't earn any money but I have to work.

All of the above quotes show that across generations, socio-economic status, and occupational types, the desire to have a sense of personal identity holds strong for all participants. In fact, the ability to have one's own identity was a strong expectation from work. As a result, these women derive meaning in work by work's ability to meet this expectation. Madhura (55), who after years of raising her daughter and working for her husband's business, started a school for the blind 12 years ago, perhaps best summarizes this sentiment when she says, "I wanted to be something, somewhere, someone in life."

Work as Providing Learning Opportunities and Intellectual Engagement

Women find meaning in their work when it provides them learning opportunities and keeps them intellectually engaged. Sachi (28), a classical dancer, considers her profession a passion. When she performs, she says, she gets to meet and learn from people with diverse backgrounds and communities, which she believes opens the world to her. Vanaja (33), a free-lance interior designer who also teaches design, says, "To teach is to learn twice. I'm constantly doubling my knowledge and knowledge in any form is not wasted." The opportunities she gets to learn while teaching her students makes her work meaningful and her own need for professional fulfillment is

met by her independent design work on the side. By actively scouting learning opportunities and using them to her advantage, she defines meaning in
her work as the ability to build her knowledge.

It is important for participants that time, education, abilities, as well as
their senses are being utilized in their work, which in turn makes that work
meaningful. Avantika (39) works as a financial product analyst for an information technology company and she says, "I work because it gives me immense satisfaction of utilizing my brains. I need to use my knowledge and
education, not so much housework. Need to put education to good use"
(*kartavya* orientation). Pooja (50), the principal of an international school,
says, ". . . my work is something that keeps my mental abilities ticking all the
time. I need to be mentally stimulated." Like Avantika and Pooja, Sukanya
(32), an agricultural consultant, also works to engage her faculties, "All the
money won't fulfill the need of my intelligence or my brain so to fulfill the
need of my intelligence, I have to work." Bhavana (38), the controller of
finance at a multinational company, finds that her work has meaning because
she is able to contribute on multiple levels. She says her work includes:

> Contribution to my own development and satisfaction and contribution to
> creating something better from whatever it is. If I am able to do my job well
> here and that helps my boss and helps my department and helps the company
> that is more important for me than just coming to office one day and finishing
> of the day and going back home.

Thus, work becomes meaningful when participants are able to engage their
abilities, skills, as well as academic knowledge. This theme resonated almost
exclusively among middle and high-income earning participants. None of the
participants in the low-income category mentioned intellectual fulfillment or
learning opportunities as the reasons why they work or as most meaningful
about their work.

Work as Fulfilling a Higher Purpose

Women in high-income occupations frequently construct meaning in their
work in terms of satisfaction, enjoyment, fulfilling a passion, and finding
happiness. Despite work's ability to provide women in the low-income occupations with a sense of fulfillment in gaining financial independence and
meeting familial responsibilities, they did not specifically construct their
meanings of work in terms of happiness. These feelings were the prerogative
of women in the middle- and high-income occupational groups. Anita (31), a
corporate secretary, believes her work gives her fulfillment and a sense of
accomplishment.

[Work is] Fulfilling. Every time there is a new thing that needs to be done, you do it, it makes me feel nice. There is a target to be achieved, you achieve it, it is nice. There is a deadline to be achieved, you meet it, that is nice. It can be anything. It can be a small deadline on doing a particular activity, or a huge thing of acquiring a particular company, or it may be getting that contract across to the next guy and getting him to sign it and negotiate before a deadline whatever. You have to complete it.

Vijaya (48), a journalist and editor of a newspaper, finds fulfillment in her work through the stories she chooses to investigate and the issues she raises through her newspaper. She explains:

See work is creativity and letting out something which is very deep in your heart. Like for a painter it is painting, you know he lets out that whole fusion of colors. It, you know, gives him so much of inspirational happiness mainly. It's the same thing with me. For me the creation of something which is useful to a society you know gives me a lot of happiness. Like when I receive letters from my readers or people call me up and tell me this that and for this also this story—that Dow story today's I got so many e-mails. So I feel a sense of fulfillment, and what I feel is very nice—is that in my everyday life I feel very . . . my heart cries because I see corruption. I see I told you I see casteism, and I see this thing of one upmanship. But because I'm doing this genuine work, I find that if you're doing that which is actually not the norm of the society, there is appreciation. Which means that although people may have a bad attitude towards life or they may be doing bad things, but if somebody's doing good they have that kind of a respect. And I'm happy that I formed that oasis. You know I call this an oasis of a genuine workplace—where it is untarnished.

For Anuja (44), a gynecologist, the meaning of work is finding satisfaction in the everyday engagement of varied professional activities, as is the case with Aparna (55), a leprosy technician; Chaitali (62), a priest; Meha (27), supervisor at a multi-national company; and several other women. While for women in middle- and high-income occupations, work was a way to meet self-actualization needs, for women in low-income occupations; meanings of work depended on fulfilling their dreams of a better future for their children, consistent with information revealed in previous chapters.

Kavita, a maid, explains that she has reconciled to her circumstances which necessitate her occupation as a maid due to a lack of education that consequently also affect her own job opportunities. With that acceptance, she was not going to let the same thing happen to her children. She says, "Only if I work can I educate my children, only if they get an education will they be able to do something about their future." Shanti (35), a school peon, also hopes to do the same for her son: "My son is brilliant. I have a great desire to make him *a somebody*."

For Vanaja (33), an interior designer, the meaning of work lies in maintaining relationships, "work not only for money, if I had everything in life, life would be boring. With the money, I can buy everything but I cannot buy someone's nature, I can't buy someone's love, I can't buy someone's friendship." Finally, for Anahita (53), a landscape designer, work is not only contentment, it is an unleashing of her creativity, and serving her community by landscaping spaces that generations of people can use. The meaning of work for Anahita also includes the sense of achievement and material comforts that are only possible through earning one's own money. She explains:

> See at one stage I was not working for economic needs but when it started doing well then I realized that I could buy a lot more of things, I could have a different type of lifestyle and I could also have a lot of creature comforts you know. So at some stage when you start earning well, your life changes. You become a lot more used to a certain amount of luxuries you know which you can do without but then you find that you can afford them so why not you know. So working, it has not been that I had to do it you know. I do not need the kind of money to run my home since I was already married so whatever I was earning after paying off all the labor and everybody else it was not a whole lot but it was mine you know. Something I had achieved on my own.

Even though work fulfills higher level needs, more practically, money was also important. In fact, having money enables the women to aim for those higher purposes and needs.

DISCUSSION

This study deliberately explored a variety of occupational engagements and income categories to develop a comprehensive understanding of what work means to the study's participants. Even though a practical viewpoint would suggest that work essentially becomes meaningful because it helps take care of financial responsibilities, among these participants that financial aspect did not always attain primacy. Of course earning an income helped but beyond that, work had meaning because it helped fulfill a number of intrinsic and extrinsic objectives, for self, family, and society. For example, the diverse meanings that participants reveal show that women strongly believe themselves to be part of a collective. Work as serving one's society and community emerged as one of the strongest themes across income and occupational categories. This shows how even though the meanings we draw from work may be individually determined, for Indian working women they are socially constructed and communally motivated.

The discourses that direct the narratives of women's work are abundant with somewhat conflicting notions of work, life, and balance. Yet, the women seem to derive a crystallized understanding of what work really means to them on a personal level. Women across categories of occupations and incomes are able to explain what work means to them. A noteworthy point is the way participants speak of their "non-working" counterparts, housewives. There is a negative vibe to the ways in which they choose to frame what housewives do. Clearly, for women who are engaged in paid employment, the work of women not earning an income through their work is inferior. In fact, the work that women who stayed at home did, looking after their families and households, amounted to "nothing" when woman after working woman commented on how they could not imagine their lives "sitting at home and doing nothing." There was condescension and rarely, some appreciation on part of a number of participants toward housewives or non-working women. When appreciation did become a part of their discourse, it was conveyed in terms of—"of course they do a lot of work too (and that is why they deserve appreciation) but I would never be able to do it (because I am better—not obviously stated but strongly implied)." This "working-non-working" tension among Indian women is deserving of further exploration in future studies.

Even though Indian women have been part of the paid workforce since the early 20th century, it is only now that their entry has been accepted as normal to what was an anomaly even a couple of decades ago. The themes discussed above are representative of participants' voices, descriptions, and explanations.

This study foregrounds Indian women's phenomenological experiences and explanations of their world of work in their own words and in doing so shatters the traditional organizational boundaries within which work typically gets situated and defined. Even though a number of participants worked in such organizations, except Bhavana, for whom the meaning of work was contributing to her company, none of the other participants mentioned anything about their workplace as being of any significance when it came to their subjective meaning-making. However, as is indicative of a collectivistic orientation in the communally-focused meanings participants derived from work, Bhavana's comment too can be interpreted as contributing to the collective well-being of her organization.

Participants' narratives redefined a generic understanding of what constitutes a workplace because participants' places of work included the streets, employers' houses, outdoor construction sites, and others typically considered outside the purview of "organizational" studies. By reassessing what constitutes meaningful work and by giving primacy to workers engaged in these non-organizational occupations also capable of meaning-making, scholars can develop better qualitative insights into the macro constructs of work itself as envisioned by Cheney et al. (2008).

(RE)DEFINING CAREERS

In addition to inquiring about how participants construct meanings of work, they were asked to define a "career" as they understand the concept. The following discussion reveals participants' responses to the question.

Career Communication in Context

> Everybody understands what *career* is. The trouble with it, though, is that it is so broad and vague. It is an everyday word used by a variety of people, in a variety of contexts, from a variety of perspectives, for a variety of purposes, and with various levels of specificity or generality, focus or breadth. (Collin, 2007, p. 558)

Even though people usually have an intuitive grasp of the concept of career, the word itself is often subject to a definitional dilemma (see Collin & Young, 2000). However, Western scholars who examine careers generally agree on some version of Hall's (1976) definition which views career as "the individually perceived sequence of attitudes and behaviors associated with work-related experiences and activities over the span of the person's life" (p. 4). While beginning this research project, I used Arthur et al.'s (1989) definition of a career as "the evolving sequence of a person's work experiences over time" (p. 8) as my starting point. The findings of this study indicate that neither of the definitions completely capture the essence of what a career means to Indian women. Even though there are some similarities between Western framing of the word, "career," this study contributes uniquely by first, explaining the themes surrounding Indian women's definition of a career and then by proposing one that captures participants' interpretation of what it means to engage in a *career.* The following themes were apparent in participants' definitions of career.

Career Defers to Family

In the opinion of Indian women, families always come first. Pursuing a career at the negligence of family was unimaginable to the women. As Meeta (40), an accountant, says, "First women need to pay attention to the children at home, attend to the health of family members that is main. Career comes later." Mukta (25), a fashion designer, concurs: "Career is definitely the next priority after your house [family] . . . like if you are married, as a person I would definitely like to handle both, my house and my career. I won't be a careeristic woman definitely. I will definitely like to keep my house very nice and homely." Thus career is something that follows family on a list of individual priorities. Even single women like Mukta have already planned for what a career should look like vis-à-vis balance, and they have no doubt in their minds about which one of the two—career or family—comes first (also see chapter 4). In other words, career is that which does not interfere with familial responsibilities and duties. Career is something that may be pursued but only after family needs and wants are taken care of first.

The above definitions run contrary to Indian media representations of working women as indulging in guilt-free materialism, renegotiating parental ties, disregarding norms of an appropriate marital age, and pursuing single-minded careerism (*BusinessWeek*, 2005) and may actually be more hyped than a reflection on reality—examples of exceptions—than typical behavior. This study found that whether women are renegotiating parental ties or re-evaluating norms, they are doing so remaining mindful of parental concerns and acceptance. Following customs and traditions are important to the women because they are important to their parents, whom they respect. This does not mean that they passively observe those norms. Parents and their daughters openly converse about ancient wisdom and co-construct knowledge about traditions they will and will not follow. This study did not find single-minded careerism in any of the participants. The importance of their family was apparent throughout their narratives and in all their career-related decisions. In fact, women willingly compromised on aspects of their careers so that their family was not disadvantaged by their ambitions.

Career Is Not a Nine-to-Five Job

Participants are clear on what careers are not. They believe that a true career does not fall into specific time schedules. Work that had time restrictions are jobs not careers, in their opinion. They also consider careers as having long term orientations while jobs, by definition, were termed temporary. Participants said that jobs that are nine to five are not done because people enjoy them; they are done because they meet a financial need. Participants also said that jobs are done reluctantly and out of compulsion due to a lack of better alternatives while careers were engaged in willingly, by choice. As Anahita (53), a landscape designer, summarizes,

> It [career] is something one takes up for a whole lifetime. It is not a job which you take for a few months or a few years but it is an ongoing process where from scratch you develop the career, you refine the finer points. You find ways of doing things in a better way and then you try to do [it].

Careers not only have a lasting quality, but they involve a process of continuous individual initiatives.

Careers Are Personally Meaningful; Money Is Secondary

Participants present contradictory discourses regarding money as an outcome of career. While some state that being financially independent is required of a career, the general consensus was that careers are those work engagements that provide tremendous inner satisfaction while also helping women "stand on their own feet" with onus being on the former. A career was also described as "pursuing something of your interest," "a search for self, knowing yourself, having an identity," "something that you are committed to," "happening outside the home," "something I accomplish on my own merit," "a matter of discovery," "something one is passionate about," "benefits future generations," "makes life meaningful," and "makes you a positive element for your family and people near you." Participants also said that a career should be of personal significance to them by enabling the fulfillment of self-actualization needs. Careers should also have the ability instill pride in the individual about her work and benefit society (see Meanings of Work discussed earlier in this chapter).

Career Involves Linear Progression and Growth

Linear models of career have typically dominated the rhetoric of professional work. Even though these models have been critiqued (e.g., Buzzanell & Goldwig, 1991), metaphors such as "career ladder," continue to be seen as a linear one-way path measuring career success by Indian women. As Shalini (32), an attorney, says,

> To work well, to earn a good living, to earn a good name for yourself and I guess to reach . . . to try and keep on climbing up the ladder. That is my definition of a career. The career graph should always be up and you know, you have to just keep on and on working . . .

Growing into a career from a lower level position to higher positions was preferred by Bhavana (38), controller of finance at an MNC.

> Career according to me is what I have personally experienced. I believe in growing into a career from the base and that is what has happened to me also. I think that strengthens your roots so much into what you have been doing that the comfort level and the ease with which you grow subsequently is far better than if you did not have the roots. After taking the right opportunity when you get it, with the full confidence of whatever you have learnt and experienced up until now . . . That is the most important point of the whole thing.

Participants' answers indicate a strong sense of agency. Their narratives make them the architects of their own career paths. Women in the study are certain that a career meant overall growth, not just in their specific work lives, but also spiritually and personally by providing learning opportunities and helping them give back to the community. Therefore, for Indian women, the definition of a career includes a linear progression at work but growth itself has to be at all levels of personhood, not just professional. Sakshi (29), a radio host, summarizes,

> A career is something which must take you to a higher level where you can grow with it and at the same time give something back to society. It is not just a one way process for me. It is not just *my* career. If it is my career, I need to affect people around me in some or the other way which I am sure I am.

CONCLUDING THOUGHTS

In conclusion, a career defers to family responsibilities, is distinctive from a job, is personally meaningful, provides financial independence, and enables individual initiatives toward progression and growth. With regard to women's careers, the concept of linearity and equating of organizational success with advancement has been found untenable by Western scholars. However, outside of academia and in the Indian context, women continue to associate success with climbing up professional ladders. This does not mean that Indian women are unaware, immune, or not disadvantaged from career discontinuities, shorter ladders, or the glass ceiling. This does mean, however, that the rhetoric of measuring career success by linear progression is so strongly embedded within the developing work cultures of India, that its impact is all-pervasive. Examining meanings of work is a better indicator of what work itself signifies to Indian women but when work is framed as embedded within careers, the meaning of the word "career" gathers new connotations as explained above. In light of the discussion above, I propose a definition of career as follows:

> *Career involves active engagement in long-term activities that are personally meaningful, that provide some financial remuneration, and offer consistent growth opportunities while enabling quality of (work)life for self, family, and society.*

The above definition of career includes personal agency, an individually interpreted meaning of work, compensation, preferred work outcomes such as professional and personal growth, and makes room for family. In the Indian context, women in low-income occupations think of a "career" as conceptualized in the West, as incompatible with their own lives. In fact, even definitions provided by Indian women in middle- and high-income occupations that speak of progression and growth, project an elitist perception of what a career should constitute. For women in low-income groups, this concept of career is inconceivable given that the "jobs" they do at places such as other people's houses or on the streets, redefine "organizational careers." The definition above developed out of the answers of middle- and high-income categories of women also does not completely do justice to the work lives of women in low-income categories. Perhaps, narcissistic definitions of career need a complete overhaul if they are to include all kinds of work, workers, and work arrangements. Perhaps, a new, all-inclusive word that captures the essence of human activity or paid work should be developed instead; a word that appreciates and accounts for the hard physical labor done by millions of workers who are systematically and socially marginalized.

This study shows that in addition to career being a gendered construct (see Chang, 2003; Wilson, 1998), it is also culturally determined. "Career" is a communicatively (co)constructed term that is defined in terms of the values considered most significant to a given culture. For example, in India, Sinha (1990, cited in Kapoor, 1997) has examined the role of *nishkam-karm* or the idea that "work should be performed as a duty in the service of others without any desire for outcomes or reciprocity" (p. 218) as a powerful socializing message in Hindu families. This may explain why Indian women not only hold the ability to serve their society as important to the meanings they draw from their work, but their definitions of career also include giving back to society as a crucial element. Other explanation for participants' meanings in work may be related to Hindu Indian concepts of *dharma* and *karma* (Shenoy-Packer & Buzzanell, 2013).

In the next and concluding chapter, I summarize the major findings and contributions that this study, the first of its kind, has made to the different intersecting disciplines it represents as well as to our general understanding of Indian women, work, and career discourses.

NOTES

1. Due to time constraints toward the end of the interviews, I was unable to ask participants their ages.

2. I chose to code the use of the word *punya* as implying service. In reality, *punya* is a consequence of providing selfless service to one's community (as used by the participants). To achieve *punya* (opposite of *punya* is *paap* which means "sin") is often to achieve good favor and blessing from the Almighty. The specific context within which participants used *punya* was to imply that by doing this dirty work, they were earning credit toward a better reincarnated life (in their next cycle of birth). Hindus believe that our actions in this life determine the fate of our future reincarnations. As a result, the more credit you earn in this lifetime by doing good, the better your chances will be for your next cycle of birth to be one of wealth, comfort, and happiness.

3. *Warkaris* are pilgrims who descend on Pune city in large numbers every year on their way to Pandharpur, a holy city. *Warkaris* walk for 21 days as part of a procession that carries the *padukas* or sandals of the Saint they worship. Given their mobility, *warkaris* are at the mercy of the residents of Pune, who provide them with food and shelter. The city government often builds large tents for the *warkaris* to rest and sleep in at night.

Chapter Six

Conclusion

Table 6.1. Generational Representation of Women and Work

Family First	Family First, Work Next	Work First, (but) Family Matters Equally
↓	↓	↓
Mothers of the current generation of middle-aged working women (currently in their 40s-60s)	Middle-aged women and mothers of the current generation of working women who are in their 20s and early 30s	Current generation of working women in their 20s and 30s
• Mostly illiterate or semi-literate • Little formal education • Never engaged in paid employment or quit after marriage or childbirth	• Mostly educated to highly educated • Many engaged in paid employment • No model of the working woman balancing work and family • Sacrificed career opportunities to further husbands' careers and raise children • Took a break from work after childbirth but returned to employment in later years • Encouraged daughters to have careers but remain mindful of customs and traditions • Anger, resentment, and some frustration toward younger generation of women for not observing customs and traditions and spending quality time with families and getting away with it	• Educated to highly educated • Focus on individual achievement and success • Enjoy many personal freedoms and career options • Expect equal share in familial responsibilities from husbands • Believe in equal partnerships at work and home; not willing to take second place just because they are female • Willing to take risks in careers and avail of opportunities • Want to stay closer home to their parents and not hesitant to turn down career advancement opportunities to do so • Dedicated workers committed to successful careers but family is of equal and considerable importance • Often misunderstood by women of the older generation • Willing to make compromises in their careers because they choose to do so • Supported by parents and in-laws in maintaining work-life balance

This research study investigated work and career related knowledge that Indian women produce through communicative (co)(re)constructions and (re)engagement with society, and socialization, and as represented in individual agency. Thus influenced, this study also sought to learn the meanings of work Indian working women derive from their occupations and how all of their socio–cultural realities collectively appropriate a definition of "career." The ensuing discussion weaves in and out of the many strands of thoughts and perspectives presented in previous chapters. By displaying a metaphorical quilt-like interweaved analysis, the overlapping content presented in this discussion hopes to show that the lives of Indian working women are complicated by their many realities and the simultaneously contradictory and complementary influences that entrench themselves in their thought processes and work-life realities.

This study had three primary goals: (a) to inquire and reveal the implications that societal macrodiscourses (caste, class) have on India's women, directly or indirectly, in their work and life; (b) to explore the role of socializing agents (e.g., parents, extended family) as career enablers in the lives of Indian women; and (c) investigate how Indian women express agency, constrained or otherwise, in their everyday management of work-life ambiguities and negotiations. Aligned with these objectives, two secondary goals included (a) discovering what constitutes meaning of work for Indian working women and (b) how they come to understand and (re)define a "career."

This study's findings provide a snapshot of one group of 78 diverse women from a specific region of the country, hardly representative of the millions of Indian women eager to claim their rightful place in society. Even though I present the findings in a generalized tone, the observations made from this study should only be considered as applicable to the participants. When some truths find general acceptability and consensus, the reader should only interpret them after having a nuanced understanding of the specific group of women to whom she or he sees the findings applicable.

It is difficult to discuss these findings separately. To the extent that these goals could be separated, the observations from participants' narratives have been individually explained and analyzed in their respective chapters. In a more all-encompassing collage of the experiences and realities of this study's participants, the following discussion free flows in spirit just as the experiences and lived realities of my participants, but nevertheless attempts to coherently articulate the tapestries of Indian working women's lives.

SOCIETY AND SOCIALIZATION

The findings of this study indicate that women continue to be influenced by the larger society in terms of how they come to conceive of their work choices, expectations, and work-lifestyles. Women either acknowledge society's influence on their work and careers but choose to strategically ignore specific opinions, or they believe that societal impressions about working women have started to change and women need to be self-reflexive about their own priorities and be willing to negotiate those priorities and choices. Women's career choices and subsequent career decisions continue to be affected by their caste and class. However, in case of caste, it was women of the upper castes who report being discriminated against in employment. While Western organizational scholars examine discrimination on the basis of race and gender, issues of reverse discrimination when brought up become contentious and politically sensitive. Although it was not a goal of this study, findings did reveal that the social situation of reverse caste-based perceived inequities may need further investigation in the Indian context.

Social class and desire for upward mobility also influence how women, especially those in their late 40s and beyond construct knowledge about their world of work. Among the current generation of working women, social class did influence the nature of parental advice, encouragement, ability to take risks, availability of opportunities, professional connections, educated parents who appropriated guidance, kind of education they acquired, and so on. All of these influences naturally play a role, however small, in affecting career choices and decisions. Therefore, career scholars interested in understanding women's work and career development in India should make conscious efforts to include caste and class as important variables in their areas of investigations.

In addition, women's careers in India are largely determined by the extent to which families support the career pursuits of their daughters and daughters-in-law. Not only did families directly and indirectly participate in women's careers, the women actively solicit this participation. Parents and opinions of valued family members were listened to, respected, and often followed dutifully, after having also considered their own view of others' perspectives. Even though participants seldom discussed their husbands in the context of their work decisions, their spouses' willing or even reluctant support was still important for the women's general sense of identity and confidence. A majority of the women have always had husbands support their careers, and even those husbands who did not initially approve have eventually come around either for reasons of their own or because they realized they could not guilt nor force their wives into quitting. Work and career-related family communication is a dynamic, interactive process between the women and their families, and women engage in this process throughout their formative years and even after entering into the paid workforce.

Extended family members, like in-laws, uncles, aunts, and friends also influence the work and career-related knowledge that women (co)create. Findings strongly reflect women's exertion of personal, albeit somewhat constrained agency in furthering their education, career pursuits, and advancement opportunities. Finally, while still in transition and not apparent unless one reads between the lines, results represent the changing demographics of working women who now value their careers as much if not more than their family lives but strive to balance both. While older generations of working women prioritized familial obligations over every other aspect of their lives, the younger generation of women, educated and observant of the work behaviors of their parents, are categorical in their desire for balance. Women are no longer willing to quit their careers altogether. Careers are extremely important to the current generation of working women but equally important is their time with family. To that extent, women are willing to make career compromises by choice.

No matter how career minded a single woman is, she is respectful of her parents' expectations for her life, and though she may be resistant initially, is not hesitant to fulfill her role as a dutiful daughter. To their credit, parents are more accepting of daughters in non-traditional careers and in permitting them to relocate to different cities for better career opportunities. That some daughters choose to refuse advancement opportunities because they want to live with or be closer to their families goes to highlight the strong family bonds still existent in India. For women in the low-income category, educating their children to live better lives that are removed from the mothers' own struggles is the primary motivating factor for work. The everyday hard physical labor these women put up with is a strong indicator of their desire for social class mobility.

The study of women's career development is only emerging in India. This study highlights the limited number of vocational anticipatory sources that inform women of prospective career choices and opportunities. The current generation of working women is pulling all stops when it comes to accessing resources that would develop their own careers. These women know where their priorities are and what the tradeoffs of their career decisions might be. They will be better equipped to help their own children, tomorrow's generation of working adults, to navigate through career choices and guide them to more appropriate sources. More and more of the younger generation today can be seen employed in part-time employment at fast-food establishments, retail stores, and other organizations around the country. In a few years, this work experience may also emerge a significant source of vocational anticipatory socialization.

Yesterday's Indian working woman was caught between fulfilling traditional expectations and desiring self-will. Today's working woman appreciates and respects the sacrifices of the older generation but is unapologetic about living by her choices, completely aware of the consequences of those choices. Globalization has done much to affect women's work lives. Each generation of working women believe they had better work and career opportunities than the women before them. For women of this generation freedom to choose, in and of itself, is one of the biggest changes of their lifetime and wisdom lies in not misusing this freedom but using it in appropriate ways. As Sachi (28) says,

> The freedom that you get. Definitely. To choose. The society has also built up the confidence that you should be firm on what you are doing. There are a lot of opportunities but I look at it as you should choose properly. The choice is dependent on the person.

It is only a matter of time before observers and scholars alike learn how this generation of working women, having been raised amidst personal freedoms, choices, and constrained agency, (re)engages careers for the next generation of India's working women.

To reiterate, what their families say and think about their work and careers makes a significant difference to the manner in which women perceive their own work lives. Additionally, even though parents do not always dictate specific career fields for their daughters, they help develop a number of valuable skills that can be used in the workplace. Through anecdotes, storytelling, role modeling, and some direct advice, parents teach their daughters communicative strategies to manage workplace situations and co-worker relationships, make conscientious efforts in a career direction of their choice, lead resilient lives through difficult times, differentiate between priorities at work and at home, learn humility and find contentment in what they have, be independent in thought and action, and value their own families—all while providing a supportive environment conducive to confidence building, individual freedoms, and personality development. Of course a number of these outcomes only relate to women in the middle- and high-income occupations. Parents of women in low-income occupations mostly teach their daughters by direct role modeling. Participants saw their parents work extremely hard to make ends meet, and even though some reported feeling angry and upset about the decisions that were imposed upon them such as being forced out of school to look after siblings or being married at a young age, they do not blame their parents. On the contrary, they feel fortunate about some basic education they might have received and the lessons they learned observing their parents engaging in honest hard work.

MEANING OF/MEANINGFUL WORK

Meanings of work are not stagnant. Meanings are inherently volatile due to the relative interpretations individuals assign to work. In this study, I used Lair et al.'s (2008) definition of the meaning of work as "the significance and/or purpose of work, as attributed by the worker herself or himself" (p.

173) to shape the concept before presenting it to participants. The authors differentiate meaning of work with meaningful work by defining the latter as the "culturally privileged qualities of work itself" (p. 173). Findings from this study discuss how Hindu Indian women find meaning in their work if it fulfills certain intrinsic and extrinsic needs and expectations. Unlike Western cultures where individual career advancement may be the norm, women in the study, across socio-economic statuses and generations, largely express a communal orientation to their work and careers. Desire to serve the Indian society through their work or the fact that their work already did so is a strong indicator of their other-centered focus. What work means to people and how it contributes to their sense of self-worth and identity is certainly important. However, beyond that, as was explicitly narrated by the women in the study, work has to fulfill responsibilities and meet life's higher purposes. Meanings of work are strongly embedded within cultural knowledge, but negotiated between traditional expectations and individuals' phenomenological experiences. In other words, while societally appropriate codes of conduct and values may provide a framework from within which to view work lives, individuals actively negotiate with their environments in what they choose to extract as meaningful experiences. When this interaction occurs, individuals are free to associate work with those meanings that are most significant to them.

This study shows that women are highly engaged in the process of meaning making. When women in low-income occupations were asked what the meaning of work was for them, several of the women automatically framed their answers in terms of reasons for working. It was only by working that they are able to make ends meet, educate their children, and stay healthy. By explaining their reason for working as serving Indian society, these workers are actively involved in creating positive identities for themselves through the value they find in their work. When asked the same question, women in middle- and high-income occupations are quick to note how the meaning of work for them means fulfillment, satisfaction, and continued learning opportunities, in addition to serving Indian society. For the women in the study, the everyday material realities of their work lives have real consequences on meaning making. The kinds of meanings women extract from their experiences are circumscribed within the particular class privileges they enjoy (or not), access to resources, as well as potential opportunities to better their lives. Cheney and Nadesan (2008) alert researchers of meanings of work to

> consider whether individuals distinctively (and with narrative fidelity) can (re)present the senses or meanings work holds for them, or do they almost inevitably draw on socially acceptable discourses of intelligibility when pressed by (foreign) researchers to reveal the intimacies of everyday experiences? (p. 184)

In this study, participants resist simply reproducing societally approved discourses and in fact oppose any other-imposed notions of what work should mean for them. Once the question about meaning of work was asked, women deconstructed the question to situate their own lives and experiences within the question and answered candidly about the significance of work as they interpreted it.

The constructs of "meaning of work" and "meaningful work" are communicative in nature. While everyday discourses of work may be socio-culturally and historically determined, and undoubtedly shape individual worlds of work and careers to varying degrees, what individuals come to understand as *their* meaning of work is highly personal. In other words, work has to be personally meaningful (be it in terms of fulfilling familial responsibilities or self-enrichment or serving one's society) in order for it to matter. This research promotes the ideas that no work is meaning*less* or lacking in meaning and that work is never meaning-neutral. Meanings of work are highly personal yet contingent upon one's place in social hierarchies, access to resources, and other environmental factors.

In fact, meanings of work may also be religiously motivated. Elsewhere, I have argued that culture-centered meanings of work and emerging societal discourses or macrodiscourses offer insight into the pervasiveness of religious and philosophical thoughts into people's everyday lives (Shenoy-Packer & Buzzanell, 2013). For example, several of the participants referred to religiously-inspired beliefs in defining their work as service to society. They considered their work as giving them *punya* or credit toward bettering a future reincarnated life, which speaks to their belief in Hindu ideologies. They also expressed that in doing their dirty work (as maids or sweepers) and in cleaning up after other people, they consider their work as doing God's work. "We just assume we actually see Him," said Arati, a street sweeper. In directing the intrinsic value and meaning of their work toward a religious ethos, some participants evoked a popular Indian proverb that says, "Work is worship." It may then be argued that perhaps religious and philosophical ideologies act as discursive resources that "guide interpretations of experience and shape the construction of preferred conceptions of persons and groups . . ." (Kuhn et al., 2008, p. 163). The meanings individuals express about their work are thus drawn from and inform societal discourses and are culturally and religiously mediated.

India's own role as a global player may compel individuals to rethink what work has traditionally meant for them and the outcomes they now desire. Even as a mostly collectivistic India struggles to hold on to traditional family values and financial conservatism, a more consumption conscious (Das, 2002), shallow and "westoxicated" elite new generation aspires for a higher class status (D. Gupta, 2007, p. 11). Therefore, while in reply to Broadfoot et al.'s (2008) question, "Is it possible that some cultures never question the meaningfulness of work and/or would value work's meaning to society or family as more important than its value to the individual worker?" (p. 156), the findings from this study would answer in the affirmative; it is in the interest of readers to understand the changing nature of these meanings in contemporary society. The current findings and its interpretation is merely one snapshot of how Hindu Indian women from a particular city make meanings from their work at this time. These perspectives provide an added dimension to what would otherwise be a Western-European one-sided, privilege-based narcissistic, and condescending (Lair et al., 2008) interpretation of work's meanings.

AGENCY AND FEMINIST STANDPOINTS

This section situates the findings of this study within a broader conversation on feminist standpoint theorization and agency. Feminist standpoint theory provides a strong theoretical lens to view the knowledge Indian women produce regarding their work and careers. The contexts of society, socialization, and agency simultaneously free and constrain available options. Knowledge thus developed represents Indian women's (co)constructions of individual struggles, capabilities, and possibilities, grounded firmly in the material realities of their everyday existence and manifested in their work lives.

Indian women's language of everyday experiences is colored by a multilayered consciousness of their lives' challenges. Women are continually extracting cues from their environment to develop new knowledge. Therefore, the standpoints Indian women develop regarding their work, their family, and their own lives are determined by their many complex circumstances. Feminist standpoint theorists agree that theorizing from women's perspectives provides access to knowledge that is "less false" or "more accurate" than dominant ideologies. Because standpoint feminists accept the possibility of multiple knowledges, despite some criticism (e.g., Hekman, 1997, the notion of *the Truth* has been dismissed by feminist scholars. In fact, Collins (1990, cited in Stoetzler & Yuval-Davis, 2002) asserts that the different social positions that women hold can only *approximate* truth. Accepting multiple truths then essentially means that knowledges constructed from women's standpoints have to provide for common as well as diverse views. O'Brien Hallstein (2000) notes,

> from its inception, feminist standpoint theory has held a steadfast position on the commonality-diversity issue: standpoint theorists have maintained a commitment to theorizing and describing the common standpoint women occupy, even as they have begun to recognize differences among women. (pp. 3–4)

In this study, participants included women across caste, class, income-levels, and generations. Their knowledges can best be understood through the framework of intersectionality. According to Davis (2008) the concept of intersectionality is essential to feminist theory. She defines the term as "the interaction between gender, race, and other categories of difference in individual lives, social practices, institutional arrangements, and cultural ideologies" (p. 68) and explains how the construct "addresses the most central theoretical and normative concern within feminist scholarship: namely the acknowledgement of differences among women" (p. 70).

The study's findings make it apparent how women across the highly fragmented Indian society have established their personal truths. Understandably, knowledge women of the low-caste/low-class, low-income category produce have more in common with members of the same category than knowledges produced by women in other categories. With their trying circumstances as the underlying theme, knowledges created from these circumstances intertwine with their material realities, pervading every aspect of their current lives, including work. These women believe that because poor and illiterate parents who valued hard work over education raised them, they grew up imbibing similar values. Even though they do not accuse their parents of discontinuing their education or not allowing them to study at all, they rationalize their parents' decisions as outcomes of parents' own limited understanding of the importance of education. Growing up in rural India with parents who mostly worked as agricultural laborers, they learned that in order to survive, one simply had to work as a matter of fact and this was not negotiable. Education was secondary since it did not immediately and obviously help with their family's financial situation. It is only later in life and through their own observations and experiences that participants came to realize the importance of education and the opportunities it provides. These women's narratives reflect regret about their own education levels as well as somewhat guarded feelings of helplessness about it. However, all these women are extremely determined to educate their children so they do not have to lead a life of poverty or missed opportunities like their mothers. In addition to a lack of education that stymied their progress in urban India, women in the low-income category report their depressing circumstances as the root cause of all struggles in their lives. However, what the women did not mention explicitly but was evident in *all* their narratives was the extent of agency they showed in resolving to rise above those circumstances.

Women in middle- and high-income categories develop their knowledge from staying attuned to the society around them and by systematic socialization into the expected and accepted norms for behavior. As long as their chosen profession did not bring disrepute to their families, parents allowed their daughters to pick a career of their choice. White's (1995) study on the career development of successful women in the United States found that a

majority of these women held full-time positions, fitted their familial responsibilities around work, or chose to remain childless. Even though this may
eventually be a reality among the younger generation of working women in
India, as indicated by several women in their 20s and early 30s who mentioned their decision to delay marriage, and in one case, never marry, findings from this study predominately show that for successful Indian women,
"success" itself was perceived in terms of fitting their work lives around their
domestic responsibilities and not the other way around as in White's study.

I discuss the middle- and high-income categories together because there
are more similarities than differences between these groups. The few differences that do exist are that among women in the high-income category,
parents had higher levels of education including more educated and working
mothers, and the women themselves are more obviously determined and
focused on their career aspirations. The biggest difference, however, was in
the levels of agency shown by the women. Women across categories showed
personal agency but while women in the middle-income category were generally more complacent about their levels of education and had reasonable
expectations from their careers, women in the high-income category narrated
episodes of passionate academic pursuits and a continuous quest to better
themselves at work. Otherwise, women in both categories are from the middle or upper-middle classes, had educated and working fathers, and had
relative freedom of career choice.

O'Brien Hallstein (1999) posits that feminist standpoint theorists recognize women's "common experience of disadvantage" (p. 35). In my opinion,
"disadvantage" is a matter of perspective. The context in which this word is
used in feminist theorizing represents a disadvantage vis-à-vis men since
women, as a group, are known to occupy a position of exploitation, oppression, exclusion, devaluation, and dominance (O'Brien Hallstein, 1999). It is
my contention that even though the above statement is fathomable and true to
a large extent, to reproduce that rhetoric over and over again and to perceive
ourselves as the exploited, oppressed, excluded, devalued, and dominated is
to do disservice to the consistent progress women *have* made to overthrow
just such sentiments. Women's knowledge is more accurate or less false
because we are a minority demographic, world over, and because we inhabit
a dual space as outsiders within our own cultures. It is our duality then that
puts us in a unique position to view and critique our own status as situated
within the larger, male-dominated framework, and not necessarily the juxta-
position made vis-à-vis men.

Women in this study show a similar stance with regard to their own status
as women in the workforce. To quote Anita (31),

> I have never had a feedback saying that I can't do a particular thing because I
> am a woman. I don't take that. I would probably give it right back there and

then and say that if you are going to tell me this [then] you are not entitled to be my boss. So before you disown me I disown you. So where is the question [of being discriminated against]? No, I haven't ever come across that [discrimination] because I believe that I give what is equivalent to any other colleague in the organization so it does not matter what gender that person is and if I give that I expect to be paid that. I expect that payment in terms of money. I expect it in terms of respect. I expect it in terms of designation. I expect it in terms of every damn thing that comes along with it. So if ever there were an inequality I would address it and get on with it. If you come across a situation, I haven't till date but if I were ever to come across a situation where I can't make the other guy understand that he is discriminating me unnecessarily or inappropriately then I will probably move on from there. It is not the only organization in life. There are others. I make a call and move on. So you won't get a situation where you are disadvantaged. Other options are available. There are other fish in the sea.

Anita is corporate secretary at an information technology company. As a high-profile executive who handles the company's legal, financial, and administrative responsibilities, she has extreme confidence in her abilities and does not even consider her gender as barrier to career performance or advancement. What matters in the workforce is one's ability to do the job right, which she knows she can and because she is willing to do whatever it takes to get her work done, she is unapologetic about what she expects in return for her hard work. Likewise, she believes that she would never put herself in a position of disadvantage. If she suspects gender discrimination and cannot sort the matter out communicatively, she is unambiguous of what she will do; quit that job and find another; after all, as she says, "there are other fish in the sea." This statement is perhaps a preview of how a younger generation of India's working women construct gender roles in the workplace. They are highly qualified, have the requisite work experience, are not afraid to learn or relearn new ways of working, and if they suspect discrimination, exercise the option to quit, follow legal process, or find a more inclusive workplace. What is noteworthy in Anita's quote, however, is that after a failed negotiation at making the offending party realize his mistake, her next instinct is to quit that job rather than take legal action, file an official complaint, or seek third party intervention. While the "more fish in the sea" is a good position to be in a good economy, quitting may not always be the best option under all circumstances and for all women. As liberating as the option to quit and find an ideal workplace may sound, perhaps women also need to be able to stand their ground and pursue proactive steps to eliminate discrimination or at least ensure appropriate sanctions are brought upon the discriminating agent.

The question about discrimination emerged organically during my interview with Anita but did not emerge in conversations with other participants. The point is that such perspectives do exist and as more and more women educated, enabled, and empowered by literate and working parents enter the workforce, it's this kind of equitable thinking may just become the norm than the exception. After all, according to Ujwala (29), "being a woman is fun, its real fun. Where else can you get to dress up and kick ass without showing that you are kicking ass?"

The findings of this study reveal that participants exert both agency and communion having drawn from lessons imparted to them during the anticipatory socialization and work/career identities' development stage. Even though some scholars consider agency and communion as two opposite concepts women struggle to balance, in this study, women display their self-will by *choosing* to accept and adjust to their environment, thereby showcasing agency even in communion. In other words, even as women are constrained in their exertion of agency, they try to be in harmony with their family's expectations of them. Despite the seemingly schizophrenic nature of this agency, participants reflect satisfaction and acceptance of the nature of their decisions circumscribed as they are within social and cultural templates.

Participants in this study are highly attuned to what was significant in their socio-cultural environment having extracted the same from strong cultural lessons imparted to them through socialization, parents' communicative processes, actions, and messages that subtly told them to privilege family. They express a willingness to make compromises in their careers just so they can continue fulfilling familial responsibilities and obligations. This finding is similar to Bielby and Bielby's (1989) study that found working women in the United States (participants during the time of the study) gave precedence to family roles and responsibilities over work identities. Medved et al.'s, (2006) findings from a U.S. study that revealed parents "urged daughters to choose particular careers for family reasons" (p. 175) was only imparted to some women. Participants in this study are not always and categorically told to privilege family; rather, the socialization environment they grow up in, insinuate that message to them. That they *should* privilege family was a message that was interpreted by the women based on observing the role modeling happening before them. By making choices that enable a harmonious coexistence with their environment, participants believe *they* make those culturally and gender-appropriate choices and therefore accept the consequences of those decisions. This does not mean that participants lack ambition. It does, however, mean that these working women, even if they are ambitious and desiring of successful careers, are mindful of what society and their families expect out of them and ultimately want to have professional lives that align with societal, parental, and other familial expectations.

Kanungo (1990) has observed that in the Indian context, value orientations toward work are strongly influenced by culture, reference-group norms, and parental and religious training (or socialization). He asserts that, "Pressure from relevant others in a tradition-bound family culture forces the individual to sacrifice organisational and task objectives for the sake of maintaining personalized relationships" (p. 805). Even though people unfamiliar with Indian cultural nuances may question the logic of agency as displayed by these women, participants in this study are consciously trying to make the most of the opportunities provided to them and those they venture out to create for themselves. In choosing their choices and even exercising their will albeit amidst some constraints, participants are redefining what agency means and can mean across cultures. At the same time, they appear to embody the normative expectations of Indian women who take pride in living by culturally required normative behaviors, upholding family values and respectfully deferring to elderly family members in important decision-making processes even if at times this comes at personal discomfort or frustration. Participants express pride in their ability to balance traditional family roles with their dynamic professional ones.

However, as was apparent in the findings presented in chapter 4, participants' embodying of agency was often limited by their socio-cultural and familial obligations. This observation can be further understood in feminist standpoint theorists' view of agency as being constrained. According to O'Brien Hallstein (1999),

> *Constrained agency* simultaneously grants women agency *and* recognizes that that agency occurs within constraints. Constrained agency, then, also refuses the binary logic that either denies agency by viewing subjects as fully oppressed or denies oppression by viewing the subject as fully free. Instead, constrained agency recognizes that subordinate subjects have suffered systematic oppression that is damaging without condemning subjects to positions of victimhood. For example, constrained agency suggests that just because subjects are constituted by discourses does not mean that they are fully determined by those discourses. (p. 37, emphasis in original)

Herein lays the heart of agency as enacted by women in the study. Whether it was in asserting themselves in their academic pursuits or in leading fulfilling yet somewhat compromised careers by choice, the responsibilities they held as dutiful daughters, mothers, and daughters-in-law often constrained the reach and scope of their agency. Standpoints thus developed emerged from knowledge produced amidst constraints.

Even though there is research on Indian women's careers post-organizational entry, very little contemporary research has focused on pre-entry influences that affect career choices and decisions before and during work engagement. The findings of this study indicate an overwhelming parental influence on how women not only come to construct views about their worlds of work but also how they lead those work lives in reality. Values, behaviors, and attitudes toward work developed at a young age as influenced by people significant to the women empower them in becoming confident self-agents of their own work lives. That they have such a strong influence on their daughter's careers should be more actively recognized by parents who in the awareness that their daughters heed to their advice and absorb values from their verbal and non-verbal behaviors should be more cognizant of the examples they present.

Young and colleagues (e.g., Young & Friesen, 1992; Young, Friesen, & Borycki, 1994; Young, Valach, Paseluikho, Dover, Matthes, Paproski, & Sankey, 1997), among others, have investigated parental influences on individuals' careers in non-Indian contexts. In this study, parents influenced their daughters by appealing to their sense of familial responsibilities, cultural expectations, as well as by communicative (re)constructions and role modeling. Knowing this, Indian parents may choose to engage in purposeful communicative actions and other behaviors especially if they want their daughters to pursue certain paths. It is of course important to realize that while daughters will be respectful of their parents' influences and will make informed decisions about their careers, they still reserve the call to exert ultimate agency on how they choose to materialize those influences. Additionally, knowing that by giving their daughters the freedom to choose their careers, they are in fact enabling them for life; more parents may decide to support and nurture their daughters' decisions, from a young age. This study also found that women's career decisions center on their own family priorities. These attitudes are also influenced by early socialization. What parents think about their career choices and decisions is extremely important to the women. All of this information will enable better parent-daughter work/career communication, thereby opening up many new avenues and possibilities for the younger generation of India's working women.

Potential employers of a new generation of working women may also benefit from knowing what work values these women hold most significant. As this study has established, working women across generations assign great significance to their families and their desire to balance both work and careers equally well. Even though younger women generally tend to report that their careers are extremely important, they unequivocally state the importance of family, a trend seen in other countries too (Saurine, 2009; Shellenbarger, 2009). With this knowledge, employers can develop programs and opportunities for women that uphold women's desire for better balanced careers. Proactive measures such as flexible work arrangements, transparency in advancement decisions, and open communication channels are some steps that can be implemented. Also, on-site day care facilities will especially be appreciated by the new generation of working women who tend to be part of nuclear families, living separately from their in-laws. Similarly, because parents/families are so important to their female employees, organizations can invite employees' parents/families over to the workplace so they develop a better understanding of their daughters' work. In other words, unlike the "bring your daughter/son to work day" sometimes practiced in the United

States, Indian organizations can implement a quarter or half day of "bring your parents/family to work."

Many women reported having to temporarily discontinue their careers due to childbirth, more out of a desire to want to spend time with their child than health concerns. In order to help women remain in the loop of workplace activities and not be disadvantaged by their breaks, employers may offer work-from-home arrangements, job sharing, or re-training opportunities to catch up to skills lost during leaves of absence, among other things. On the subject of children, more Indian organizations can implement paid paternity leave in addition to extended maternity leave. Likewise, knowing that a woman's time with her family is time that she truly values, employers can ensure that the discontinuities do not negatively affect careers. Also, by knowing that generations of women often carry differing expectations about their work, organizations can encourage inter-generational conversations through formal channels. Finally, when women realize the amount of influence their parents and other members of the family have on their career choices and decisions, but that even within these influences, they have the prerogative to exercise agency, their decisions will be more confident and better developed. This information may also make them critical evaluators of the information they receive from socialization sources. Women in the study already know that their family and career are closely intertwined. Knowing that findings from this study also corroborate those sentiments, women may now be in a better position to negotiate and navigate through their careers. For example, female coworkers can form alliances and demand better or flexible work arrangements or other programs or practices (e.g., day care, workout equipment) that facilitate more fulfilling careers.

CONCLUDING THOUGHTS

In conclusion, Hindu Indian women who participated in this study are strongly influenced by their caste status and desires for social class/upward mobility. Despite disparate perspectives on Indian society's view of working women, participants make their own peace with its demands by either choosing to ignore the implications or working from within the discursive frame and developing personally meaningful and societally approved behaviors. Parents' socialization processes were taught through verbal messages and non-verbal communicative behaviors including role modeling. What their parents/families say and think about their work and careers makes a significant difference to the manner in which women come to perceive and approach their own work lives. Additionally, even though parents did not necessarily demand specific career fields for their daughters, it was often the daughters' own desire to live up to the career expectations that their parents, especially fathers had of them, that made them pursue specific career paths.

Participants actively participate in the interpretation process and learn how to make educated and informed career choices, develop a strong work ethic, engage in continued learning activities, and balance work-life situations, among others. Participants also strategically negotiate agency when it comes to doing what they believe in but they do so conscious of the cultural, societal, and familial sense of duty and responsibility prescribed and approved by parents and other elders. They express their willingness to make compromises in their careers but there is a generational difference seen in this regard.

While almost all participants in their 40s and older mentioned that their mothers were housewives, they believe that as long as their own family got priority, having a career was permissible by the standards set by society and their own cultural conditioning. Younger participants in their 20s and 30s display similar attachment to their families but also assert that while their families are important to them, they are uniquely positioned to focus more on their careers at present time. This study is just a glimpse into the dynamic nature of socialization and its influence on Hindu Indian's women work/career and family identities. As the first study of its kind with Hindu Indian female participants, this project was inspired by similar studies in the United States (e.g., Lucas, 2011; Medved et al., 2008). In concluding this study, it is my hope that future scholars will utilize these findings to develop more complex approaches to understanding the nature of women's work in India.

Appendix A: Research Methodology

FEMINIST INTERVIEWING

Critical of the absence of women's voices in research accounts, feminist standpoint research articulates a view that develops from women's own experiences (Harding, 2004). This can be done in the form of interviews since this method enables researchers to understand their participants' world in their own words. Similarly, interviewing women is considered a research strategy that allows for documentation of women's accounts of their own lives and experiences (Langellier & Hall, 1989). Reinharz (1992) contends that the interviewing of women and learning of their experiences in their own words acts as an "antidote to centuries of ignoring women's ideas altogether" (p. 19).

The primary method of data collection for this project, feminist interviewing, avoided controlling the interviewees' answers by first developing a sense of connectedness with them. Feminist interviewing encourages women to interview women since this promotes better understanding and leads to more open discussions of topics. Additionally, DeVault (1990) believes that women interviewing women enables both "researcher and subject [to] act on the basis of understandings about interviewing, and both follow the rules (or negotiate a shared version of the rules) associated with their respective roles" (p. 101). Feminist researchers are especially committed to the diversity in women based on their race, class, ethnicity, and so on (Langellier & Hall, 1989). However, when women interview women, it is also important that they share cultural norms otherwise these barriers lead to class and cultural divisions between women, something that feminists have worked hard to alleviate from research (Riessman, 1987).

With its focus on intimacy, including self-disclosure, openness, and engagement, feminist interviewing is considered an alternative (Reinharz, 1992) to the dominant mode of interviewing (see Foss & Foss, 1989; Oakley, 1981). By listening actively with care and caution, women researchers help their women participants develop ideas, construct meanings and use words to say what they mean (Reinharz, 1992).

Feminist interviewing uses self-disclosure on the researcher's part as an important tool to put participants at ease. However, as Kerlin (1997) notes, the timing and degree of self-disclosure significantly affects the interviewee-interviewer relationship. Therefore, I was cautious about when and how much I disclosed about myself. Reinharz (1992) recommends that when interviewing women below one's social status, researchers can build trust by downplaying the apparent status differences between themselves and their participants. I did this by talking to the participants in the local language, actively listening to their narratives with a conscious awareness, and showing genuine care for their concerns. Reinharz also recommends that in interviewing those above one's social status, the researcher should increase status and credibility, which I did by mentioning my educational background and qualifications.

I support the argument that women (and men) are all differently conscious of the societies and contexts around them due to their own experiences. Therefore, as a matter of qualitative research reality, I acknowledge the differences within the themes emerging out of my data.

Stewart (1994) concludes her seven strategies for studying women's lives by asserting;

> It is important to notice the many different voices of the women we study for the same reason it was important to notice that women had something to say at all: Silencing voices always leaves us without knowledge. Listening will leave us with more. (p. 30)

Thus, by engaging in the feminist mode of interviewing with my participants, I was not only able to establish a rapport with them, but the self-disclosure and open transgressions into each other's personal worlds made the purpose of the project genuine and as authentic as should be. Just as I was asking my participants questions, I allowed the space for them to ask me questions about myself—the field research experience is described in more detail in Appendix B.

Data Analytic Techniques

According to Holliday (2002), the point of data collection and analysis is to *"make sense of what is encountered in the field"* (p. 98, italics in original). Of my 78 interviews, 41 were conducted in Marathi and the remainder mostly in

English but also in English and Hindi or English and Marathi. In all the narratives that are quoted verbatim, I have remained true to participants' syntax and language use, whether spoken in Marathi or English. During transcriptions, it was important to me to capture not just the meaning of what they were expressing but how they were uttering the particular arrangement of words. Therefore, I have retained the integrity of their sentence structures even though at times this makes for somewhat awkward translations into English. When participants did speak in English, given that everybody spoke it as a second language (it was evident that some participants who attended Marathi schools had learned English as a subject and others had studied English as a medium of instruction throughout their schooling), some content is grammatically different from the way it would have been spoken by native speakers. Here again, I have remained true to the essence of participants' voices and kept their words exactly as they said them. Occasionally in order to clarify contexts, I have inserted meanings and relevance in brackets.

The transcriptions led to a total of 918 single-spaced pages. The 918 pages yielded a large amount of complex data, woven as they were expected to be, through the intricacies of imposed social structures and systems, and aspired work and career statuses. The technique I chose to navigate my way through my raw data is constructivist thematic analysis. I looked for coherences in knowledges produced by women in particular social locations, even as I understand that the themes might contrast as I move out of a particular group.

I chose to use a constructivist thematic analysis approach toward my data in order to help me understand my participants' experiences of their work lives. This approach consolidates constructivist grounded theory with thematic analysis. I drew primarily from the insight and guidance provided by Braun and Clarke (2006), Charmaz (2005), and DeSantis and Ugarrizza (2000).

Constructivist Thematic Analysis

Before I explain my specific data analysis procedures, I would like to reproduce here Charmaz's (2005) explanation of a constructivist approach to grounded theory. She writes,

> A constructivist approach emphasizes the studied phenomenon rather than the methods of studying it. Constructivist . . . theorists take a reflexive stance on modes of knowing and representing studied life. That means giving close attention to empirical realities and our collected renderings of them—*and* locating oneself in these realities. It does not assume that data simply await discovery in an external world or that methodological procedures will correct limited views of the studied world. Nor does it assume that impartial observers enter the research scene without an interpretive frame of reference. Instead,

what observers see and hear depends upon their prior interpretive frames, biographies, and interests as well as the research context, their relationships with research participants, concrete field experiments, and modes of generating and recording empirical materials. No qualitative method rests on pure induction—the questions we ask of the empirical world frame what we know of it. In short, we share in constructing what we define as data. Similarly, our conceptual categories arise through our interpretations *of* data rather than emanating *from* them or from our methodological practices. . . . Thus, our theoretical analyses are interpretive renderings of a reality; not objective reporting of it. (pp. 509–510, italics in original)

A framework as the above "carries with it a number of assumptions about the nature of the data, what they represent in terms of the world 'reality' and so forth" (Braun & Clarke, 2006, p. 81). A good thematic analysis, explain the scholars, makes this transparent. Braun and Clarke (2006) argue for the consideration of thematic analysis as a foundational method in its own right for qualitative analysis instead of using it as a process within other analytic traditions such as grounded theory. As a method for "identifying, analysing and reporting patterns (themes) within data" (p. 79), they believe this form of analysis provides a "rich and detailed, yet complex account of data" (p. 78). The above methodological philosophy is thus the guiding principle behind my data analysis.

I used the qualitative software NVivo to guide me along the initial stages of analyses. The latter stages of analyses were conducted manually. To begin with, all transcripts were uploaded to the software. These transcripts were then read individually and coded in order to develop free nodes. Free nodes serve as "containers for what is known about, or evidence for, one particular concept or category" (Bazeley, 2007, p. 15). Each node was given a title and provided with a description that captured the essence of the content within it. Coding at the paragraph level led to *a priori* or theoretically derived codes. For example, lessons based on work experience retold by parents to their daughters were coded as "Memorable Messages." According to Bazeley (2007), this method of data analyses is conducive to studies where researchers come into their research with an initial list of concepts they want to explore through the study.

Despite the free coding of passages into pre-determined categories that were key to the investigation, such as career advice, agency, and societal impressions in the first stage of data reduction, I used flexibility in the latter stages of analysis in recognizing, and identifying nodes that were *in vivo* or derived from data. The first stage of data analysis sorting, led to the emergence of 60 free nodes. In the second stage of analysis, these free nodes were combined into a total of 21 tree nodes. Bazeley (2007) explains that while "free nodes do not presume any relationship or connections—they serve simply as 'dropping-off' points for data about ideas you want to hang on to"

(p. 83), however, tree nodes is where data started getting connected to larger concepts under investigation. Tree nodes serve the purpose of organizing the categories initially or codes (or nodes) originally drawn into conceptual groups and subgroups. In the third stage of data management, I created meta-nodes under Tree Nodes titled after each of the research questions. I also analyzed additional Tree Nodes to investigate the women's definition of career and understanding of globalization. Subsequent tree nodes (that included the relevant free nodes) were then added to each of the meta-nodes depending upon the question that was being answered. This concluded the use of NVivo in data management.

Next, tree nodes were analyzed individually and manually to look for themes that spoke specifically to the areas of investigation and answered research questions. I read and re-read the data, all the while making notes in the margins and using loosely structured memos to park personal opinions, questions that stood out, things that did not make sense, as well as explain the contexts within which some of the answers were embedded. According to Strauss and Corbin (1990), memos are "written records of analysis related to the formulation of theory" (p. 197). To me, memoing served the same purpose as journaling. Upon completion of this stage of the analysis and after having run the data through rigorous analyses, my interpretation of the data led to the inductive development of several different themes (Charmaz, 2005) for each research question. The thematically developed answers to the research questions were presented as different chapters in this book.

Appendix B: Positionality and Field Research Experiences

Dow (1997) argues that,

> When we speak and write, we do so from social locations that are constituted by discourse and experience. Moreover, because all social locations are not equal, because some are attended by privilege and others by marginalization, our socially located voices have political implications. (p. 243)

One's social location is defined by "discourses of race, ethnicity, gender, sexuality, and class" (Dow, 1997, p. 246). In a country that is known for its multilingual, multireligious, and multicultural characteristics, the issues of caste, ethnicity, gender, sexuality, and class form the essential components of an individual's identity. Among the factors enumerated by Dow (1997), the one that applies most directly to this study is class. Other factors, perhaps unique to the Indian context, are religion and caste. In positioning myself within the goals of this study, therefore, I have to confront the realities of my caste, class, and religion upfront.

Admitting one's positionality upfront is an essential component of qualitative research, and particularly so in the case of feminist research. Deutsch (2004) explains that awareness of one's subjective experiences in relation to one's participants is "key to acknowledging the limits of objectivity" (p. 889). In this section, therefore, I provide readers with a glimpse into my background and elaborate on my field research experiences.

I am a cisgendered female born to a middle/upper-class Indian family and was 29 years old at the time of conducting this research study. I am also an upper-caste Hindu Brahmin who has enjoyed many privileges in life. My parents sent my sisters and me to English schools and allowed us the freedom to choose absolutely any career path we wanted. Despite the struggles they faced, growing up with limited means and humble beginnings, my parents never hesitated when it came to making every resource available to us. Whether they were curricular or extra-curricular activities, my parents enthusiastically and unconditionally supported our many endeavors, cheering on our successes and encouraging us through some failures. In our early childhood days, raising three daughters in India was not an easy task especially when having to deal with disappointed looks on the faces of random people and unedited rude comments made by insensitive adults at the prospect of my parents having to live a life without sons. Undeterred by societal reactions, my parents raised us to be strong, independent, and confident women who are not afraid to speak our minds and hold our own in this world. I worked my first job as a door-to-door newspaper saleswoman at 15 years of age, something unheard of for young people at the time in India. Part-time employment of teenagers from middle/upper-class families simply did not happen and oftentimes people whose homes I visited to sell newspapers wondered why I was working at my young age and if my family had fallen on hard times. That I was simply doing so to gain real-life work experience and make some money for myself did not make sense to my inquisitors. At 17, I lived and studied in Japan for a year as a Rotary International Youth Exchange Student and represented India as a cultural ambassador. After returning from Japan, while pursuing my undergraduate studies full time, I also worked full time as a journalist for almost three years, for Pune's highest selling English newspaper at the time, making my own money, paying for two years of my college education with that money, and gaining a tremendous amount of work experience meeting and interviewing people, writing news stories, and even gaining some popularity (including fan mail) by writing for and later editing a youth tabloid. When my older sister and three years later, I, decided to come to the United States to pursue advanced studies, our parents provided the financial and emotional support that was needed. I completed my master's and Ph.D. degrees here and, as of this writing, I lived and worked in the United States for 14 years. All through my own career trajectory, starting at age 15, having had the unreserved blessings and encouragement of my parents including having my mother's example before me as a role model (she was the first and only working woman on both sides of my family including among all of my parents' siblings, cousins, and relatives for the longest time), I have always only wondered about what else I could accomplish to make my parents proud. This personal story was significant to why I decided to pursue this research project.

During my doctoral program, intrigued by feminist principles, gender, and work ideologies, I decided to explore these areas further in the Indian context. The more I read, the more I realized that there were at least three distinct "types" of working women in India, and I absolutely had to hear from everybody. Having described my background briefly, it is not difficult to believe that I was most comfortable conducting research with participants of the middle-class, mid-income category. My mother, who worked at a bank for 33 years, would fall under this category as much as I would, had I been currently living in India. I was also comfortable with upper-class professional women. The reason is quite simple; Their position in the workplace and society is something I can successfully aspire to become, should I choose to follow that path. Moreover, the language of the interview with women in the high-income category was English, a language I am most comfortable expressing myself in and my preferred mode of communication despite the three other languages I speak fluently.

I expected that the most challenging part of this project would be conducting research with women in the low-income occupations. Dow (1997) explains that our social locations influence our understanding and consequently the interpretation of knowledge, truth, and meaning. In fact, Mies (1983) has termed a woman scholar's experiences of conducting value-free research as a type of schizophrenia. Because my life experiences have been nothing like those of these women, I thought I might face challenges in understanding *their* unique locations. Being the same gender as your participants is not enough as has been demonstrated by Riessman (1987). As a result, I expected some initial challenges in negotiating entry into their social and psychological spaces. I intended to manage these challenges by working to gain trust and building a rapport.

For these women who are often forgotten or ignored by policy makers, employers, and society, alike, an interest in their work lives by an "outsider" naturally evokes some curiosity or suspicion. That is why the role of an informant was key to my gaining access into their lives. Once contact was established, I used feminist methods of interviewing (Reinharz, 1992) in order to build my relationships with the participants (See Appendix A). As opposed to typical interviewing methods that are more formal and perhaps even impassioned, feminist interviewing believes in openness, and self-disclosure by the interviewer. Even though I had suspected a potential disconnect between this group of participants and me, my confidence and genuineness toward wanting to understand their work lives made them accept me as a confidante. I truly wanted to learn about the women's work lives. I also wanted to know these women as individuals and because research has always been a self-reflexive process for me as it traditionally has been in feminist research (Deutsch, 2004), I was not afraid to draw on my own experiences to make sense of the women's discourses. For this I took refuge in Krieger's (1991) contention that the self cannot be separated from one's research because, when we discuss others, we are always talking about ourselves. Our images of "them" are images of "us." Our theories of how "they" act and what "they" are like, are, first of all, theories about ourselves: who we are, how we act, and what we are like. This self-reflective nature of our statements is something we can never avoid. In social science, although we try to comprehend others, and although we may aim to depict the ways their realities are different from our own, understanding others actually requires us to project a great deal of ourselves onto others, and onto the world at large. (p. 5)

Thus, my position with my research project is a unique one where I shift between contradictory spaces of comfort and discomfort. I played the role of an outsider within my own community, asking my participants about their work lives. My credibility as a researcher going into the field came from my educational background in India and the United States, my professional background in India, and my sincerity, integrity, and genuineness toward my research and my participants.

EMOTIONS AND EXPERIENCES OF FIELD WORK

In this section, I want to produce some of my research experiences from the field. I had made some notes about my experiences while I was still in the field in India. These were written in the format of brainwriting (like brainstorming but done through writing). I let the words flow as they came, without censoring anything. Upon returning to the United States, I compiled those notes into a free flowing personal essay with some citations. I would like to reproduce the same here to give readers an insight into my actual frames of mind during this eventful journey called fieldwork:

It was the first day of my fieldwork in India. One of my father's acquaintances had organized a meeting with some maids in her neighborhood for my research purpose and had invited me over to her house to conduct those interviews. Off I went on my way to my first "international" field experience. Just the use of the word international in the previous sentence is reason for pause. Is it really considered international research if one conducts research within one's own culture? Own country? I had left for the United States as a 21 year old who had just graduated with a bachelor's degree in English. I did not understand the nuances of research or even what it meant to complete a research study until I started my doctoral program at Purdue University. As a result, all of my research activities had focused on people in the United States. This was the first time I was conducting research among my own people. I took it for granted that because I am an Indian among Indians I would not have any problems going about my research study. Fortunately for me, the problems that arose were never too big to be of any real cause for concern. I was ready to embark on my first field experience.

Camera—check, digital audio recorder—check, consent forms—check. I was ready. But wait, I had to take what is known as a "stamp pad" in India, an inkpad that India's majority illiterate population uses to sign their names, rather print their thumb impression on legal paper. This last detail was almost an afterthought. It would never have occurred to me to carry an inkpad with me in the United States because I would not have needed one. In the Indian case, had I not carried the stamp pad this day, I would not have been able to conduct any of the interviews I did since the participants would not have been able to fingerprint their consent forms.

My first day of fieldwork entailed interviewing a lot of maids. Maids, although often taken for granted, are an invisible yet solid backbone of most Indian families. These women are sometimes single handedly responsible for the smooth running of others' households. My father's contact had informed her maid about my research interests who had then informed a number of other maids working in that neighborhood that someone from America was going to interview them.

As nearly seven of them huddled into a small office room to be interviewed, there was curiosity writ large on their faces. Several of them looked at me with skepticism. I was careful how to dress for this interview. I wore a pair of jeans and a long tunic known as *kurta*—a traditional Indian top over my jeans. I did not want to come across as too modern in their terminology lest they did not feel comfortable talking to me. I also made sure I wore a black-beads and gold chain around me known as the *mangalsutra*— a chain that represents a woman's marital status. I wore this for two reasons; first, I wanted these women who were almost all married to feel comfortable to open up to me as a married woman; and second, I wanted them to know that even though I live in America, I am an Indian first and believe in traditions and customs. These reactions were important to me because I wanted to be accepted as well as trusted by these women.

As I began introducing myself and explaining the interview protocol, I was interrupted. "What is in it for us?" I heard the clear but somewhat hesitant voice. I was surprised and I was impressed with what had just happened. In a simple question, a participant had re-negotiated the researcher-participant relationship. I had always known Indian women to be talkative and eager to talk about their experiences, which these women were after some initial uncertainty about what I was going to do with their information, but the question regarding whether their being interviewed was going to help them in any way brought a smile to my face even as I searched for the right thing to say. This was whole new territory for me. Any researcher-held notions of who has power and who does not got dispelled that day with that simple question. Traditionally qualitative research was the Western world's attempt at gaining an understanding of the colonized, non-White, exotic "Other." It was the power-wielding White researcher who entered into the natural settings of the "powerless" Other to "study" them (Denzin & Lincoln, 2005). But how do the dynamics of power play out when native insiders interview their own? Agreed I was not really an insider into their worlds but I was still a part of it! What was I supposed to tell them? That indeed I can do something for them and then actually try to do so—which would mean talking to each one of their employers and ask them to increase these maids' wages (which was what they wanted me to do) or be honest and say no, I really cannot do anything for you. I chose to be honest and upfront about my intentions since the goal of my project was interpretive. I was merely there to understand their world of work.

I told them that I could not do anything for them monetarily. Paying participants for their interviews was not a part of my research protocol or else I could have expressed that arrangement to them. I had to once again explain the intention of this interview session. Remorsefully yet selfishly, I had to tell them that I was interviewing them for my research study, but not without a sense of guilt and helplessness. Everything seemed to be about me even though this research was supposed to be about them. This thought continues to affect me, and I am still trying to find the right solution out of this dilemma. What is one to make of such situations? I keep wondering about the maids' helplessness, the extent of which extended to asking anybody, even a random stranger as myself for help with increasing their wages.

My mental state at that time was again, quite selfishly, the hope that they do not refuse to be interviewed because of my inability to help them. As I struggled with this thought, I wondered if it would mean compromising on my research if indeed I promised them help and then actually talked to their employers about their wages. My research did not have a critical-activist agenda. I was in the field as an interpretive-qualitative scholar and first and foremost I wanted to understand their work/lives. Besides, there are always two sides to an argument and without doubt, their employers would have a different story to tell. I let that matter rest by being forthright about my intentions and reiterating that if as a result they wanted to withdraw from the study, I would respect their decision. Everybody stayed. In fact, perhaps gauging from my facial expressions and stammering as I tried to recover and explain what I could not do, perhaps sensing that they had already shown me my place by putting me in a tight spot and shown who was boss, some of them immediately reprimanded the woman who had raised the question and then turning toward me said that it was okay that I could not help them. They were just curious if I could, that was all. Interviews followed.

The above experience strengthened my resolve on what I had decided early on in my research: that come what may, I was not going to compromise on the project's integrity. Then again, the dilemma still strikes me—would it really have been a compromise if I had indeed spoken to their employers? Would the employers have accepted my intervention on their maids' behalf?

I was in India for a short period. As such, I was not invested in their wages negotiation. Would I have made their lives more difficult in having approached their employers? Who was I anyway to have a say in their individual employer-employee relationship?

As I sat there interviewing all of them, one by one as they spoke of their lives and their circumstances, it really did not matter that there were at one time at least 12 people in the room. They did not care much about the interview per se and they did not care that they were being recorded. They also did not care that the other maids were keenly listening to their stories. Talking of compromises, at 12 participants, I had already surpassed the recommended number of focus group members. This concern was immaterial to the women who sat in the room with me, some of them who sat on the chairs around the table I sat at but most of whom who sat cross-legged on the floor. They wanted to talk about their lives, they wanted me and the other women in the room to listen, and they wanted empathy from others with similar situations. I asked my questions and I tried to maintain a certain amount of organization among the maids but that was not meant to be. They had developed their own little conversational culture. Someone would say something and almost in unison others would agree and add their own experiences to the tally. It was a very new experience for me. To the participants, it almost appeared a cathartic occasion to vent their frustrations, gain empathy, learn from others' experiences, and have patient and respectful listeners.

Had it not been for this research project, I would never have had the opportunity to speak to so many women regarding their work. Why else would they have gathered around me the way they did and pour their hearts out? Of course several of them were there just curious to find out what was going on while others had been told to meet me. My contact person in charge of coordinating this meeting had told (not asked or requested) all these women to meet me and get interviewed. I made sure I told the women that this interview was strictly voluntary and they could choose to leave or withdraw from the interview at any time. A few of the women left during the conversations since it was time for them to show up to work at their employers' home. I was extremely uncomfortable at the manner in which my contact had bragged to me her ability to get so many women together. I also did not like her behavior or method of recruiting for me. Of course I was appreciative but in my US-educated mind this was not the way research is supposed to be conducted.

Once the women had collected in that little room, my contact walked in again and told them to answer all my questions without fear, after all she was going to be interviewed too so it was okay for them to be interviewed by me. I had told this woman a number of times earlier that day and the day we had first met that her role ended with providing me with the contacts and that she was not supposed to know who was actually being interviewed. To ensure this was of course my concern, not hers. She had provided me with the participants, and she was going to make sure they spoke to me. After all, I was an acquaintance's daughter and she had to maintain her reputation in society as someone who stuck to her word and helped people.

Perhaps I consider this woman's unwanted interruption as unnecessary and unprofessional from my vantage point developed through my sensibilities by living and studying in the United States. Her behavior was wrong because of what I know to be right having studied the rules and ethics of qualitative research in the United States. Perhaps, in the Indian context, an interruption by a familiar figure ensures safety as well as helps build trust with the researcher. For this reason, even while I sat there cringing at the woman's interruptive presence at the beginning of the interviews and wanting her to just go away, there was a part of me that just wanted to take it in my stride as my research experience. I did tell the maids after my informant left that they should feel free to talk to me since the content was confidential and that they would all be assigned pseudonyms. Of course since the interviews were now being conducted as huge focus groups, I could no longer ensure individual confidentiality anyway. I had also realized by then that I was the only one who had become uncomfortable with the woman's presence. Everybody else just treated the situation matter-of-factly.

Confidentiality

Through my coursework and research projects in the United States, I had been trained such that informants and people who provide contacts should not be aware of who is being interviewed. Their work ends at providing me with potential participant information and the rest of the efforts are up to me. Alas, like most things, things just work differently in India. Many times people blatantly asked who else I was interviewing. I firmly said that I could not reveal names of my participants. Some understood, some were offended, some were surprised, while some others simply wondered aloud why I was being so rigid about it. What was the big deal after all?

Women from the low-income category were amused at the entire idea of confidentiality. They did not care either way because they believed theirs was a universal story. "Whatever I am telling you is nothing new. All of us go through it," was how one woman explained her lack of interest in maintaining her confidentiality. In fact, a few of the maids I interviewed actually wanted their tales to be revealed to as many people as possible so that their employers would hear about their hardships and everyday struggles and increase their wages. They even asked me if their interviews would be broadcast on television and at what time, even though there were no video cameras in the room.

My participants considered confidentiality, a key element of research in the United States, as well as a top priority with all Institutional Review Board forms as unnecessary and too much paperwork for no reason. Statements such as "Oh you can use my real name," "I have nothing to hide," "No big secrets in my life," and "My life is an open book" were common among my participants, especially in the middle- and high-income categories. Several of the women even told me to use their real names because they wanted everybody to know what they had to say. These women were confident in themselves, had a stable sense of personal identities, and comfortable of their standing in society. While some were vocal with their intentions, others made no such declarations but visibly did not care whether their real names were used or not. I even had a woman sign the consent form but dismiss confidentiality by saying, "This is all in your America because everybody sues. In India, we don't care." To stay consistent, I decided to use pseudonyms for all my participants.

Audio Recording

The personalities of my participants impressed me in different ways. I interviewed 78 women belonging to a cross section of society and across income levels. A few were quiet, answered to the point, and were generally reserved. At the other end of the spectrum I had women who were very vocal and had a lot to say. I stayed true to the ideals of feminist interviewing and decided to let my participants write their own scripts. I made sure I asked some of the questions pivotal to my research but other than that, I generally let them lead the way. According to Reinharz (1992), this method of interviewing is particularly important when the participants are women. She contends that the interviewing of women and learning of their experiences in their own words acts as an "antidote to centuries of ignoring women's ideas altogether." (p. 19).

All women allowed me to audio record our sessions. Quite naturally some were cautious, skeptical, or sensitive with the presence of a microphone and recording device. One woman asked me to pause the recording during the times she did not understand particular questions. Once paused, she asked me to explain exactly what my question meant and only after she had mentally prepared an answer, would she let me turn the recorder back on. Another woman was so impressed with my little digital recorder that she actually asked details of the make and model and immediately emailed her son in the United States to buy her one.

Language

As a result of almost every state in India having its own language, it is no surprise that most Indians speak at least two languages, more if they have moved from state to state. The language in which all interviews with low-income women and some middle- and high-income women were conducted was Marathi, the language of Maharashtra, a state in Western India. Interviews with most of the middle-income women and almost all the high-income women were conducted in English. Code switching between languages comes as a natural skill to many Indians used to shifting effortlessly between a primary language and a secondary language in their day-to-day conversations. Having lived in the United States for as long as I have and speaking almost exclusively in English, I took a few days to adjust to speaking in the local language. Also, because the local language is not my native language or mother tongue, I was often left searching for the right words to convey the right meaning. In such situations, I went about a roundabout manner of asking a question, asking the same question but with many more words than necessary. At other times, my participants helped out. For example, I did not remember the Marathi word for "definition" and so I asked one of my participants, a Marathi teacher at an English-medium school, and she helped me out. The biggest challenge for me, however, was in trying to figure out the Marathi word for "career" and the English word for "*punya*" since many women mentioned their work as helping them get *punya*. In case of career, all of my participants had an intuitive grasp of the meaning of the English word "career" and no translation was required. The English translation of the word *punya* was a little complicated. Several words such as righteousness, good deed, benevolence, and others were proposed but none of them captured the essence of the word "*punya*." In the end, the idea that made most sense was one of "earning credit for a future reincarnated life" since that was in essence what the participants were implying.

Not all of my participants were literate. A majority of the low-income women could not even write their names but the few who could automatically became leaders of the groups they were part of for the interview. They read aloud the consent forms written in Marathi and even explained to the other women who I was, where I came from, and the purpose of our interview session. They proudly signed their own names and some even helped me spell and write others' names next to their thumb impressions in Marathi.

Handling Emotions

The face-to-face interviews with my participants lasted anywhere from seventeen minutes to over two hours, which helped me grasp human nature in many different ways. My participants opened up to me, sometimes revealing episodes of their lives they have not told anybody else. They have taken me on a ride with them through their emotional journeys as well as many a celebratory moments. Our conversational spaces were at times filled with laughter and pleasant reminiscences, while at other times they were overwhelmed by painful memories of the past. I shall eternally be grateful to my participants for sharing intimate details of their selves with me. Riding those emotional roller coaster journeys with my participants was an extremely humbling experience for me.

One of the biggest challenges of my field experiences, however, came precisely from this experience—handling emotions. No matter how many research experiences one has, nothing can prepare or train you to handle raw human emotions, as genuine as they come. The nature of my study's questions took the women back to their childhood experiences. Reliving that childhood with me released many emotions. There were a number of women who got teary eyed during the course of our interview; some wept while others were quick to check themselves. The memories that brought tears were moments that were part of their lives, forever etched and frozen in that special time, the loving absences felt from dear departed family members especially parents, and those crucial and resilient phases of their lives that made them all the more determined to emerge stronger and succeed. At such times I mostly chose to be quiet and let them calm themselves down. Sometimes I offered tissues, and at other times I held their hand. I always asked if they were okay, if they needed to take a break, and if they were ready to want to continue. The women regained composure within a matter of seconds and we continued our interviews. Some women got emotional but fought back tears and continued with the rest of the interview. At these times I was humbled to see the participants manage their emotions stoically as they lay bare their lives wide open for me. How difficult it must have been for them to talk about some of the things and yet they willingly shared them with me! I learned that no matter what the situation in one's life, we eventually end up dealing with it in the best possible way that we can under the circumstances. Their faith and resilience further strengthened my belief that we are never given more grief than we can handle.

The Self as Researcher

Qualitative research is a very personal experience. It was even more personal for me being a woman interviewing women I could relate to on many different levels. Being a middle/upper-class woman belonging to the upper caste in Indian society, social experiences wise I had little in common with women in the low-income category as I had expected. As I sat talking to them, I would often feel a surge of sympathy and helplessness. My sympathy, however, was of little use to them and my helplessness was just that, helpless. There was not much I could do to alleviate their situation. These women have accepted their circumstances as fate even though they call themselves victims of these very circumstances. I found in all these women a certain acceptance of the cards they had been dealt with. At the same time I found in them a strong resolve that their next generation would not go through what they had. Things would change for their children and grandchildren, and they would make sure of that.

I became very conscious of my life and the privileges and opportunities I have had. An important observation that I made when I interviewed low-income women was the sense of a distinct discomfort they felt as a result of the differences in our social statuses. This did not happen all the time but the few times that this discomfort was apparent, it was noteworthy. When I insisted on carrying my own chair to our interview location or when I just sat on the floor next to them, these participants appeared visibly uncomfortable with my behavior. To my egalitarian ideals, carrying my own chair was just the natural thing to do. For these women who constantly embody societal norms relegating them to a lower position, my behavior was atypical of upper-class women such as the women for whom they worked and an anomaly from their day-to-day experiences. I knew going into the field that my numerous identities, relevant only in Indian contexts, such as social class and caste, were going to be important in my fieldwork. These identities did not matter with the other categories of women I interviewed. It was only with the women mentioned above that I felt the difference. Then again the differences mattered only on a very superficial level. We were women first, and there was an unspoken bond that was instantly apparent between most of my participants and me that transcended all other societally imposed rules.

Another very personal experience I had was the way in which some of the women reacted to my *mangalsutra*. As explained earlier, I wore the chain when I went to interview the maids. I also wore it when interviewing street sweepers and some women belonging to the middle- and high-income category. There is often an understanding among women that comes with the adorning of this piece of jewelry around one's neck—that of knowing that you are married, that you have responsibilities, that of empathy, that of realizing that you are just another woman like them working for a living, for independence, for knowledge, for whatever your individual pursuits may be. There is no need to be vocal about it, but the understanding is genuinely there. None of the women in the low-income category asked me about my *mangalsutra* or my marital status. I assumed that they simply quietly acknowledged it. Among the middle-income, middle-class women, several expressed a curiosity about me.

Some wanted to know my background—who am I and where I did my education in India, where in the United States did I live, how was it possible that I was in India for my research—is that acceptable to my United States university? What do I hope to achieve by talking to Indian women if I work in the U.S.? The more curious questions, however, were regarding my marriage. No one asked me if I was married; it was assumed because of the *mangalsutra.* So what does your husband do? Is he a student? One wondered if my husband was an American while another woman, out of nowhere, especially since we had not discussed my marriage at all, provided me with some unsolicited advice. She told me that it was easy to dismiss one's family when one is on a strong career path. She advised me to have a couple of children and basically have a family and not get too involved in my career— an advice she said she gives all the young girls of today. Such questions are an accepted part of social interactions in India and have been experienced by other US-educated Indian scholars while conducting fieldwork in the country (e.g., Chawla, 2004). Most of the questions they asked were personal, but there is a very thin line that differentiates between the public and personal in India. Unlike in the United States, most people do not think much of asking or answering personal questions and neither did I. Of course once I am back in the United States, I again embody my Americanized persona and neither ask nor compel myself to answer such questions unless the nature of the relationship with the person allows for that. I was always honest with my answers to the women perhaps because I felt it was the right thing to do since they had revealed their entire life stories to me. Had it been some other context, I may have responded differently.

Finally, because I wanted to discover how women's outlook toward me would change or if it would, toward the second half of my fieldwork, I decided to no longer wear my *mangalsutra.* The reaction I got this time was that of indifference. I continued to have the same kind of rapport with my participants as before, but somehow, somewhere I sensed that the women were now looking at me as part of the new generation of Indian women who chose to stay single to pursue their careers. Not that it in any obvious way change the dynamic of our participant-researcher relationship, but it did make me feel like I was being somewhat judged by them, almost all of whom were married. Perhaps I was wrong, I will never know. One woman assumed I was single and when asked about her opinion about the new generation of Indian working women, said, "So many women like you are single today because they are such careerists." Where previously there was a quiet understanding of my marital status, this time some women actually asked me if I was married and my answer seemed to comfort them on some level.

One of the hardest things to do during my field research was holding back my personal opinion on the different issues I was questioning my participants. I had to remind myself that I was there to listen to them, to develop an understanding of their lives, from which obviously their opinions stemmed. A simple lesson in social interaction and personal values came from casual observation. During the course of my fieldwork I have visited the homes of those for whom poverty is just a way of life. These women welcomed me warmly into their homes and never hesitated to offer me a cup of coffee or tea—a common gesture in most Indian households. I almost always graciously declined the offer while thanking them for their hospitality. On the other hand, women sitting in air-conditioned homes and offices with maids and office assistants to make and serve tea or coffee did not bother to offer me anything until the end of the interview when they suddenly remembered their lack of hospitability. In these cases, I always refused their last-minute offer. Did I really care for tea or coffee—no, indeed, I did not. I did not enter the field with any of these expectations and yet these observations were too obvious to be ignored. Indeed in none of interviews conducted in the United States have I been offered as much as a glass of water, and it never bothered me. It did not bother me in India either. However, the above observation exercise was a good indication of human nature. It taught me how it does not take too much to give but it takes a lot to become the kind of person who wants to give.

There are several other lessons I take away from this experience. Talking to my participants has taught me lessons in humility and an even greater appreciation for what I have. It has shown me how one can lead a life of quiet dignity, make do with less, overcome hardships and stay resilient, instill strong values in one's own life, and make conscious efforts at becoming a different and better person, stronger, more content and more confident. Most importantly, I have realized that life teaches, every day, and for those who take them, these teachings are lessons for a lifetime.

I collected data over three months after which I returned to the United States. Since then, friends and colleagues alike have asked about my summer. I tell them it was interesting, but only I know the true depth and context in which I use that word. The lessons I have learned are mine for a lifetime. I learned a lot through my international-Indian experience. I played the outsider-insider role within my own culture. People identified with me but were skeptical of my intentions until a rapport was established. At my end, I looked like them and I spoke like them but as was the case with many of my participants, I did not always think like them. My participants at once impressed me and inspired me. The stories they shared with me; stories for the rest of us—real life for the people who lived them will forever remain a part of my life. Many times during the course of my fieldwork I have wanted to pinch myself, not believing that I am actually getting the opportunity to meet so many amazing women from all walks of life, the chance of a lifetime to enter into someone else's personal and professional space and learn from it. How many people get to do what I did! How fortunate am I! Had I not had the credibility of a researcher and the integrity of my intentions, this experience would never have been possible.

I entered my research field naïve, having taken for granted that being an Indian, this kind of fieldwork would be relatively "easy" compared to my research experiences in the United States In many ways it was but in many other ways, it was the complete opposite of how I had imagined it to be and I am better off for it. I remember every interview as if it was yesterday. This was the first time I undertook a project of such mammoth proportions. Just as well. I made my own decisions, and I made my own mistakes.

CONCLUSION

While I was in the field, I was completely immersed in my data and my participants' stories. Whether it was while taking a bumpy rickshaw ride to a participant's preferred interview location or returning home exhausted late evening, sometimes after collecting five interviews in five different and scattered locations, my participants' stories were always on my mind. I became reflective of everything that was happening in my own professional life as enabled by my personal realities. Even when I spent time with family, I was many a times mentally arguing over points that a participant may have uttered. I had already started seeing themes by the time data had started to reach saturation. I kept going for a few more interviews, especially with the low-income category of women, curious to find out if there might emerge something else that would contribute to the preliminary themes. By the time I had all the transcriptions done, I was energized by the discoveries that lay ahead of me. The months of reading, analyzing, and interpreting the data, immersed in a project that is fuelled by my passionate intellectual endeavor to understand the worlds of work of the women of my country, enabled by my American education and training, have been extremely gratifying. This book is but an honest attempt at (re)presenting my participants' positions, perspectives, experiences, and realities as they live it, every day.

Appendix C: Interview Guide

EARLY EXPERIENCES/CHILDHOOD/ADOLESCENCE

Tell me about your childhood.
  Sample Topics and Probes:

  Memories of work and working growing up
  Nature of parents' work
  Stories/anecdotes about work
  Definition of "career"
  Career aspirations and ambitions as a child
  Definition of career
  Schooling/Education
  Career preparation/Vocational Training, etc.
  Media influences—movies, television shows, etc.
  Role models

SOCIETAL/CULTURAL EXPERIENCES AND CAREERS

What were the expectations for women's work in your family growing up?
Societal expectations? Contemporary expectations?
  Sample Topics & Probes:

  Influence of religion on career choice
  Influence of larger society on career choice
  Parents'/others' support of career/language of reprimand/encouragement
  Parents' education/Careers
  Specific stories of parents'/others' work or careers
  Neighborhood career stories

WORK/CAREERS

Tell me your work history—all the different places you've worked at and the
different jobs you've had.
   Sample Topics & Probes:

   Current job/occupation
   Current definition of career/ideal career
   Turning Points, Critical incidents

Meanings of Work
   Why do you work?—Motivations? Reasons?
   How do you find meaning in your work?
   Would you continue to work even if you had all the money in the world?
   What do you find most meaningful about your work?

ON-THE-JOB EXPERIENCES/GENDER

Sample Topics & Probes:

   Everyday challenges
   Career advancement/discrimination
   Work-family balance
   Gender issues at work
   Perceptions of Indian society toward working women

GLOBALIZATION/INDIA/CULTURE/WOMEN

How do you define globalization?
   Sample Topics & Probes:

   Influence of globalization on work/career and life
   Status of women in India
   Concluding thoughts

Appendix D: Profiles of Participants

Table D.1: Profiles of Women in the Low-Income Category

Pseudonym	Occupation	Age	Tenure (in years)
Anusha	Maid	55	17.5
Anusya	Incense Sticks Maker	21	2
Arati	Sweeper	NA	NA
Asha	Maid	NA	NA
Bharati	Maid	45	33
Bhumika	Maid	NA	NA
Chaitali	Priest	62	3
Dhanashree	Maid	NA	NA
Ganga	Sweeper	NA	NA
Gunjan	Maid	NA	NA
Jayanti	Sweeper	NA	NA
Kavita	Maid	NA	NA
Leela	Maid	32	7
Manisha	Priest	49	8
Meeta	NGO Accountant	40	8
Meghana	Maid	NA	NA
Prajakta	School Peon	40s	2
Priya	Sweeper	NA	NA
Rati	Maid	NA	NA
Rekha	Maid	19	10
Reshma	Maid	NA	NA
Savita	Receptionist	21	1.5
Seema	Live-in Nanny	20	2
Shanti	School Peon	35	5
Shobana	Maid	NA	NA
Sonali	Maid	18	15
Sulaja	Maid	NA	NA
Suleka	Incense Sticks Maker	24	4
Sulochana	*Masala* Maker	62	39
Varsha	Maid	NA	NA
Veena	Sweeper	NA	NA
Vidya	Maid	45	3
Usha	Maid	NA	NA

NA: Not Available. Many of the participants either did not know their age or were unsure of the right age.

Table D.2: Profiles of Women in the Middle-Income Category

Pseudonyms	Occupation	Age	Tenure (in years)
Anahita	Landscape Designer/Owner of Company	53	23
Anjusha	Social Worker	50s	NA
Anuja	Anesthesiologist	44	18
Aparna	Leprosy Technician	55	24
Avni	Ayurveda Doctor	27	4
Harsha	Physiotherapist	29	8
Jagruti	Radiologist	34	7
Jaya	Social Worker	48	10
Madhura	Runs a School for the Blind	55	12
Manjula	Dietician	51	20
Maya	High-Ranking Police Officer/ Administrator	51	27
Meena	Teacher	57	13
Mohini	Judge	63	12
Mukta	Fashion Designer	25	2
Nutan	Government Employee	39	15
Priyanka	Teacher	40s	NA
Rakhi	Sales Manager	27	4.5
Ramya	Teacher	47	14
Sachi	Dancer	28	15
Sandhya	Government Employee	45	25
Sonal	Visual Merchandizer	24	2.5
Sukanya	Agricultural Consultant	32	5
Tanushree	Make-Up Artist/Model	22	4
Ujwala	Journalist	30	8
Vanaja	Interior Designer	33	11
Vijaya	Journalist	48	21
Yamini	Architect	31	8

NA: Not Available. Participants either did not remember or did not know

Table D.3: Profiles of Women in High-Income Occupations

Pseudonym	Occupation	Age	Tenure (in years)
Anita	Corporate Secretary	31	12
Anjana	CEO/Co-Owner, Manufacturing Company	48	22
Avantika	IT Product Analyst	39	7.5
Bhavana	Controller of Finance, MNC	38	18
Bindiya	Actress/Producer	40s	8
Charulata	Owns Nurseries	61	35
Manjushree	Director, Performing Arts Academy	59	6
Meha	IT Supervisor	27	9
Padmini	Physicist	36	11
Pooja	Principal of an International School	50	2
Rajani	HR Recruiter	42	13
Sakshi	Radio Jockey	29	6.5
Shalini	Lawyer	32	8
Shipta	Insurance Company Branch Manager	32	6
Shraddha	IT Quality Control Manager	27	7
Vaishali	Ayurveda Doctor & Yoga Professional	37	14
Vedha	General Manager, MNC	49	30
Vidisha	Project Director, Risk Management	29	7

References

Abele, A. E., & Wojciszke, B. (2007). Agency and communion from the perspective of self versus others. *Journal of Personality and Social Psychology, 93*, 751–763.

Acharya, J. (2003). Women's well-being and gendered practices of labor and workspace in traditional craft productions in Orissa, India. *Gender, Technology and Development, 7*, 333–343.

Aga, A. (January 15, 2006). What will it take to increase the number of women in our workforce, *Business Today*: ABI/INFORM Global.

Agrawal, S. (March 12, 2006). Women rising: India Inc. is still largely a men's club. But an increasingly large number of companies are taking steps to make it more gender-diverse, *Business Today* (pp. 88): ABI/INFORM Global.

Ahmad, N., & Lahiri-Dutt, K. (2006). Engendering mining communities: Examining the missing gender concerns in coal mining displacement and rehabilitation in India. *Gender, Technology and Development, 10*, 313–339.

Ali, M. M. (2006). India's booming economy poses challenges as well as opportunities [Electronic Version]. *The Washington Report on Middle East Affairs, 25*, 36–37. Retrieved January 22, 2008, from ProQuest database.

Ali, A., & Al-Shakhis, M. (1989). The meaning of work in Saudi Arabia. *International Journal of Management, 10*, 26–32.

All India Radio. (n.d.). Retrieved from, http://allindiaradio.gov.in/default.aspx.

Altschuler, J. (2004). Beyond money and survival: The meaning of paid work among older women. *International Journal of Aging and Human Development, 58*, 223–239.

Andrade, C., Postma, K., & Abraham, K. (1999). Influence of women's work status on the well-being of Indian couples. *International Journal of Social Psychiatry, 45*, 65–75.

Aptheker, B. (1989). *Tapestries of life: women's work, women's consciousness, and the meaning of daily experience* Amherst, MA: University of Massachusetts Press.

Arthur, M. B., Hall, D. T., & Lawrence, B. S. (Eds.). (1989). *Handbook of career theory.* Cambridge, UK: Cambridge University Press.

Ashcraft, K. L. (2005). Feminist organizational communication studies: Engaging gender in public and private. In S. May & D. K. Mumby (Eds.), *Engaging organizational communication theory & research: Multiple perspectives* . Thousand Oaks, CA: Sage.

Astin, H. S. (1984). The meaning of work in women's lives: A sociopsychological model of career choice and work behavior. *The Counseling Psychologist, 12*, 117–126.

A tryst with destiny (August, 1997). *India News On-Line.* Retrieved from https://www.indianembassy.org/inews/aug15.pdf

Baker, S. (1990). *Caste: At home in Hindu India.* London, England: Jonathan Cap Ltd.

Bala. B. (2003). 'Love for my father spurred me to do my duty by him.' *Tribune India.* Retrieved from http://www.tribuneindia.com/2003/20030914/herworld.htm#1

Bamzai, K. (2006, April 24). *Mistress of choices.* Retrieved from http://www.indiatoday.com/itoday/20060424/cover.html&SET=T

Bandura, A. (2001). Social cognitive theory: An agentic perspective. *Annual Review of Psychology, 52,* 1–26.

Banerjee, N. (2002). Between the devil and the deep sea: Shrinking options for women in contemporary India. In K. Kapadia (Ed.), *The violence of development: The politics of identity, gender and social inequalities in India* (pp. 43–68). London: Zed Books.

Bardhan, K. (1993). Work in South Asia: An inter-regional perspective. In S. Raju & D. Bagchi (Eds.), *Women and work in South Asia: Regional patterns and perspectives* (pp. 39–98). London: Routledge.

Barrett, M., & Davidson, M. J. (Eds.). (2006). *Gender and communication at work.* Hampshire, UK: Ashgate.

Basu, S. (May 4, 2006). Odd-hour woes: BPOs offer diet chart. Retrieved March 4, 2008, from http://timesofindia.indiatimes.com/articleshow/1516763.cms

Bazeley, P. (2007). *Qualitative data analysis with NVivo.* Thousand Oaks, CA: Sage.

Beinhocker, E. D., Farrell, D., Zainulbhai, A. S. (2007). Tracking the growth of India's middle class. *The McKinsey Quarterly, 3,* 51–61.

Berger, P. L., & Luckmann, T. (1967). *The social construction of reality: A treatise in the sociology of knowledge.* New York: Anchor Books.

Bernstein, P. (1997). American work values: Their origin and development. Albany, NY: SUNY Press.

Bharadwaj, A. (2007a, April 16). *A taste of freedom.* Retrieved from http://www.indiatoday.com/itoday/20070416/cover3.html

Bharadwaj, A. (2007b, April 16). *Daring to be different.* Retrieved from http://www.indiatoday.com/itoday/20070416/cover4.html

Bhogle, S. (1999). Gender roles: The construct in the Indian context. In T. S. Saraswathi (Ed.), *Culture, socialization and human development: Theory, research and applications in India* (pp. 278–300). New Delhi, India: Sage.

Bidwai, P. (2006, June). India: Bringing the caste-aways on board. *Asia Times.* Retrieved from http://www.atimes.com/atimes/South_Asia/HF02Df01.html

Bielby, W. T., & Bielby, D. D. (1989). Family ties: Balancing commitments to work and family in dual earner households. *American Sociological Review, 54,* 776–789.

Bijapurkar, R. (2007, September 8). The new Indian woman. Retrieved January 8, 2008, from http://www.businessworldindia.com/mar1907/column03.asp

Blustein, D. (2006). *The psychology of working: A new perspective for career development, counseling, and public policy.* Mahwah, NJ: Lawrence Erlbaum Associates, Inc.

Bradford, L., Buck, J. L., & Meyers, R. A. (2001). Cultural and parental communicative influences on the career success of white and black women. *Women's Studies in Communication, 23,* 194–217.

Braun, V., & Clarke, V. (2006). Using thematic analysis in psychology. *Qualitative Research in Psychology, 3,* 77–101.

Breman, J. (1999). The study of industrial labour in post-colonial India—The informal sector: A concluding review. *Contributions to Indian Sociology, 33,* 407–431.

Broadfoot, K.J., & Munshi, D. (2007). Diverse voices and alternative rationalities: Imagining forms of postcolonial organizational communication. *Management Communication Quarterly, 21,* 249–267.

Broadfoot, K. J., Carlone, D., Medved, C. E., Aakhus, M., Gabor, E., & Taylor, K. (2008). Meaningful work and organizational communication: Questioning boundaries, positionalities, and engagements. *Management Communication Quarterly, 22,* 152–161.

Budget 2013-2014 Special. (2013). *Latest income tax slabs for FY 2013-2014.* Financeminister.in. Retrieved from http://financeminister.in/latest-india-income-tax-slabs

Budhwar, P. S., & Baruch, Y. (2003). Career management practices in India: An empirical study. *International Journal of Manpower, 24,* 699–719.

Budhwar, P.S., Saini, D.S., & Bhatnagar, J. (2005). Women in management in the new economic environment: The case of India. *Asia Pacific Business Review, 11,* 179–193.

BusinessWeek. (August 22, 2005). Online Extra: India's new worldly women. Retrieved March 3, 2008, from http://www.businessweek.com/magazine/content/05_34/b3948530.htm

Butalia, U. (2007, April 16). *Living the dream.* Retrieved from http://www.indiatoday.com/itoday/20070416/cover1.html

Buzzanell, P. (1994). Gaining a voice: Feminist organizational communication theorizing. *Management Communication Quarterly, 7,* 339–383.

Buzzanell, P. (1995). Reframing the glass ceiling as a socially constructed process: Implications for understanding and change. *Communication Monographs, 62,* 327–354.

Buzzanell, P. M. (Ed.). (2000). *Rethinking organizational and managerial communication from feminist perspectives.* Thousand Oaks, CA: Sage.

Buzzanell, P. M., & Goldzwig, S. R. (1991). Linear and nonlinear career models: Metaphors, paradigms, and ideologies. *Management Communication Quarterly, 4,* 466–505.

Bowie, N. E. (1998). A Kantian theory of meaningful work. *Journal of Business Ethics, 17,* 1083–1092.

Carr, M., Chen, M. A., & Tate, J. (2000). Globalization and home-based workers. *Feminist Economics, 6,* 123–142.

Chaffee, S. H., McLeod, J. M., & Wackman, D. B. (1973). Family communication patterns and adolescent political participation. In J. Dennis (Ed.), *Socialization to politics: A reader* (pp. 349–364). New York: Wiley.

Chanana, K. (1994). Social change or social reform: Women, education, and family in pre-independence India. In C. C. Mukhopadhyay and S. Seymour (Eds.), *Women, education, & family structure in India* (pp. 37–57). Boulder, CO: Westview Press.

Chanana, K. (2003). Visibility, gender, and the careers of women faculty in an Indian university. *McGill Journal of Education, 38,* 381–389.

Chandrashekhar, C. P., & Ghosh, J. (2011, August). Women's work: Has anything changed? *Business Line.* Retrieved from http://www.thehindubusinessline.com/opinion/columns/c-p-chandrasekhar/womens-work-has-anything-changed/article2337066.ece

Chang, T. F. H. (2003). A social psychological model of women's gender-typed occupational mobility. *Career Development International, 8,* 27–39.

Charmaz, K. (2005). Grounded theory in the 21st century: Applications for advancing social justice studies. In N. K. Denzin & Y. S. Lincoln (Eds.), *The SAGE Handbook of qualitative research* (pp. 5–7–536). Thousand Oaks, CA: Sage.

Cheney, G. (2000). Thinking differently about organizational communication. *Management Communication Quarterly, 14,* 132–141.

Cheney, G., & Ashcraft, K. L. (2007). Considering "The Professional" in communication studies: Implications for theory and research within and beyond the boundaries of organizational communication. *Communication Theory, 17,* 146–175.

Cheney, G., & Nadesan, M. H. (2008). Forum conclusion: A response to these essays and a prologue to further investigations. *Management Communication Quarterly, 22,* 181–189.

Cheney, G., Lair, D., Ritz, D., & Kendall, B. (2010). *Just a job? Communication, ethics & professional life.* New York: Oxford University Press.

Chester, N. L., & Grossman, H. Y. (1990). Introduction: Learning about women and their work through their own accounts. In H. Y. Grossman & N. L. Chester (Eds.), *The experience and meaning of work in women's lives* (pp. 1–9). Hillsdale, NJ: LEA.

Census of India (2011). Primary census abstract: Figures at a glance. Retrieved from http://www.censusindia.gov.in/vital_statistics/SRS_Reports.html

Ciulla, J. (2000). *The working life: The promise and betrayal of modern work.* New York: Three Rivers.

Clair, R. P. (1996). The political nature of the colloquialism, "a real job": Implications for organizational socialization. *Communication Monographs, 63,* 249.

Collin, A. (2007). Contributions and challenges to vocational psychology from other disciplines: Examples from narrative and narratology. *International Journal of Education and Vocational Guidance. 7,* 159–167.

Collin, A., & Young, R. A. (2000). *The future of career.* Cambridge, UK: Cambridge University Press.

Combs, G. M., & Nadkarni, S. (2005). The tale of two cultures: Attitudes towards affirmative action in the United States and India. *Journal of World Business, 40,* 158–171.

Corbridge, S., Harriss, J., & Jeffrey, C. (2013). *India Today: Economy, politics, and society.* Cambridge, UK: Polity Press.

Crabtree, S., & Pugliese, A. (2012, November). China outpaces India for women in the workforce. Retrieved from the Gallup World website: http://www.gallup.com/poll/158501/china-outpaces-india-women-workforce.aspx

Crites, J. O. (1969). *Vocational psychology: The study of vocational behavior and development.* New York: McGraw-Hill.

Crosby, F. J. (1990). Divorce and work life among women managers. In H. Y. Grossman & N. L. Chester (Eds.), *The experience and meaning of work in women's lives* (pp. 121–142). Hillsdale, NJ: LEA.

Dallimore, E. J. (2003). Memorable messages as discursive formations: The gendered socialization of new university faculty. *Women's Studies in communication, 26,* 214–265.

Dalmia, S. (April, 2010). India's government by quota. *The Wall Street Journal.* Retrieved from   http://online.wsj.com/news/articles/SB10001424052748703871904575215810722146240

D'Aluisio, F., & Menzel, P. (1996). *Women in the material world.* San Francisco, CA: Sierra Club Books.

Das, G. (2002). *India unbound: From independence to the global information age.* New Delhi, India: Penguin Books.

Das, G. (2006). The India model [Electronic Version]. *Foreign Affairs, 85,* 2–16. Retrieved January 22, 2008 from ProQuest database.

Dasgupta, K. (1998). Women as managers of libraries: A developmental process in India. *IFLA Journal, 24,* 245–249.

Datta, A. (2005). MacDonaldization of gender in urban India: A tentative exploration. *Gender, Technology and Development, 9,* 125–135.

Datta, D., Krishnamurthy, A., David, S., & Sen, S. (June 11, 2007). Overstretched dads. Retrieved September 10, 2007, from http://www.indiatoday.com/itoday/20070611/society.html

David, R., & Alexander, G. S. (2011, June). Top women at Indian banks prove ICICI CEO factory gender neutral. *Bloomberg Markets Magazine.* Retrieved from http://www.bloomberg.com/news/2011-06-22/top-women-in-india-banking-proving-icici-s-factory-for-ceos-gender-neutral.html

Dhawan, N. (2005). Women's role expectations and identity development in India. *Psychology and Developing Societies, 17,* 81–92.

Department of School Education & Literacy (2012). Ministry of Human Resource Development, Government of India. Retrieved from http://mhrd.gov.in/rte

Derr, B.C., & Laurent, A. (1989). The internal and external career: A theoretical and cross-cultural perspective. In M.B. Arthur & D.T. Hall (Eds.), *Handbook of career theory* (pp. 454-471). Cambridge, UK: Cambridge University Press.

DeSantis, L., & Ugarriza, D. N. (2000). The concept of theme as used in qualitative nursing research. *Western Journal of Nursing, 22,* 351–372.

Deshpande, A. (2011). *The grammar of cast: Economic discrimination in contemporary India.* New Delhi, India: Oxford University Press.

Desai, N., & Krishnaraj, M. (2004). An overview of the status of women in India. In M. Mohanty (Ed.), *Class, caste, gender* (pp. 296–319). New Delhi, India: Sage

Deetz, S. (1992). Democracy in an age of corporate colonization: Developments in the communication and the politics of everyday life. Albany, NY: SUNY Press.

Deutsch, N. L. (2004). Positionality and the pen: Reflections on the process of becoming a feminist researcher and writer. *Qualitative Inquiry, 10,* 885–902.

DeVault, M. L. (1990). Talking and listening from women's standpoint: Feminist strategies for interviewing and analysis. *Social Problems, 37,* 96–116.

Devi, M. (2004). *Socialization of women in India.* New Delhi: Concept Publishing Company.

Dirks, N. B. (2001). *Castes of mind: Colonialism and the making of modern India.* Princeton, NJ: Princeton University Press.

Divakaruni, C. B. (2005, April 04). *Power goddess.* Retrieved February 4, 2008, from http://www.indiatoday.com/itoday/20050404/cover.shtml

Dow, B. J. (1997). Politicizing Voice. *Western Journal of Communication, 61,* 243–251.

Dow, B. J., & Wood, J. T. (Eds.). (2006). *The SAGE handbook on gender and communication.* Thousand Oaks, CA: Sage.

Dube, L. (2001). *Anthropological explorations in gender.* New Delhi, India: Sage.

Eapen, M. (2004). Women and work mobility: Some disquieting evidences from the Indian data. *Centre for Development Studies, Trivendrum Working Papers* Retrieved January 23, 2008, from http://econpapers.repec.org/paper/indcdswpp/358.htm

Eapen, M., & Kodoth, P. (2004). Family structure, women's education, and work: Re-examining the high status of women in Kerala [Electronic Version]. *The International Development Research Centre.* Retrieved February 10, 2008 from http://www.idrc.ca/en/ev-58040-201-1-DO_TOPIC.html.

Factbox—Caste-based quota system in India. (2008). Retrieved from http://uk.reuters.com/article/2008/04/10/uk-india-caste-idUKB51468920080410

Fat air-hostesses out, but portly pursers fly [Electronic (March 8, 2008). Version]. *The Times of India,* 2008 from http://timesofindia.indiatimes.com/Fat_air-hostesses_out_but_portly_pursers_fly/articleshow/2846556.cms.

Feldman, D. C. (1981). The multiple socialization of organization members. *The Academy of Management Review, 6,* 309–318.

Fernandes, L. (2000). Restructuring the new middle class. *Comparative Studies of South Asia, Africa and the Middle East, XX,* 1 & 2.

Fernandez, J. P. (1981). *Racism and sexism in corporate life.* Lexington, MA: DC: Heath and Company.

Flores, L. Y., & O'Brien K. M. (2002). The career development of Mexican American adolescent women: A test of social cognitive career theory. *Journal of Counseling Psychology, 49,* 14–27.

Foss, K. A., & Foss, S. K. (1989). Incorporating the feminist perspective in communication scholarship: A research commentary. In K. Carter & C. Spitzack (Eds.), *Doing research on women's communication: Perspectives on theory and method* (pp. 65–94). New Jersey, US: Ablex Publishing Corporation.

Freeman, C. (2001). Is local: Global as feminine: Masculine? Rethinking the gender of globalization. *Signs: Journal of Women in Culture and Society, 26,* 1007–1037.

Friedman, T. L. (2005). *The world is flat: A brief history of the twenty-first century.* New York: Farrar, Strauss and Giroux.

Ganesh, K. (1999). Patrilineal structure and agency of women: Issues in gendered socialization. In T. S. Saraswathi (Ed.), *Culture, socialization and human development: Theory, research and applications in India* (pp. 235–254). New Delhi, India: Sage.

Ganguly-Scrase, R. (2003). Paradoxes of globalization, liberalization, and gender equality: The worldviews of lower middle class in West Bengal, India. *Gender & Society, 17,* 544–566

Ghatak, A. (2006). Faith, work, and women in a changing world: The influence of religion in the lives of *beedi* rollers in West Bengal. *Gender & Development, 14,* 375–383.

Gibson, M. K., & Papa, M. J. (2000). The mud, the blood, and the beer guys: Organizational osmosis is blue-collar work groups. *Journal of Applied Communication Research, 28*(1), 68–88.

Global Employment Trends report. (2013). International Labour Organization. Retrieved from http://www.ilo.org/wcmsp5/groups/public/---dgreports/---dcomm/---publ/documents/publication/wcms_202326.pdf

Grossman, H. Y. (1990). The pregnant therapist: Professional and personal worlds intertwine. In H. Y. Grossman & N. L. Chester (Eds.), *The experience and meaning of work in women's lives* (pp. 57–81). Hillsdale, NJ: LEA.

Grossman, H. Y., & Stewart, A. J. (1990). Women's experience of power over others: Case studies of psychotherapists and professors. In H. Y. Grossman & N. L. Chester (Eds.), *The experience and meaning of work in women's lives* (pp. 11–33). Hillsdale, NJ: LEA.

Gentleman, A. (2007, June). Indian shepherds stoop to conquer caste system. *The New York Times*. Retrieved from http://www.nytimes.com/2007/06/03/world/asia/03india.html?_r=0

Goodnow, J. J., & Lawrence, J. A. (2001). Work contributions to the family: Developing a conceptual and research framework. *New Directions for Child and Adolescent Research, 94*, 5–22.

Gupta, D. (2007). Mistaken modernity: Indian between worlds. New Delhi: HarperCollins

Gupta, N., & Sharma, A. K. (2003). Gender inequality in the work environment at institutes of higher learning in science and technology in India. *Work, employment and society, 17*, 597–616.

Gupta, A., Koshal, M., & Koshal, R. K. (1998). Women managers in India: Challenges and opportunities. *Equal Opportunity International, 17*, 14–31.

Hall, D. L. (1976). *Careers in organizations*. Santa Monica, CA: Goodyear Publishing Company, Inc.

Hancock, M. E. (1999). *Womanhood in the making: Domestic ritual and public culture in urban South India*. Boulder, CO: Westview Press.

Haq, R. (2013). Intersectionality of gender and other forms of identity: Dilemmas and challenges facing women in India. *Gender in Management: An International Journal, 28*, 171–184.

Harding, S. (1997). Comment on Hekman's "Truth and Method: Feminist standpoint theory revisited": Whose standpoint needs the regimes of truth and reality? *Signs: Journal of Women in Culture and Society, 22*, 382–391.

Harding, S. (2004). Introduction: Standpoint theory as a site of political, philosophic, and scientific debate. In S. Harding (Ed.), *The feminist standpoint reader: Intellectual and political controversies* (pp. 1–15). London: Routledge.

Harris, G. (October, 2012). Is it time to retire India's quota system? The New York Times International Edition: India Ink. Retrieved from http://india.blogs.nytimes.com/2012/10/08/is-it-time-to-retire-indias-quota-system/?_r=0

Hussmanns, R., & Mehran, F. (n. s.). Statistical definition of the informal sector- International standards and national practices. from www.gdrc.org/informal/huss0772.pdf

Hegde, R. (1995). Recipes for change: Weekly help for Indian women. *Women's studies in communication, 18*, 177–188.

Heikkila, P. (2012, April). Indian women scale heights of the workforce. *The National*. Retrieved from http://www.thenational.ae/business/industry-insights/economics/indian-women-scale-heights-of-the-workforce.

Hekman, S. (1997). Truth and method: Feminist standpoint theory revisited. *Signs: Journal of Women in Culture and Society, 22*, 341–365.

Hill Collins, P. (1997). Comment on Hekman's "Truth and method: Feminist standpoint theory revisited": Where's the power? *Signs: Journal of Women in Culture and Society, 22*, 375–381.

Hoffner, C. A., Levine, K. J., & Toohey, R. (2008). Socialization to work in late adolescence: The role of television and family. *Journal of Broadcasting & Electronic Media, 52*, 282–302.

Holder, T. (1996). Women in nontraditional occupations: Information-seeking during organizational entry. *Journal of Business Communication, 33*, 9–26.

Holder, D. P., & Anderson, C. M. (1989). Women, work, and the family. In C. M. A. F. W. M. McGoldrick (Ed.), *Women in families: A framework for family therapy* (pp. 357-380). New York: W. W. Norton & Company, Inc.

Holliday, A. (2002). *Doing and writing qualitative research*. Thousand Oaks, CA: Sage.

Hudson, P. (2001). Women's work. Retrieved August 27, 2007, from http://www.bbc.co.uk/history/british/victorians/womens_work_01.shtml

Ilavarasan, V. P. (2006). Are opportunities equal for women in the IT workplace? Observations from the Indian software industry. *IEEE Technology and Society Magazine, Winter*, 43–49.

Inderfurth, K. F., & Khambatta, P. (2012). *India's economy: The other half* (Vol. 2, Issue 2). Retrieved from Center for Strategic & International Studies website: http://csis.org/files/publication/120222_WadhwaniChair_USIndiaInsight.pdf

India joins list of 135 countries in making education a right (April, 2010). *The Hindu.* Retrieved from http://www.thehindu.com/news/national/article365232.ece

India passes free education bill. (August, 2009). *BBC News.* Retrieved from http://news.bbc.co.uk/2/hi/south_asia/8184779.stm

India re-assesses menstrual forms. (2007). British Broadcasting Corporation website. Retrieved from http://news.bbc.co.uk/2/hi/south_asia/6547909.stm

India Today. (April 4, 2005). Retrieved from http://www.indiatoday.com/itoday/20050404/

India Today. (April 24, 2006). Retrieved from http://www.indiatoday.com/itoday/20060424/cover.html

India Today (April 16, 2007). Retrieved from http://indiatoday.intoday.in/calendar/252/2007/magazine.html

Inkson, K. (2004). Images of career: Nine key metaphors. *Journal of Vocational Behavior, 65,* 96–111.

Jablin, F. M. (1985). An exploratory study of vocational organizational communication socialization. *The Southern Speech Communication Journal, 50,* 261–282.

Jablin, F. M. (2001). Organizational entry, assimilation, and disengagement/exit. In F. M. Jablin & L. L. Putnam (Eds.), *The new handbook of organizational communication.* (pp. 732-818). Thousand Oaks, CA: Sage.Jain, Ratnam, & Venkata, 1994

John, M. E. (1998). Feminism in India and the West: Recasting a relationship. *Cultural Dynamics, 10,* 197–209.

Kaila, H. L. (2004). Indian women managers: Their stresses, health and coping behavior—A survey in Mumbai. *Journal of Health Management, 6,* 147–161.

Kakad, K. (2002). Gender discrimination in the construction industry: The case of two cities in India. *Gender, Technology and Development, 6,* 355–372.

Kakar, S., & Kakar, K. (2007). *The Indians: Portrait of a people.* New Delhi, India: Penguin Books India, Pvt. Ltd.

Kala, A. V. (July 25, 2013) How to read India's poverty stats. *Wall Street Journal Blog: India Realtime.* Retrieved from http://blogs.wsj.com/indiarealtime/2013/07/25/how-to-read-in-dias-poverty-stats/.

Kantor, P. (2002). A sectoral approach to the study of gender constraints on economic opportunities in the informal sector in India *Gender & Society, 16,* 285-302.

Kanungo, R. N. (1990). Culture and work alienation: Western models and eastern realities. *International Journal of Psychology, 25,* 795–812.

Kapadia, S. (1999). Self, women and empowerment: A conceptual inquiry. In T. S. Saraswathi (Ed.), *Culture, socialization and human development: Theory, research and applications in India* (pp. 255–277). New Delhi, India: Sage.

Kapadia, K. (2002a). Translocal modernities and transformations of gender and caste. In K. Kapadia (Ed.), *The violence of development: The politics of identity, gender and social inequalities in India* (pp. 142–179). London: Zed Books.

Kapadia, K. (2002b). Introduction: The politics of identity, social inequalities and economic growth. In K. Kapadia (Ed.), *The violence of development: The politics of identity, gender and social inequalities in India* (pp. 1–40). London: Zed Books.

Kapoor, P. (1997). Work: Its meaning and socialization in the Indian context. *Trends in Social Science Research, 4,* 217–229.

Karmali, N. (2013, April). Ambani brothers are back in business together. *Forbes Online.* Retrieved from www.forbes.com/search/?q=+Ambani+brothers+are+back+in+business+together.

Kessler-Harris, A. (1981). *Women have always worked—A historical overview.* New York: The Feminist Press.

Ketkar, S. V. (1909). *The history of caste in India: Evidence of the laws of Manu on the social conditions in India during the third century A. D. interpreted and examined* (Vol. 1). Ithaca, NY: James B. Lyon Company.

Key features of the budget 2008-2009. (2008). India budget. Retrieved from http://indiabudget.nic.in/ub2008-09/bh/bh1.pdf.

Kishwar, M. P. (May-June 2006). Diagnosing and remedying backwardness: English education defines the new Brahmins and the new Dalits of India. *Manushi, 154,* 4–10.

Knapp, M. L., Stohl, C., & Reardon, K. K. (1981). "Memorable" messages. *Journal of Communication, 31,* 27–41.

Knudson-Martin. (1995). Wild (powerful) women: Restorying gender patterns. *Contemporary Family Therapy, 17*(1), 93–107.

Kolenda, P. M. (1964). Religious anxiety and Hindu fate. *The Journal of Asian Studies, 23,* 71–81.

Krieger, S. (1991). *Social science and the self: Personal essays as an art form.* New Brunswick, NJ: Rutgers University Press.

Kreiner, G. E., Ashforth, B. E., & Sluss, D. M. (2006). Identity dynamics in occupational dirty work: Integrating social identity and system justification perspectives. *Organization Science, 17,* 619–636.

Kuhn, T., Golden, A. G., Jorgenson, J., Buzzanell, P. M., Berkelaar, B. L., Kisselburgh, L. G., Cruz, D. (2008). Cultural discourses and discursive resources for meaning/ful work: Constructing and disruption identities in contemporary capitalism. *Management Communication Quarterly, 22,* 162–171.

Lair, D. J. (2007, November). Rethinking the "organizational" in organizational socialization research: From ontological agent to discursive domain(s). Paper presented at the National Communication Association annual meeting, Chicago, IL.

Lair, D., Shenoy, S., McClellan, J. G., & McGuire, T. (2008). The politics of meaning/fulwork: Navigating the tensions of narcissism and condescension while finding meaning in work. *Management Communication Quarterly, 22,* 172–180.

Laird, J. (1989). Women and stories: Restorying women's self-constructions. In M. McGoldrick, C. M. Anderson and F. Walsh (Eds.), *Women in families: A framework for family therapy* (pp. 427–450). New York: W. W. Norton & Company, Inc.

Lalmalsawma, D. (April 18, 2013). Thirty-three percent of the world's poorest live in India. Reuters Blog: India Insight. Retrieved from http://blogs.reuters.com/india/2013/04/18/thirty-three-percent-of-worlds-poorest-live-in-india/.

Langellier, K. M., & Hall, D. L. (1989). Interviewing women: A phenomenological approach to feminist communication research. In K. Carter & C. Spitzack (Eds.), *Doing research on women's communication: Perspectives on theory and method* (pp. 193–220). Norwood, NJ: Ablex.

Lebra, J., Paulson, J., & Everett, J. (1984). *Women and change in India: Continuity and change.* New Delhi, India: Promilla & Co., Publishers.

Lee, K. S. (2006). Gender beliefs and the meaning of work among Okinawan women. *Gender & Society, 20,* 382–401.

Liddle, J., & Joshi, R. (1989). *Daughters of independence: Gender, caste and class in India.* New Brunswick, NJ: Rutgers University Press.

Littleton, S. M., Arthur, M. B., & Rousseau, D. M. (2000). The future of boundaryless careers. In A. Collin & R. A. Young (Eds.), *The future of career* (pp. 101–114). Cambridge, UK: Cambridge University Press.

Lucas, K. (2006). *No footsteps to follow: How blue-collar kids navigate postindustrial careers* Unpublished Dissertation, Purdue University, West Lafayette, IN.

Lucas, K. (2011). Anticipatory socialization in blue-collar families: The negotiation of contradictory messages of social mobility and reproduction. *Western Journal of Communication, 75,* 95–121.

Luck, M., & d'Inverno, M. (1995). *A formal framework for agency and autonomy.* Paper presented at the Proceedings of the First International Conference on Multiagent Systems.

Madgavkar, A. (2012, December). India's missing women workforce. Livemint & *The Wall Street Journal.* Retrieved from http://www.livemint.com/Opinion/dd8OFniJdurubBOoNJeoHK/Indias-missing-women-workforce.html.

Marshall, J. (1989). Re-visioning career concepts: A feminist invitation. In M. B. Arthur, D. T. Hall, & B. S. Lawrence (Eds.), *Handbook of career theory* (pp. 275–91). Cambridge, UK: Cambridge University Press.

Mathew, A. (2005). Awareness of social issues among Indian women construction workers. *International Social Work, 48,* 99–107.

Mazumdar, I. (2007). *Women workers and globalization: Emergent contradictions in India.* Kolkata, India: Bhatkal and Sen.

Medved, C. E., Brogan, S., McClanahan, A. M., Morris, J. F., & Shepherd, G. J. (2006). Work and Family Socializing Communication: Messages, Gender, and Power. *Journal of Family Communication, 6,* 161–180.

Menon, U. (2000). Does feminism have universal relevance? The challenges posed by Oriya Hindu family practices. *Daedalus, 129,* 77–99.

Merton, R. K. (1957). *Social theory and social structure.* Glencoe, IL: Freepress

Mies, M. (1983). Towards a methodology of feminist research. In G. Bowles & R. D. Klein (Eds.), *Theories of Women's Studies* (pp. 117–139). Boston: Routledge Kegan Paul.

Mitra, A. (2005). Women in the urban informal sector: Perpetuation of meagre earnings. *Development and Change, 36,* 291–316.

Mize, L. K. (1995). Ritual experience and its emergence with story: An experience in meaning. *Contemporary Family Therapy, 17*(1), 109–125.

Mohan, S. (1999). Career development in the Indian context. In S. Mohan (Ed.), *Career development in India: Theory, research, and development* (pp. 29–52). New Delhi: Sage.

Mohanty, C. T. (1984). Under Western eyes: Feminist scholarship and colonial discourses. *Boundary 2, 12,* 333–358.

Mohanty, M. (2004). Introduction: Dimensions of power and social transformation. In M. Mohanty (Ed.), *Class, caste, gender* (pp. 14–44). New Delhi: Sage.

Moskowitz, D. S., Suh, E. J., & Desaulniers, J. (1994). Situational influences on gender differences in agency and communion. *Journal of Personality and Social Psychology, 66,* 753–761.

Mukherjee, R. (1999). Caste in itself, caste and class, or caste in class. *Economic and Political Weekly, 3,* 1759–1761.

Mukhopadhyay, C. C., & Seymour, S. (Eds.). (1994). *Women, education and family structure in India.* Colorado: Westview Press.

Nagaich, S. (1997). *Changing status of women in India.* New Delhi, India: Anmol Publications Pvt. Ltd.

Narayan, U. (2004). The project of feminist epistemology: Perspectives from a nonwestern feminist. In S. Harding (Ed.), *The feminist standpoint reader: Intellectual and political controversies* (pp. 213–224). London: Routledge.

Narayan, U. (2005). Contesting cultures: "Westernization," Respect for cultures, and Third-World feminists from disclocating cultures: Identities, traditions and Third World feminisms. In W. K. Kolmar & F. Bartkowski (Eds.), *Feminist Theory: A reader* (pp. 542–550). New York: Mc-Graw Hill.

Nath, D. (2000). Gently shattering the glass ceiling: Experiences of Indian women managers. *Women in Management Review, 15,* 44–52.

Nath, S. K., & Rastogi, P. (1993). *Workshop on using statistics for gender-responsive policy analysis and advocacy.* Bangkok, Thailand: UNESCAP/UNIFEM.

Nigam, A. (2002). In search of a bourgeoisie: Dalit politics enters a new phase. *Economic and Political Weekly, 37,* 1190–1193.

Nijman, J. (2006). Mumbai's mysterious middle class. *International Journal of Urban and Regional Research, 30,* 758–775.

Oakley, A. (1981). Interviewing women: A contradiction in terms. In J. Roberts (Ed.), *Doing feminist research* (pp. 30–61). London: Routledge & Kegan Paul.

O'Brien Hallstein, D. L. (1999). A postmodern caring: Feminist standpoint theories, revisioned caring, and communication ethics. *Western Journal of Communication, 63*(1), 32–56.

O'Brien Hallstein, D. L. (2000). Where standpoint stands now: An introduction and commentary. *Women's Studies in Communication, 23,* 1–15.

O'Leary, V. E., & Ickovics, J. (1990). Women's supporting women: Secretaries and their bosses. In H. Y. G. N. L. Chester (Ed.), *The experience and meaning of work in women's lives* (pp. 35–56). Hillsdale, NJ: LEA.

O'Neil, D. A., & Bilimoria, D. (2005). Women's career development phases: Idealism, endurance, and reinvention. *Career Development International, 10,* 168–262.

Online Extra: India's new worldly women (2005, August 21). Retrieved from http://www.businessweek.com/magazine/content/05_34/b3948530.htm.

Ostendorf, L. (1997). *The meaning of work in women's lives: A developmental perspective.* Unpublished Dissertation, The California School of Professional Psychology, Almeda.

Pai, A., Krishnamurthy, A., & Sen, S. (2007, April 16). *Her own space.* Retrieved February 3, 2008, from http://www.indiatoday.com/itoday/20070416/cover2.html.

Pal, M., & Buzzanell, P. M. (2008). The Indian call center experience: A case study in changing discourses of identity, identification.

Pande, R. (2007). Gender, poverty and globalization in India. *Development, 50,* 134–140.

Parikh, I. J., & Engineer, M. (2002). Women at the workplace: The journey of three generations of women. *IIMA Working Papers* Retrieved February 3, 2008, from http://www.iimahd.ernet.in/publications/data/2002-10-03IndiraJParikh.pdf

Parliament passes sexual harassment at workplace bill (February, 27, 2013). The Times of India. Retrieved from http://articles.timesofindia.indiatimes.com/2013-02-27/india/37330220_1_physical-contact-and-advances-conduct-of-sexual-nature-sexually-coloured-remarks.

Patton, M. Q. (2002). *Qualitative research & evaluation methods.* Thousand Oaks, CA: Sage.

Pausch, R., & Zaslow, J. (2008). *The last lecture.* New York: Hyperion.

Poverty estimates for 2011–2012 (July 2013). Government of India Planning Commission. Retrieved from http://planningcommission.nic.in/news/press_pov2307.pdf.

Powell , G. N., & Graves , L. M. (2003). Women and men in management (3rd edition). Thousand Oaks, CA: Sage.

Prasad, G. (2006). The great Indian family: New roles and old responsibilities. New Delhi: Penguin Books.

Pringle, J. K., & McCulloch Dixon, K. (2003). Re-incarnating life in the careers of women. *Career Development International, 8,* 291–300.

Purie, A. (March 27, 2006). Overcoming the Indian divide [Electronic Version]. *India Today,* 19. Retrieved January 22, 2008 from ProQuest database.

Raju, S. (1993). Introduction. In S. Raju & D. Bagchi (Eds.), *Women and work in South Asia* (pp. 1-36). London: Routledge.

Raju, S., & Bagchi, D. (Eds.). (1993). *Women and work in South Asia* London: Routledge.

Reinharz, S. (1992). *Feminist methods in social research.* New York: Oxford University Press.

Riessman, C. K. (1987). When gender is not enough: Women interviewing women. *Gender & Society, 1,* 172–207.

Qayum, S., & Ray, R. (2003). Grappling with modernity: India's respectable classes and the culture of domestic servitude. *Ethnography, 4,* 520–555.

Raina, T. (December 11, 2005). In the driving seat. Retrieved February 7, 2008, from http://www.tribuneindia.com/2005/20051211/society.htm#3.

Raju, S., & Bagchi, D. (Eds.). (1993). *Women and work in South Asia* London: Routledge.

Raman, S. A. (2009). *Women in India: A social and cultural history—Volume I.* Santa Barbara, CA: Praeger.

Rao, N. (1996). Empowerment through organisation: Women workers in the informal sector. *Indian Journal of Gender Studies, 3,* 171–197.

Rayman, P. (1987). Women and employment. *Social Research, 54,* 355–376.

Ritzer, G. (2004). *The McDonaldization of society: New century edition.* Thousand Oaks, CA: Pine Forge Press.

Ruddick, S., & Daniels, P. (Eds.). (1977). *Working it out.* New York: Pantheon Books.

Ruether, R. R. (2005). Women and globalization: Victims, sites of resistance and new world views. *Feminist Theology, 13,* 361–372.

Ruiz-Quintanilla, A. S., & England, G. W. (1996). How working is defined: Structure and Stability. *Journal of Organizational Behavior, 17,* 515–540.

Sandhu, H. S., & Mehta, R. (2007). Personal and organizational correlates affecting attitudes of women executives towards their job. *Global Business Review, 8,* 135–151.

Saraswathi, T. S. (1999). Introduction. In T. S. Saraswathi (Ed.), *Culture, socialization and human development: Theory, research and applications in India* (pp. 1-42). New Delhi, India: Sage.

Saurine, A. (April 04, 2009). Women putting career on hold. Retrieved April 3, 2009, from http://www.news.com.au/dailytelegraph/story/0,,25287110-5001021,00.html.

Schwartz, S.H. (1999). A theory of cultural values and some implications for work. *Applied Psychology: An international review, 48,* 23–47.

Sengupta, S. (December 21, 2007). India overturns law banning women bartenders. Retrieved from http://www.nytimes.com/2007/12/21/world/asia/21india.html?n=Top/Reference/Times%20Topics/Subjects/L/Labor.

Shenoy, S., Williams, E., & Linvill, J. (2008, May). *Anticipatory socialization in family businesses: (co)Constructions of career and agency among successors.* Paper presented at the International Communication Association annual conference, Montreal, Canada

Shenoy-Packer, S. (2013). Her holiness—The purohitas of Pune, India: Female Hindu priests as embodied, emotional spiritual, and aesthetic (performative) laborers. *Journal of International and Intercultural Communication.*

Shenoy-Packer, S., & Buzzanell, P. M. (2013). Meanings of work among Hindu Indian women: Contextualizing meaningfulness and materialities of work through *dharma* and *karma. Journal of Communication and Religion, 36,* 149–176.

Shenoy-Packer, S., & Myers, K. K. (2013). Challenges to organizational assimilation: Experiences of White women and people of color in the U.S. workforce. *International Journal of Organizational Diversity, 12, 2,* 1–15.

Shellengarger, S. (February 4, 2009). No waiting: Younger women are saying yes to motherhood Retrieved April 7, 2009, from http://online.wsj.com/article/SB123371049941845977.html.

Sheth, D. L. (1999). Secularisation of caste and making of new middle class. *Economic and Political Weekly, 34,* 2502–2510.

Shome, R. (2006). Thinking about the diaspora: Call centers, India, and a new politics of hybridity. *International Journal of Cultural Studies, 9,* 105–124.

Singh, B. N. (1989). Women workforce: Problems and prospects. *Yojana, 33,* 4, 15–17 and 34.

Singh, P. (2002). Women in the corporate world in India - Balancing work and family life. *Alva Myrdal's Questions to our Time conference* Retrieved February 4, 2008, from www.pcr.uu.se/conferenses/myrdal/pdf/singh.pdf.

Sinha, D. (1984). Some recent changes in the Indian family and their implications for Socialization. *The Indian Journal of Social Work, 45,* 271–286.

Sloan, D. K., & Krone, K. J. (2000). Women managers and gendered values. *Women's Studies in Communication 23,* 111–130.

Smith, D. E. (1997). Comment on Hekman's "Truth and method: Feminist standpoint theory revisited." *Signs: Journal of Women in Culture and Society, 22,* 392–398.

Smyer, M. A., & Pitt-Catsouphes, M. (2007). The meanings of work for older workers.*Generations, 31,* 23–30.

Sonawat, R. (2001). Understanding families in India: A reflection of societal changes. *Psicologia: Teoria e Pesquisa, 17,* 177–186.

Song, S. (2006). *Defining the meaning of work for minority older adults: A comparative study between Korean Americans and African Americans.* Unpublished Dissertation, Columbia University.

Srinivas, M. N. (1978). *Caste in modern India and other essays.* Bombay, India: Media Promoters and Publishers Pvt. Ltd.

Stewart, A. J. (1990). Discovering the meanings of work. In H. Y. Grossman & N. L. Chester (Eds.), *The experience and meaning of work in women's lives* Hillsdale, NJ: LEA.

Stewart, A. J. (1994). Toward a feminist strategy for studying women's lives. In C. E. Franz & J. Stewart (Eds.), *Women creating lives: Identities, resilience, and resistance* (pp. 11–35). Boulder, CO: Westview Press.

Stoetzler, M., & Yuval-Davis, N. (2002). Standpoint theory, situated knowledges, and the situated imagination. *Feminist Theory, 3*(3), 315–333.

Stohl, C. (1986). The role of memorable messages in the process of organizational socialization. *Communication Quarterly, 34,* 231–249.

Strauss, A., & Corbin, J. (1990). *Basics of qualitative research: Grounded theory, procedures and techniques.* Newbury Park, CA: Sage.

Suriya, M. (2003). Gender issues in the career development of IT professionals: A global perspective. Retrieved March 6, 2008, from http://www.gisdevelopment.net/proceedings/mapasia/2003/papers/i4d/i4d2002.htm.

The changing nature of work. (n.d.) International Development Research Centre. Retrieved March 7, 2008, from http://www.idrc.ca/en/ev-83654-201-1-DO_TOPIC.html.

The meaning of working: MOW International Research Team. (1987). London: Academic Press, Inc.

The state of the poor: Where are the poor and where are they poorest? (April, 17, 2013). The World Bank. Retrieved from http://www.worldbank.org/content/dam/Worldbank/document/State_of_the_poor_paper_April17.pdf.

Thomas, J. J. (2013, January). A woman-shaped gap in the Indian workforce. *The Hindu.* Retrieved from http://www.thehindu.com/opinion/op-ed/a-womanshaped-gap-in-the-indian-workforce/article4287620.ece.

Townsley, N. C. (2006). Love, sex, and tech in the global workplace. In B. J. Dow & J. T. Wood (Eds.), *The SAGE handbook on gender and communication* (pp. 143–160). Thousand Oaks, CA: Sage.

Tryst with destiny (2008). Retrieved from https://www.youtube.com/watch?v=1wUcw8Ufx_Y.

Uberoi, P. (April, 04, 2005). The invisible help. Retrieved February 3, 2008, from http://www.indiatoday.com/itoday/20050404/cover3.shtml.

Vajpeyi, N. (2003). Social monitor: Breaking religious barriers. *Tribune India.* Retrieved from, http://www.tribuneindia.com/2003/20030914/herworld.htm#1.

Van Maanen, J. (1976). Breaking in: Socialization to work. In R. Dubin (Ed.), *Handbook of work, organization & society.* Chicago, IL: Rand McNally.

Varma, P. (1998). *The great Indian middle class.* New Delhi, India: Viking.

Vasudev, S. (2005, April 4). She wants more. *Women & Relationships.* Retrieved February 3, 2008, from http://www.indiatoday.com/itoday/20050404/cover6.shtml.

Westwood, R., & Lok, P. (2003). The meaning of work in Chinese contexts: A comparative study. *International Journal of Cross-Cultural Management, 3,* 139–165.

White, B. (1995). The career development of successful women. *Women in Management Review, 10,* 4–15.

Whitemarsh, L., Brown, D., J., C., Hawkins-Rodgers, Y., & Wentworth, D. K. (2007). Choices and challenges: A qualitative exploration of professional women's career patterns. *Career Development Quarterly, 55,* 225–236.

Willis, P. (1977). *Learning to labor: How working-class kids get working-class jobs.* New York: Columbia University Press.

Women taxi drivers make their way to Indian roads. (2009, June 3). Retrieved February 8, 2010, from http://rt.com/news/women-taxi-drivers-make-their-way-to-indian-roads/

Wood, J. T. (2005). Feminist standpoint theory and muted group theory: Commonalities and divergences. *Women and Language, 28,* 61–72.

Yadav, Y., & Kumar, S. (2007). The challenge of change: Women emerge champs [Electronic Version]. *IBNLIVE.COM.* Retrieved from http://www.ibnlive.com/printpage.php?id=57441&section_id=19.

Young, R. A., & Friesen, J. D. (1992). The intentions of parents in influencing the career development of their children. *Career Development Quarterly, 40,* 198–207.

Young, R. A., Friesen, J. D. & Borycki, B. (1994). Narrative structure and parental influence in career development. *Journal of Adolescence* 17: 173–191.

Young, R. A., Valach, L., Paseluikho, M. A., Dover, C., Matthes, G. E., Paproski, D. L., et al. (1997). The joint action of parents and adolescents in conversation about career. *The Career Development Quarterly, 46,* 72–86.

Index

About the Author

Suchitra Shenoy-Packer is assistant professor of organizational and multi-cultural communication at DePaul University, Chicago, USA. She can be reached at suchitraspacker@outlook.com. Follow her on Twitter @suchitrashenoy.

Lightning Source UK Ltd.
Milton Keynes UK
UKOW05n0007060814

236391UK00001B/11/P